Black Americans

and the

Evangelization of Africa, 1877–1900

Black Americans
and the
Evangelization of Africa
1877–1900

Walter L. Williams

The University of Wisconsin Press

Published 1982

The University of Wisconsin Press
114 North Murray Street
Madison, Wisconsin 53715

The University of Wisconsin Press, Ltd.
1 Gower Street
London WC1E 6HA, England

First printing

Printed in the United States of America

For LC CIP information see the colophon

ISBN 0-299-08920-7

Publication of this book was made possible in part by a grant from the Charles Phelps
Taft Memorial Fund, the University of Cincinnati.

Dedicated to my parents,
Opal Chester Williams
and
Walter B. Williams

Contents

Illustrations

Acknowledgments

Most of a historian's research is necessarily done in libraries, and I can only begin to suggest the debt I owe to the staffs of the following institutions: University of North Carolina Library, Library of Congress, National Archives, New York Public Library's Schomburg Center for Research in Black Culture, Arnett Library of Atlanta University, Interdenominational Theological Center Library of Atlanta University, Moorland Collection of the Howard University Library, Theological Library of Howard University, Lincoln University Library, Livingstone College Library, Fort Valley State College Library, Emory University Theology Library, Duke University Library, and the Houghton Library of Harvard University.

I also owe a great deal to the following missionary agency archives: Presbyterian Historical Foundation, at Montreat, North Carolina; Board of Global Ministries of the United Methodist Church, at New York City; United Methodist Commission on Archives and History, at Lake Junaluska, North Carolina; Evangelical United Brethren Division of the United Methodist Commission on Archives and History, at Dayton, Ohio; Foreign Mission Board of the National Baptist Convention at Philadelphia, Pennsylvania; and Southern Baptist Historical Commission, at Nashville, Tennessee. The registrars of the following institutions kindly provided information about their black alumni who were involved with Africa: Fisk University, Livingstone College, Alabama A and M University, and Yale University.

Many people generously assisted me by sharing perspectives and references from their own research, including Josephus Coan of Atlanta University, Blyden Jackson of the University of North Carolina, Frederick McEvoy of Marshall University, Jane Herndon of DeKalb College, David Foley of the University of Georgia, Abna Aggrey Lancaster of Livingstone College, Donald Roth of the University of Texas, Sylvia Jacobs of North Carolina Central University, and A.M.E. Zion Bishop Jacob Walls. I have greatly benefited from the readings and critical comments of all or parts of the manuscript (at various stages in its development) by a number of scholars, including Frank W. Klingberg, Joel Williamson, Roberta Ann Dunbar, and Donald Mathews, all of the University of North

Carolina; and by my colleagues at the University of Cincinnati, Roger Daniels, Herbert Shapiro, Zane Miller, William Aeschbacher, William Seeman, and Amuzie Chimezie. Others include August Meier of Kent State University, Willard Gatewood of the University of Arkansas, and John Hope Franklin of the University of Chicago. My editor at the University of Wisconsin Press, Brian Keeling, has been most helpful. To all of these, and to any others I may have neglected to mention, I express heartfelt thanks.

The Journal of Negro History kindly permitted me to reprint the part of chapter 8 of this book that first appeared in their summer 1980 issue.

I am also most grateful for generous financial support from the Woodrow Wilson Fellowship Foundation, the Charles Phelps Taft Fund of the University of Cincinnati, and the American Council of Learned Societies. Lastly, I wish to thank my family and close friends for their continuous moral support while I wrote this book.

W.L.W.

Cincinnati
1981

Introduction

The year was 1900 and the place was London. As the black men and women filed into the Westminster meeting hall, they may have realized that they had reached a turning point in their history. The busy city scarcely noticed their presence, but the delegates had arrived from the United States, the West Indies, Africa, and Europe, with their purpose clearly in mind: "to bring into closer touch with each other the peoples of African descent throughout the world."[1] The name of the assembly suggested its newness: the First Pan-African Conference.

"Pan-Africanism" embodied the concept that black people in both the Old and New Worlds had a common identity and should struggle together for their mutual interests. It reflected a feeling of racial solidarity and cultural unity of all blacks. These sentiments were best expressed by an American delegate to the Conference, a young Atlanta University professor named W. E. B. Du Bois. In his speech Du Bois predicted that, throughout the world, the most serious controversies of the forthcoming century would be related to "the problem of the color line." As an Afro-American, he recognized that this problem existed in the United States, but he saw a similar situation in Africa. On both continents the basic problem involved white subjugation of blacks. Du Bois appealed to the colonial powers to restrain themselves, to treat Africans justly, to train the people in self-government, and to respect the independent black nations of Liberia and Ethiopia. He warned European rulers:

> Let not the natives of Africa be sacrificed to the greed of gold, their liberties taken away, their famiy life debauched, their just aspirations repressed, and avenues of advancement and culture taken from them. Let not the cloak of Christian Missionary enterprise be allowed in the future, as so often in the past, to hide the ruthless economic exploitation and political downfall of less developed nations.[2]

Du Bois' concern for the welfare of Africa, plus his subsequent stimulation of contacts between Africans and Afro-Americans, has made him known as the "father of Pan-Africanism."[3]

Since the organized Pan-African movement began in 1900, most historians have seen it as a twentieth-century phenomenon. The nineteenth-century antecedents of Pan-African ideology have consequently been largely ignored. Those scholars who have searched for the origins of Pan-African sentiments among black Americans have generally concentrated on "back-to-Africa" emigration movements.[4] While these studies are valuable, they do not tell the whole story. It will be argued in this book that the mission movement, by encouraging an interest in Africa among the masses of black Americans, was even more important.

A study of the missionary movement reveals much more about Afro-American life than simply church history. It demonstrates one mechanism by which black Americans adapted to their low status in post-Reconstruction America—by building their own independent churches and extending those institutions abroad. This study also shows the assimilation by black Americans of the dominant Western attitudes of the era, and the conflict between those values and the emerging feelings of closeness to the fatherland.

This book is written as a case study of inter-ethnic relations between two culturally distinct peoples who happened to have a common racial identity. By focusing on the churches, the most influential institutions among late nineteenth-century Afro-Americans, this study attempts to show that black people were taking an active interest in determining United States–Africa relations. They were not merely acted upon by whites, but were developing their own ideas and actions to bring about changes in their own position as well as that of Africa.

Nineteenth-century Afro-Americans had passed a watershed in their history during the years of the Civil War and Reconstruction. Their enslavement had finally ended, and during the late 1860s and early 1870s substantial gains had been made in education, civil rights, and political participation. The potential for continued progress was curtailed over the next decades, however, largely because there was very little acceptance of social equality on the part of whites, and because only a few black people managed to gain economic independence. The change in white/black relationships was not as great as the freedmen had hoped. Occupationally, most black southerners had merely exchanged the bondage of slavery for the peonage of sharecropping.

By 1877, with the abandonment of the remaining Reconstruction state governments by the federal government, it was clear that black rights would be sacrificed to a period of reunion and reaction. The commitment to racial equality by white northerners had never been more than half-hearted, and they had never accomplished basic economic changes in the South. Once federal protection for blacks was withdrawn, the recently freed slaves did not have enough economic power to guarantee their political and civil rights. Reconstruction was indeed a "tragic era," because it left the ex-slaves with a status far below that enjoyed by whites.

Nevertheless, there was some progress. Black families could no longer be broken up and sold on the whim of a master; freedmen had chances to migrate in search of better conditions; black sharecroppers usually won the right to farm their own family plots; and many blacks took advantage of the chance to get at least a rudimentary education. Some even obtained advanced education, and with it rose to higher-status occupations, which increased class stratification within Afro-American society. But the biggest change of the post-emancipation decades was the emergence of an independent black community organization. In the rural South, where the majority of black people lived before 1900, the central institution of this community organization was the church.

The decades after Reconstruction were times of both hope and discouragement: the small cadre of successful blacks prided themselves on "pulling themselves up by their own bootstraps," but there was much despair at continued white domination. The rise of institutionalized discrimination, disfranchisement, the convict lease system, lynching, and the general curtailment of black economic opportunity were the things which most aroused Afro-American dissatisfaction. Over it all hung the realization by blacks that if they protested too much, were "uppity," and did not "stay in their place," they could lose everything. They had to work out their own relation to the nation of their birth, without assistance from the government of that nation.

While most black people felt a strong attachment to the South, the region where their families had lived for many generations, migration movements emerged among them by the late 1870s. Some moved west, joining frontier settlements, seeking refuge with various Indian nations, or establishing their own separate communities. But others doubted that there was a hopeful future for them anywhere in the United States. Because of racism and the economic failures of the Reconstruction era, they were kept as a separate caste in a supposedly casteless society. Black Americans had to decide if they were really Americans at all.

If they could not fully accept the United States as their birthright, the only place they could turn to was their ancestral home: Africa.

But identification with a distant place which they had never seen, and which was stereotyped by whites as "savage," was difficult for blacks who were struggling for acceptance as bona fide Americans. For those who were educated, and were promoting their self-concept as "civilized people," identification with "savage" Africa was even more strained.

The problem of identification with Africa was enhanced by the fact that black Americans who wondered about Africa in the late nineteenth century found it difficult to obtain information about it. While many retained oral traditions of family origins in Africa, by this time hardly any native-born Africans were still alive in the United States. It was not until the twentieth century that a Western-educated African intelligentsia established substantial intercontinental communication with black Americans. Thus, at a time when Afro-Americans were most in need of an identity with the fatherland, they had relatively few direct contacts. To gain information about Africa they often had to depend on accounts by whites.

The late nineteenth century was an era when the Western world had Africa much in mind. Advances in medical practices allowed whites to survive more readily in the tropical climate. Fueled by increasing nationalistic competition, Western nations sent out wave after wave of explorers, traders, missionaries, and conquerors. Their reports increased excitement about a vast area of the world previously unknown in the West. This new interest in Africa by whites had an impact on Afro-Americans, who also showed increased interest in the continent, even though their major sources of information were white-authored.

The "opening of the dark continent" had even more impact on Africa itself. The previous history of Africa had been marked by the same mixture of continuity and change that typified European history, but its peoples were extremely dissimilar. Parts of the continent were peopled by preliterate tribal villagers or nomadic herdsmen, while other parts were dominated by large centralized kingdoms with great universities and wealthy cities. The continent was made even more diverse because of the impact of European trade and settlements on the western and southern coasts, and especially because of the spread of Islam into most of West Africa, the Sudan, and the east coast. On the west coast, Afro-American colonists had established their own settlements in Liberia and Sierra Leone. This varied continent could hardly be stereotyped as primitive, yet Europeans justified their scramble for colonial control on the basis of Africa's need for "civilization." Victorian imperialists saw their conquest of Africa as inevitable, and they naively expected Africans to abandon their own ways of life and adopt Western culture.

African societies were undergoing considerable internal change during the nineteenth century. The continuing expansion and consolidation of Islam sparked political/religious revolutions and interethnic unification. The end of the Atlantic slave trade disrupted coastal kingdoms, which for the previous three centuries had built their economy upon the slave trade. Material trade with Europe did not fill the vacuum left by the end of slave exportation. While the coastal kingdoms were in this weakened economic position, European merchants and missionaries, followed by soldiers and administrators, forced their way into more territories. While these circumstances produced revolutionary changes, African peoples successfully held onto their cultural institutions and mitigated the disruptive impact of change.

By the late nineteenth century, Africans and Afro-Americans were two peoples, separate in culture but united by color and by struggles to control their own lives. Both peoples were diverse, and had experienced tremendous changes during their lives. The attitudes of black Americans toward Africa reflect this diversity. The structure of their society meant that many of these attitudes would be expressed in a religious context, through missionary evangelization.

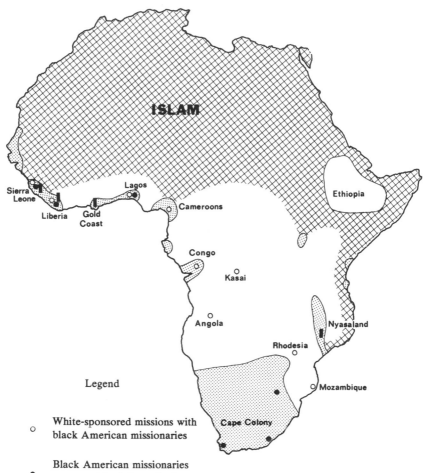

ISLAM

Sierra Leone

Liberia

Lagos

Gold Coast

Cameroons

Ethiopia

Congo

Kasai

Angola

Nyasaland

Rhodesia

Mozambique

Legend

○   White-sponsored missions with black American missionaries

●   Black American missionaries sponsored by independent black American churches

❙   Africans educated in black American schools, who returned to Africa as missionaries

Extent of Christian missionary activities by 1880

Islamic areas of Africa by 1880

Cape Colony

Black American Christian Missionary Locations in Africa, 1877–1900

xviii

Part One
People of God:
The Rise of Mission Sentiment
among Black Americans

1

Sources of Afro-American Mission Sentiment

The rise of Christian missionary sentiment among black Americans was at least partly due to the influence of evangelism among whites and the impact of white churches upon black religious activism. Despite their own distinctive modification of Christianity to make it more compatible with their African heritage, black people in nineteenth-century America followed a religion that remained basically part of the European cultural tradition. They absorbed much of their religious interest, organization, and ritual from white churches, and in some cases consciously emulated the white ideal, in attempt to gain respect from whites through Christian brotherhood. For example, most of the missionary songs in black-compiled church hymnals were written by whites, and mission boards were modeled on those in white churches.[1]

The rise of interest in missions reflected expansionist Christian ideology. Christianity, unlike most of the world's religions, has been strongly expansionistic, which has caused its followers to feel a duty to convert people of other faiths. This ideology originated in Jesus' last commandment to his disciples: "Go ye therefore, and teach all nations . . . to observe all things whatsoever I have commanded you," and "Go ye into all the world, and preach the Gospel to every creature."[2] The Roman disciple Paul extended this sense of duty by proclaiming that all Christians were ambassadors for Jesus, as though God were acting directly on other peoples through them.[3] Black missionaries in particular never tired of quoting the Old Testament prophesy of David, that "Ethiopia shall soon stretch out her hands unto God."[4]

Yet through most of its history Christianity was more or less confined to people of European descent. The expansionist ideology remained mere rhetoric until after 1800, when Christian expansion became a world-wide phenomenon. Never before had any religion spread to as large an area as Christianity did in the nineteenth century.[5]

The reasons for this expansion were many, and involved large-scale European developments. Europeans were going through a series of evangelical "awakenings." The idea of the perfectibility of a unified humanity produced a new social consciousness. Parts of this trend which related specifically to Africa were the antislavery and mission movements. The new missionary efforts in many ways were the embodiment of Western nationalism. In fact, mission sentiment and European nationalism followed similar courses.[6] The late nineteenth century was the heyday of Christian missions, and even during the era of imperialism the average person in Europe and America knew more about mission expansion than about colonial acquisitions.[7] Mission growth was phenomenal: in 1876 there were only two thousand Christian missionaries in service in the world, yet by 1900 this number had increased to over fifteen thousand.[8]

The rise of the mission movement in the United States paralleled and drew inspiration from the movement in Europe. Before 1880, mission sentiment concentrated on American Indians, but after that date the movement began to have a sense of world-wide destiny. In 1885 a Congregationalist minister named Josiah Strong wrote *Our Country: Its Possible Future and Its Present Crisis*. The book, which became one of the bestsellers of the century, dramatically reflected the realization by Americans of their growing power in the world. They had survived their most crucial test in the Civil War, and they had subdued a continent. This very progress caused new problems, said Strong, because with the West filled up and the nation industrialized there would be new need for expansion in order to avoid catastrophe. The development of a new Anglo-Saxon Christian world empire, he felt, would at last bring about the coming of Christ's kingdom. This empire would be distinctively American, and missions were the first step.[9]

Strong's book sparked mission enthusiasm in many of the nation's colleges and seminaries, and by 1888 the Student Volunteer Movement was organized with over 2,000 volunteers for foreign missions. Their bombastic slogan, "The evangelization of the world in this generation," held a new immediacy that was lacking in previous mission attempts. Much of the moral fervor that had previously been channeled into continental Manifest Destiny or against southern slavery slackened with the subjugation and nominal Christianization of frontier Indians and the end of slavery. As Americans looked beyond their own continent for moral causes, the international missionary movement answered their need. With increasing wealth, Americans could now afford to finance more foreign missions. By the 1890s this cultural imperialism evolved into support for American political expansion abroad, which was in imitation of Europe's "New Imperialism" of the same era.[10]

Perhaps the best indication of the rise of mission interest by the late nineteenth century is the number of missionaries sent out by American churches. The number of missionaries backed by the Congregationalist American Board of Commissioners for Foreign Missions, one of the largest sponsoring organizations, for example, reached a peak of about 350 in the 1840s. A decline in strength set in during the Civil War years, and the previous record was not again matched until 1877. During the last two decades of the century the number of Congregationalist missionaries continued to grow until by 1900 it surpassed five hundred.[11] The total number of American missionaries of all denominations nearly doubled during the last fifteen years of the century alone, from 2,465 to 4,728.[12] These missionaries had a stern sense of Christian duty, and endeavored to lift the unconverted to what they felt to be a higher and better plane of spiritual life. The missionaries were characterized by a strong belief in the superiority of their own way of life. Sometimes they were alarmed by the decline in spiritual values which marked their rapidly changing secular age, and some missionaries went abroad to escape modern industrial society. Nevertheless, they remained so convinced of the need for Christian civilization that they sought to spread their culture to all the people of the world.[13]

These tenets meant that the missionary actually went into an area with two goals: to teach the Christian religion, and to westernize the way of life. Everything Western was sanctioned as the will of God, while everything belonging to the indigenous culture was evil. A mission, therefore, could bring great disruption into a non-Western society. The introduction of Western values and Western technology and material culture rapidly challenged the traditional order of life.[14]

Christian denominations saw Africa as one of the major areas of the world to be converted, but the first missionaries sent to Africa had little resistance to the many tropical diseases. The continent

became known as a "white man's grave." Faced with a lack of
white volunteers, several mission boards hit upon the idea of sending
black missionaries. It was believed that, because they were descended
from Africans, Afro-Americans could better adjust to the climate.
Blacks also would not cost as much for expensive European furloughs, and they could be paid a smaller salary. In its 1874 report,
the Southern Baptist Convention concluded:

> The history of the mission exertions has demonstrated that
> white missionaries, as a general thing, cannot succeed in laboring
> long as missionaries in Africa. Nearly every white missionary
> has either fallen a victim on the field, or has been compelled
> to return to America [because of disease]. If Africa is evan-
> gelized, colored men must be the agents of that great work. . . .
> Young colored brethren should be encouraged to prepare for
> the work of preaching the gospel to people of the same color
> in Africa. At present they are our only hope of success.[15]

In 1877, after they had begun to support an Afro-American missionary in Lagos, who was reported doing outstanding work among
the Yoruba, the Convention concluded that black Americans were
the "best fitted" for mission work in the tropical climate of Africa.[16]

White churches therefore endeavored to increase black interest
in African missions. One method of arousing support was by articles
in black religious publications. For example, the *A.M.E. Church
Review* contained an article in 1885 that called for the "redemption"
of Africa. The writer (who was white) stated that missionaries
could help end the slave trade in Africa, and open the continent
to the products and trade of the West. Such a development, he
claimed, would allow Africans to rise to full manhood and would
mean black elevation throughout the world.[17] This combination
of idealism and self-interest obviously appealed to blacks who were
worried about gaining white acceptance.

White missionaries trooped to black campuses to speak about
Africa. In an address to the student body of Atlanta University in
1888, for example, a white missionary began his lecture with the
standard Biblical prophesy that "Ethiopia shall soon stretch out
her hands unto God." He claimed that God had ordained slavery
as the mechanism for raising a new African elect into civilization
and Christianity. Once blacks had been civilized in America, he
reasoned, God caused slavery to be ended and Africa to be opened
so that Afro-Americans could "bring Africa to Christ." It was their
destiny to "cover Africa with homes and schools and churches and

Christian States"; God gave them authority to take the continent "for their *work* and *reward*." With God's help, this missionary foresaw, the Afro-Americans would be able to overcome "the ignorance, the animalism, and the barbarism of the African tribes."[18]

The concept of Afro-American history exemplified by the above ideas was known as the "Theory of Providential Design." It originated with supporters of colonization who were looking for theological justification for their movement. By the late nineteenth century, the mission advocates had adapted this theory for their own uses, and it became a facet of the Afro-American mission movement. The fact that black Americans, rather than Africans themselves, became the means for the redemption of the continent, typified mission assumptions that progress had to come from outside the "dark continent." Mission supporters thought that only civilized westerners, whether white or black, could bring about a regeneration of Africa. Consequently, they saw it as their duty to take over the leadership of indigenous Africa.[19] The concept of "duty" was used as a justification for expansion in the same way that it was used to justify white colonialism. For example, white mission supporters organized a "Congress on Africa" at the 1893 Chicago World's Fair, its goal being the arousal of the Afro-American's "nobler self to the duty to his kin beyond [the] sea."[20] This call for black American expansionism amounted to an adapted form of Manifest Destiny, and it typified thought during the era of imperialism. "The white man's burden" was merely broadened in nonracist terms to become "the civilized man's burden."

Another route of white influence in the rise of black mission interest was through white-sponsored schools. No white denomination exerted more influence on black education than the northern Methodist Episcopal Church. Ante-bellum white Methodists had split on the slavery question, and it was with feelings of vindication that northern missionaries entered the South after 1865 to bring back their departed southern brethren. But few white southerners were interested in coming under the denominational dominance of northerners, so abolitionist-oriented missionaries turned the Methodist Episcopal Church's attention to the recently freed slaves. Attracted by respectful treatment and financial resources to support schools, many black Methodists abandoned the southern church for the northern one. In 1866 northern church leaders formed the Freedman's Aid Society, and within four years it was sponsoring over a thousand schools in the South. In 1883 a northern Methodist philanthropist established the Gammon Theological Seminary in Atlanta, to train black Methodist Episcopal clergymen. As a result, by 1890 the church had 300,000 black members and 1,700 black clergy, making it the white church with the largest black membership in the nation.[21]

Methodist officials in Freedman's Aid schools encouraged their black students to take an active interest in African missions. For example, in 1890 a white bishop encouraged the organization of a "Friends of Africa" club at New Orleans University, one of the Methodist Episcopal schools. Within a few years, a black Methodist clergyman was able to write that "all the schools under the direction of the Freedman's Aid Society have at least one organization of Friends of Africa, and both the organization itself and the thought which directed it have spread among schools and Young People's Societies and Churches. As a result there is today among all educated Negroes in the South an increasing interest for Africa's Evangelization."[22]

Additional interest was sparked in 1894 by the formation of the Stewart Missionary Foundation, set up by a prosperous white Methodist preacher specifically to train black missionaries for Africa. The foundation became part of the Gammon Seminary, and encouraged missions by sponsoring essay- and hymn-writing contests, sending speakers on tours of black churches, collecting a library on African subjects, and providing fellowships for missionary trainees. Under the direction of the white president of Gammon and a black professor there, John W. E. Bowen, the foundation's most dramatic moment came in December 1895 when it sponsored a much larger Congress on Africa than had ever been held in America. In accordance with the ideals of racial equality held by the leaders of Gammon, the conference was fully integrated and included notable black as well as white speakers. Its purpose was to spread accurate information on Africa for black Americans. Some African students in the United States, as well as black nationalist and former U.S. diplomat to Liberia John H. Smyth, were among the speakers. In general, despite some positive views of Africa, the majority of speakers repeated the standard picture of "pathetic heathens" that was common among missionaries.[23]

This publicity about Africa had a dramatic effect on black Methodists. Professor Bowen, writing to the American Colonization Society for literature on Africa, noted that books on the continent were "in constant demand and use. . . . An enthusiasm in research and for endeavor touching that land is taking possession of our students."[24] The Colonization Society itself had done much to encourage Afro-American interest in missions, principally by paying the ocean passage to Liberia for black clergymen.[25]

The major influence of the white churches on Afro-American mission interest was to attract missionary volunteers. Their ability to do this marked the degree of success of their efforts at publicizing Africa through meetings, speakers, publications, and schools.

Afro-American missionaries were sent by white churches only to tropical areas of western and central Africa, where disease took a greater toll on white missionaries. Consequently, there were no white-sponsored black churchmen in healthy areas like the Kenya highlands or South Africa. This distinction points out the self-serving nature of white church use of Afro-Americans: blacks were not deemed to be of worth unless health factors prevented the use of white clergy. But within tropical areas, black missionaries were often used. Before 1880 almost all black evangelists working among indigenous Africans were supported by white churches.[26]

The trend of sending black missionaries was especially true with regard to Liberia, the small West African colony for emancipated American slaves. Liberia was founded in 1822 by the American Colonization Society, led by a varied group of whites whose concern was to get black people out of the United States.[27] Many of the founders of the Society were clergymen who, besides wanting a place to resettle black Americans, also saw the situation as an opportunity to spread the Gospel. This connection led anti-colonizationist black leaders to avoid involvement with African missions. In Liberia, however, the influence of missions was pervasive, since the churches were the main social institution among the Americo-Liberian settlers. Missions fulfilled an important financial role as well, since their educational and social welfare programs were the only ones available.[28]

Despite the presence of white missionaries, after Liberian independence in 1847 the white churches came to depend more and more on black emigrants as their missionary representatives in Africa. By 1893, for example, the Massachusetts Colonization Society reported that of the fifty-two missionaries it was supporting in Liberia, only two were specifically sent as missionaries. The remainder were Americo-Liberians.[29] This trend was understandable, but it meant that most of the "missionary" work was among Americo-Liberians rather than indigenous Africans. By the end of the nineteenth century only small inroads had been made in the evangelization of the tribal population of interior Liberia.[30]

Most of the clergymen who served as "missionaries" to the already Christianized black American settlers were merely preachers who wished to go to Liberia as emigrants themselves. They did not really care much about converting non-Christians, and they often had relatively little exposure to indigenous Africans. Because they were permanent emigrants, they did not return to the United States to publicize their work. For these reasons, Americo-Liberian preachers had less impact on the development of black American mission sentiment than missionaries to aboriginal Africans.

Several white churches used black Americans as their representatives in Africa. In 1835, the Protestant Episcopal Church became the first white denomination to turn over its African mission work to blacks. Mr. and Mrs. James M. Thompson, the church's first black missionaries in Liberia, served until 1865.[31] The most important Episcopalian in Liberia, however, was Alexander Crummell. Born free in New York City in 1819, and ordained as an Episcopal clergyman in 1844, he became despondent about the future of black people in the United States and moved to England. After graduating from Queen's College of Cambridge University in 1853, Crummell was sent by the British Anglican Church as a missionary to Liberia.

Alexander Crummell quickly became one of Liberia's leading intellectuals, and his speeches and writings were internationally known. Nevertheless, his mission work did not go well in Liberia, due to his health problems and personality conflicts. Even though he remained in Liberia for twenty years, by the 1870s Crummell had become caught in political cross-currents and was disillusioned with Liberia. In 1873 he decided to return to America.[32]

Despite his disappointment with emigration, Crummell continued to support African mission efforts for the remainder of his life. Even though he was a member of a white denomination, his influence on black churches, and on Afro-American thought in general, was considerable. The major emphasis of his writings was on the need for black people to gain "civilization," by which he meant the education typical of refined Anglo-Saxons. In 1897 he founded the American Negro Academy to promote black intellectual and artistic development in opposition to the ideas of "industrial" vocational education propounded by Booker T. Washington.[33] Crummell's last major address before his academy was appropriately titled "Civilization the Primal Need of the Race."[34]

Crummell's emphasis on "civilization" pertained to Africans as well, and he stressed that "Gospel Missions are the only hope of the heathen of Africa" ever becoming civilized.[35] He continued to encourage missionary zeal, for example, in an 1887 tract for the American Colonization Society and in a speech he gave at the 1895 Atlanta Congress on Africa.[36] His most serious effort in support of missions was in his 1891 book *Africa and America*, which explained the relationship of missions to his ideas of civilization. He wrote that if Africa "is ever regenerated the influences and agencies to this end must come from *external* sources. Civilization . . . never springs up, spontaneously, in any new land. It must be transplanted."[37]

Reverend Crummell never questioned his assumption that Africa should be civilized along Anglo-Christian lines. The only problem he faced was deciding how best to civilize it. For this problem he had a clear solution: Africa could only be civilized by black missionaries from the United States. The first qualification of the Afro-American missionary, in Crummell's view, was the same one given by white churchmen, physical adaptability to the climate. The black American, wrote Crummell, "is indigenous, in blood, constitution, and adaptability [to Africa]. . . . There is a tropical fitness, which inheres in our constitution, whereby we are enabled . . . to sit down under an African sun; and soon, and with comparative ease, feel ourselves at home."[38] More important than physical ability, however, was a second qualification: God's special mission for black Americans. Crummell elaborated upon the "Theory of Providential Design," seeing Afro-Americans as an elect group who had been exposed to Christian civilization, tested by the "sorrow, pain, and deepest anguish" of slavery, and freed so that they could take civilization to Africa. In common with other evangelists, Crummell concluded that the time was right for the redemption of Africa: "The hand of God is on the black man, in all the lands of his distant sojourn, for the good of Africa. This continent is to be reclaimed for Christ. The faith of Jesus is to supersede all the abounding desolations of heathenism."[39]

Even after Crummell's return to America in 1873, his influence continued to be felt in Liberia. Samuel David Ferguson, one of his students, had taken over the Episcopal mission after Crummell's departure. Ferguson, born in South Carolina in 1842, had emigrated to Liberia with his family when he was six years old. After being educated under Crummell's direction, he became a preacher among the Grebo people of southern Liberia and also served as an agent there for the American Colonization Society. In 1885 Ferguson was chosen as the first black bishop in the Episcopal Church. Under his direction the mission made much progress, so that by 1898 a United States diplomat to Liberia could acknowledge that the Episcopalians had "done more than any denomination in lifting the heathen into civilization and Christianity."[40]

Besides the Episcopalians, another major white denomination to use black missionaries early in its African work was the Presbyterian Church. Their first notable black representative was James M. Priest, who arrived in Liberia in 1843 and continued his missionary service for the next forty years. His long service reinforced white beliefs that black missionaries could adapt better to the tropical climate. This belief was undermined and the Presbyterian effort was hampered, however, when four of the six black graduates of the denomination's Lincoln University who were sent to join Priest died soon after their arrival.[41]

By the 1860s leadership of the Presbyterian work in Liberia passed to an Americo-Liberian, Edward Wilmot Blyden, who exerted even more influence on black thought than did Alexander Crummell. Although Crummell reflected and enlarged upon the theories of African heathenism and Providential Design, Blyden developed his own ideas of black nationalism. Blyden, in fact, so alarmed his white sponsors that Presbyterian efforts in Liberia were disoriented for the remainder of the century. His increasing radicalism offers a striking contrast to Crummell's conservatism, and demonstrates the varied impact of white-sponsored black missionaries in Africa.

Blyden was born in 1832 in the Danish West Indies to a family of educated free blacks who were proud of their pure African ancestry. A white Presbyterian missionary educated him and in 1850 sent him to the United States for theological training, but he was refused admission to Rutgers College because of his race. Blyden's closest Presbyterian associates, who were members of the American Colonization Society, encouraged him to go to Liberia. Attracted by the idea of helping to shape the future of the newly independent nation, Blyden accepted an offer by the colonizationists to pay his way to Africa.

After his arrival in Liberia in 1851, Blyden made rapid progress in completing his education. He became a teacher, and in 1861 was appointed professor of Greek and Latin at the new Liberia College, where he began to build an international reputation as an authority on classical studies. That same year he and Crummell were sent to America by the Liberian government to attract more settlers. For the remainder of the century Blyden periodically held important government posts and was a leading West African intellectual. He made eight speaking tours of America during his lifetime, and with the assistance of the American Colonization Society his influence was spread among Afro-Americans.[42]

Blyden's greatest influence occurred after the 1887 publication of his book, *Christianity, Islam and the Negro Race*. He followed that with several articles in the *A.M.E. Church Review*.[43] On an 1889 visit to America, he spoke at numerous black churches, and at the South Carolina General Conference of the African Methodist Episcopal Church. His plea for the evangelization of Africa by black Americans was, according to the church newspaper, warmly welcomed by the conference. A.M.E. Bishop Benjamin Arnett stated that Blyden had an intellectual status "attained by no other Negro in the world."[44]

As his influence grew in the 1880s, however, Blyden's relations with his Presbyterian sponsors deteriorated. According to his biographers he was often tactless and difficult to work with, but conflict began due to his hatred of mulattoes. Blyden argued that their European genetic background made mulattoes less able than pure blacks to withstand the African climate, and he also felt that mulattoes were less sympathetic to Africans. He therefore insisted that the Presbyterian Church send only pure black missionaries in the future.[45]

An even greater conflict between Blyden and his church centered on the question of Islam. As he was exposed to the Islamic nations of interior West Africa, and after an 1866 visit to Egypt and Syria, Blyden became increasingly respectful of the followers of Mohammed. Although he did not himself become a convert, the white Presbyterians watched with horror as he moved away from denominational teachings toward a more universalistic deism. Blyden encouraged African Christians to secede from their white sponsors and set up their own independent churches, drawing as much from Islam as from Christianity. Finally, in 1886 Blyden resigned from the Presbyterian ministry to become a "minister of truth." The Presbyterian Mission Board was so disillusioned with their use of black missionaries that they did not appoint another one to Liberia until 1895.[46]

The next white denomination to send Afro-American missionaries to indigenous Africans in Liberia was the northern Methodist Church. Methodists had been involved in the colony since its early settlement, but their work had been restricted to the Americo-Liberian population. Mission work among Africans began in 1882 with the arrival of Amanda Smith in Liberia. Though she had come on her own, financed by individual contributors who were impressed with her evangelistic camp meetings in America, she soon affiliated herself with M.E. Bishop William Taylor. Miss Smith ministered to some Africans, but she stayed within the settled areas of Liberia and Sierra Leone. After meeting with emigrant sexism and resistance to her strict campaign against alcohol, she returned to America in 1890. In 1887 Bishop Taylor sent another Afro-American woman, Miss Susan Collins, to Angola. A graduate of the Chicago Missionary Training School, Collins was still in Angola in 1893, but no other black Methodist missionaries were sent to join her and her efforts remained isolated.[47]

After Bishop Taylor retired in 1896, Joseph Hartzell was appointed as the new Methodist Bishop of Africa. Hartzell was a white northerner who had first become interested in Africa during his 1880s work with the Freedman's Aid Society in the South. A strong advocate of racial equality, he made many contacts with black southerners and was impressed by their religious zeal. Because of the high death rates among his denomination's white missionaries in tropical Africa, and his belief in colonization, he encouraged the use of Afro-Americans.[48]

Under Hartzell's direction, ten black missionaries were sent to Liberia before the end of the century. The first of these were Mr. and Mrs. Alexander Priestly Camphor. A product of Freedmen's Aid schools in Louisiana, Alexander Camphor graduated from New Orleans University and Gammon Theological Seminary in Atlanta, then did postgraduate work at Columbia University and Union Theological Seminary in New York. In 1897 Bishop Hartzell chose him as Principal of the denomination's dilapidated Monrovia Seminary. Under the inspiration of Edward Blyden, he changed the name to the College of West Africa, reflecting a more Pan-African orientation. Within a year the Camphors built up an enrollment of 140 students, thirty of whom were indigenous Africans. By the end of the century Blyden complimented them for making the college "one of the most important agencies for the regeneration and upbuilding of our people."[49]

Camphor repeatedly expressed his pleasure at being in Liberia, and his hopefulness for the future impact of his school. He was complimentary of the climate, which was not as "roasting hot" as he had expected, and he wrote that "the reception given us by the people, both native and Liberian, was everything desired."[50] Bishop Hartzell was so pleased by Camphor's progress that he decided to send eight other black American missionaries in 1898. The first of these were Mr. and Mrs. J. A. Simpson from Atlanta. Simpson had graduated with excellent recommendations from Gammon Seminary. He and his wife were sent to Greenville in southern Liberia, and served there until they had to return to America in 1908 for health reasons.[51]

The remaining missionaries were attracted through the influence of Joseph C. Sherrill, a black Methodist minister in Little Rock, Arkansas. In 1898 he and his wife volunteered to go to Liberia, and began choosing others to recommend to Hartzell. Sherrill did a thorough job of arousing missionary sentiment among black Methodists in Arkansas, and he soon had more volunteers than he could accept. All of the final choices were college graduates, and one of them, F. M. Allen, was a printer.[52] By 1899 the new group of missionaries was established in Liberia, and Allen had established a newspaper called *New Africa*. According to Camphor, who served as an editor, "The paper is enthusiastically received by all the people. It is becoming a very helpful factor in our educational and religious work."[53] After he had been in Liberia for two years, Allen wrote to the Methodist Mission Board that he had ten African boys in training as printers. He showed evidence of his satisfaction with the mission work in Africa when he wrote, "Under the administration of Bro. Sherrill whom we all love and understand, the work has moved on smoothly. We have enjoyed the past year the good-will and coperation [*sic*] of all the workers. . . . The longer I stay the better I like the work; and the better I like it, the more I am able to do."[54]

The Methodist mission, although in practical terms only a few years old, closed out the century in good form. With a school, a newspaper, and ten active black missionaries, the Methodists must be reckoned one of the most influential denominations in Liberia at the turn of the century. Sherrill retained the loyalty of his volunteers and made a good impression on the Africans as well. Alexander Camphor summed up the situation when he reported in 1899 that "every interest of the Church is taking on new life" in Liberia.[55] By the end of the century the Methodist mission represented one of the most successful white-sponsored black missions in Liberia.

While the major white American denominations generally deferred mission work in the British colony of Sierra Leone to the British branches of their churches, this trend did not apply to small distinctively American sects like the United Brethren in Christ. They began missions in Africa in 1855, working closely with the American Missionary Association.[56] In 1880 the United Brethren sent two black American missionaries, Mrs. and Mrs. Kelley M. Kemp, to Sierra Leone. Mr. Kemp was a recent seminary graduate from Pennsylvania's Lincoln University, and was highly recommended by the faculty. The Kemps did effective mission work on Sherbro Island until 1885, when both of them died of "fever."[57]

The most famous black missionaries to Sierra Leone who were sent by the United Brethren were Mr. and Mrs. Joseph Gomer. Because the church was having difficulty attracting white missionaries, in 1870 they accepted the application of the Gomers. These missionaries had good relations with the white church leaders and with the Africans.[58] One of the United Brethren's white missionaries in Sierra Leone felt that the Africans liked having a missionary of their own color. He wrote that Gomer "was very earnest, tactful and energetic. He settled many differences among the people."[59] Besides developing a reputation in the church as a skilled arbitrator of disputes among the Africans, Gomer was also noted as being "industrious" and "a man of intellectual strength and power."[60]

The main reason the Gomers were so highly esteemed by the church was that they obtained more converts than any other U.B. missionaries. Gomer himself, perhaps out of modesty, attributed the improved record of conversions to a smallpox epidemic which caused the Africans to become more receptive to Christianity. The local chieftain also welcomed the mission in order to obtain a school for his people. Nevertheless, Gomer seems to have established a remarkable rapport with the Mendi people in Sierra Leone, as evidenced by the testimony of another Afro-American missionary, who wrote that Gomer had few equals in his "fatherly sympathy and love for the poor heathen" and was "the grandest black missionary" in West Africa.[61] The United Brethren newspaper noted that Gomer had so fully "ingratiated himself into the affections of the [African] people as to be able to exert a wonderful and highly salutary influence over them. . . . [He] fully identifies himself with all their interests, civil, social, and financial. . . . The people believe in him, and the chiefs are often greatly influenced by his counsels."[62] His success prompted Gomer to remark in 1881 that the future of his mission "never looked more hopeful." He devoted the remainder of his life to the mission and died of apoplexy in Sierra Leone in 1892. Mrs. Gomer, who was equally devoted to the work, remained at the mission for two years after her husband's death. She returned to America reluctantly, and sorely missed her African home.[63]

James A. Evans was another U.B. missionary who went to Sierra Leone in 1870, but he returned three years later to serve as a missionary to the ex-slaves in Virginia. While there he met and married Rachel Allen. In 1880 they both decided to volunteer as missionaries to Sierra Leone, and they remained there for the rest of their lives, despite their bad health in the tropical climate. Evans became noted for making long journeys into the interior of Sierra Leone, and he was able to operate among the Africans without the large caravans which white missionaries usually required. He lost none of his missionary zeal, and at the time of his death in 1899 he was the acting Superintendent of the entire United Brethren mission in Sierra Leone.[64]

Even though they were not as famous as Crummell or Blyden, the Methodist and United Brethren Afro-Americans in West Africa do represent the successful long-term missionary cooperation which many black missionaries contributed to white church missions. In contrast to Blyden's conflicts, their relations with the white church leaders were mutually respectful and pacific. They were deeply committed to evangelization, and they seemed grateful that whites would support them financially in their personal endeavors for Africa.

The area around Liberia and Sierra Leone had been the traditional focus for American missions, but by the mid–nineteenth century U.S. churches had begin to expand into other areas of Africa. This was especially true of the Baptists, who periodically used black personnel in their missions. Because black missionaries would later play such prominent roles in arousing African interest among Afro-American Baptists, their initial involvement with white churches tells us much about the origins of the black American missionary movement.

Southern white Baptists were the first organization to use black missionaries in Nigeria. Having broken away from their northern brethren over the question of slavery, the Southern Baptist Convention established its separate station in southern Nigeria in 1850. During a successful first decade its missionaries became famous in religious circles, but after 1860 a series of local wars in Yorubaland hampered evangelical efforts. Missionary work was practically forgotten by southerners during their own crisis in the American Civil War, and it was not until 1875 that the church felt recovered enough to send reinforcements to its Yoruba mission. In that year

William W. Colley, a Virginia mulatto, volunteered as a missionary. Although born as a slave in 1840, Colley was educated at the Richmond Theological Seminary during Reconstruction. His education and interest in Africa caused the white church leaders to send him to their Nigerian mission stations in Lagos and Abeokuta. During his first years there his white superintendent (a necessary propriety for southern Baptists) was in England much of the time recuperating from illnesses, so Colley was left in defacto control. In this situation he reported that he was "much pleased and encouraged with the work." Nevertheless, Colley gradually became dissatisfied with his lower salary and other forms of racial discrimination by the white missionary.[65] In 1879 he decided to return to America, having become more discouraged because of his own bad health, and because continuing warfare in Yorubaland made mission work difficult there. He complained that among Africans "wives are slow to leave their husbands, servants their masters, and people their chiefs" in order to accept Christianity. But during a stop in Liberia on his return trip to America, Colley was reinspired. He reported the baptism of a group of indigenous Africans who, he hoped, would "form a native church of Baptists at a large interior town" in Liberia.[66] The experience no doubt had much to do with Colley's later leadership in independent black Baptist mission work in Liberia.

The other Afro-American Baptist who had a significant part in arousing black interest in African missions was Thomas L. Johnson. Born a slave in Virginia in 1836, after the Civil War he moved to Chicago and became a Baptist preacher. By the mid-1870s Johnson developed such a strong desire to become a missionary in Africa that he persuaded an agent of the British Young Men's Christian Association to take him to England to receive missionary training. After a year of training by the Y.M.C.A., Johnson left England in 1878 for the Cameroons. He and his wife were sponsored by the Baptist Missionary Society of Great Britain to work among the unconverted Bakwalli Kpé people. However, the Johnsons did not do much effective missionizing because they were ill much of the nine months that they were in the interior. In July, 1879, Mrs. Johnson died of malaria, and her husband returned to England five months later in such a poor state of health that doctors advised him not to go back to Africa. After his return to the United States in 1880, Johnson lived the remainder of his life in Chicago. He tried to be appointed as U.S. diplomat to Liberia nine years later, but was not successful.[67]

Even though he could not go back to Africa himself, Thomas Johnson retained his strong feelings about Africa's need for missions. He lamented the fact that he was unable to accomplish his goals, and he poured forth prodigious energy to attract other mission volunteers. Since he was working independently of white churches, Johnson's subsequent effort to increase mission interest is best reserved for a later chapter on Afro-American Baptists. However, the missionary volunteers that Johnson attracted were supported in Africa by the white American Baptist Missionary Union—an indication of the close association of mission sentiment between black and white churches.

Johnson realized that black Baptists did not have enough financial resources to support a large group of missionaries. On the other hand, the white church had money but needed more personnel for its Congo mission. Thus was born a notable example of interracial partnership between white and black churches in the late nineteenth century. By this means Johnson was able to claim the prestige of heading an active missionary effort in Africa without having to maintain it financially.[68]

The American Baptist Congo mission was founded in 1881 when overextended English Baptists offered to turn over their three-year-old "Livingstone Inland Mission" to their American brethren. Despite heavy rates of sickness and death among the missionaries, by 1894 the American mission had grown to ten stations, forty-six missionaries, and over 1,200 converts. Among these missionaries, fourteen were black. Supported by white Baptists but coordinated by Thomas Johnson, these Afro-Americans had few problems with the dual organizational arrangement.[69]

The first black missionary in the Congo, Theophilus E. Samuel Scholes, was sent by English Baptists in 1882 to join the American mission. Scholes was from Jamaica, but he studied medicine in England, and became a medical missionary. It was his belief that missionaries should be trained in practical subjects to help Africans. After several years in the Congo, he furloughed in Wales, where he attended a mission training institute which emphasized practical skills. In 1894 he went to Nigeria to head a school which was sponsored by the Welsh institute.[70] While he was in the Congo, Scholes kept in close touch with Johnson by mail. Even though they had never met in person, the two men grew to depend on each other for moral support in their work. For example, in 1887 Johnson reported that Scholes had "an inexpressible delight in his work of holding forth the word of life to that [Kongo] people, who possess

many noble qualities that have not been entirely obliterated by
the long darkness that has enveloped them, nor the debasing superstitions and heathenism to which they have been subjected for centuries." Using this rather disparaging report as an opportunity to
increase missionary interest among black Baptists, Johnson asked
his ministers: "Are *we*, the sons and daughter of Africa, doing *all*
we can to evangelize and lift up her millions to the high plane of a
Christian civilization?"[71]

The second black missionary in the Congo was John E. Ricketts,
who worked in the American Baptist Mission from 1887 to 1893.
During the last three years of his service he was joined in the Congo
by his wife. Mr. and Mrs. Ricketts were respected by Africans,
as evidenced by an offer which they received to serve in the independent United Native African Church in Nigeria. After they became
missionaries there, the Ricketts led the Nigerians to unite with the
independent black American denomination, the National Baptist
Convention.[72] Thus, they were another example of black missionaries
who originally went to Africa as part of a white mission, but who
later exerted influence on the independent Afro-American church
mission movement.

Some of the most far-flung African missions in which black
American missionaries worked were sponsored by the American
Board of Commissioners for Foreign Missions. The A.B.C.F.M.,
or American Board, was a Congregational mission society centered
in Boston. It was one of the major American missionary agencies
of the nineteenth century, and had ministered to Hawaiians, American Indians, and Chinese. By the late 1870s the Board had decided
to open operations in the highlands of interior Angola. The area
was healthful and relatively accessible, but the Ovimbundu chiefdoms
there had been unreached by previous mission operations.[73]

The first three missionaries sent by the American Board to Angola
in 1880 were an Englishman, a white American, and an Afro-
American named Samuel T. Miller. A graduate of Hampton Institute,
Miller was a teacher and a local Baptist church leader in his native
Virginia. The English missionary, upon meeting the very dark-
skinned man, remarked to the mission board that Miller seemed
simple-minded and dependent. Miller's letters, however, reveal him
to have been an articulate and well-educated person.[74]

Once they arrived in interior Angola, away from Portugese colonial
control, Miller was anything but dependent. He was impressed with
the Ovimbundu people and quickly settled into an easy comfortable-

ness with the Africans that left the white missionaries isolated. Because he learned the language faster than the whites, he was able to act more authoritatively among the Africans. Within a few years conflicts emerged between Miller and the whites. The Hampton graduate caused resentment by rejecting a white-authored grammar book as too full of errors, and writing a text himself. He also insisted that no mission station be established without the invitation of the local chief, while the whites concentrated on gaining permission from the Portuguese officials.[75]

Even though he loved his work with the Africans, in 1884 Miller returned to America because of his conflicts with his white co-workers. A year after his return to his teaching position in Virginia, he was still concerned about the progress of the Angola mission. He wrote that he had received letters from some of his Ovimbundu students, asking why he did not return to Africa. Miller was complimentary of their writing ability and Christian sentiments and was anxious to keep in touch with them. But he never returned to Africa because the Board would not allow him his own separate station.[76]

Despite these conflicts, the Board decided to accept the application for Africa work by two other black Americans, Benjamin F. and Henrietta Ousley. Both were natives of Mississippi and graduates of Fisk University, and Benjamin attended the Oberlin College Theology school to prepare himself as a missionary. In 1884 the board sent them to a newly established mission at Inhambane, on the southeast coast of Africa in Portuguese Mozambique. Reverend Ousley immediately began studying the local language, Sheetswa, in order to write a translation of the Bible.[77]

The Ousleys soon ran into trouble with Portuguese colonial officials, and with white missionaries as well. Most of the missionary disagreements centered on administrative details and financial methods, but some of the objections to the Ousleys were put in racist terms. When Ousley appealed to the Board for justice, the officials admitted that prejudice by white missionaries was a factor in the disagreement, but their solution to the problem was to appoint no more black missionaries! By 1892 the Inhambane mission was falling apart. Ousley's disgust with the situation in the mission, plus his poor health, caused him and his wife to resign.[78] Thus another attempt to use black American missionaries failed because of racial conflicts in the New England–based American Board.

The fourth black missionary sent to Africa by the American Board was Miss Nancy Jones. A native of Memphis, Tennessee, she was a friend of Henrietta Bailey Ousley while they were both students at Fisk. After joining the mission at Inhambane in 1888, she often reported her pleasure at being in Africa, and she worked well with the Ousleys. In 1893, however, conditions changed radically for her. Following the departure of the Ousleys, whom she greatly missed, Jones was transferred to a new mission in eastern Rhodesia, near a Boer-English settlement. Jones was the only black person on the mission staff, and the white influence was overwhelming. She wrote to the Board that she was "unable to work in harmony with the mission," because some of her white co-workers were "filled with prejudice." She obviously was not using the charge of racism as an excuse to leave Africa, because she wrote, "I don't like leaving the [African] people here. They have a deep place in my heart." Furthermore, she offered to continue serving as a missionary in a station that was too unhealthy for whites. But after finding no hope of change from the Board, she resigned and returned to America in 1897.[79]

By the end of the century all black American missionaries sponsored by the American Board had resigned. It is noteworthy that there were more black resignations because of racism by these New England Congregationalists than in the case of any other white missionary agency. Because of this factor, the American Board missionaries probably had less influence on black thought about Africa than any other group of missionaries.

In contrast to the Congregationalists, the white southern Presbyterians had remarkably good success with their Afro-American missionaries. Like other Protestant denominations, the Presbyterian Church had split because of the Civil War. After the war the southern Presbyterians refused to relinquish local control to their black congregations, and as a result the number of black Presbyterians declined sharply, from 14,000 in 1861 to only 1,300 by 1892. Still, southern Presbyterian leaders believed that they should exert a paternalistic influence over blacks, in order to keep out "subversive" northern influences. Thus, in 1877 they established Stillman College in Alabama, to educate black preachers and missionaries.[80]

This attempt to control the black masses through their influence on an educated black elite was not the only reason that the southern Presbyterians supported black missionaries. Paternalistic whites sometimes encouraged restless blacks to emigrate to Africa as a way of depriving the masses of potential protest leaders. In addition, Alabama Senator John T. Morgan and other influential whites encouraged the Presbyterians to begin a mission as a base for a black American colony. They believed that such a colony, in Belgian King Leopold's "Congo Free State," would provide markets for expanding American commerce.[81] Interdenominational rivalry to stake claims on newly "opened" Africa finally prompted Presbyterian concern, but no action would likely have taken place as soon as it did if it had not been for the pressure put on the mission board by William Henry Sheppard.

Sheppard is a prime example of the influence of an individual Afro-American on a white church's mission efforts. A native of rural Virginia, Sheppard had attended Hampton Institute before resolving to become a missionary and going to Stillman College. After his ordination he began preaching in Montgomery, Alabama, and later in Atlanta, Georgia. He did not adapt well to the strict segregation of the urban South, and in 1887 he petitioned the mission board to send him to Africa. The Presbyterian leaders refused to allow a black man to head one of their missions, so they delayed Sheppard's request until a white missionary could be found.

It was difficult to find a white volunteer to devote himself to Africa, and had Sheppard not kept pressuring the mission board, the effort probably would have been abandoned. But in 1890 Samuel Norvell Lapsley, from a prominent Alabama family of former slave-owners, volunteered. His family had strongly supported Presbyterian missions in China and Brazil, and he had decided on a missionary career during seminary. He felt comfortable with the idea of working with blacks, and he got along well with Sheppard. Lapsley absorbed a particular interest in the Congo from his father's law partner, who was none other than Senator Morgan. Therefore, the black-white team was soon assigned to establish the American Presbyterian Congo Mission.[82]

Sheppard and Lapsley arrived in the Congo in 1890, but it was a year before they established their mission. The mission board directed them to choose a site in the interior, well removed from other missions, in a densely populated area. The missionaries' choice, at Luebo in the Kasai Valley of southern Congo, met all these conditions. Since Luebo was nine hundred miles in the interior, and there were fewer than a thousand westerners in the whole Congo, Sheppard and Lapsley were almost isolated from outside contact.[83]

Upon leaving America Sheppard expressed some reluctance "to leave home, friends and native land and seek a home among strangers."[84] Yet his attachment to America was soon overcome, for Shepphard wrote back to the Presbyterian *Missionary* soon after arriving in the Congo, "I am certainly happy in the country of my forefathers."[85] After a year he reported, "We have on the whole been treated very kindly by all the [African] people. We have received many nice and useful presents from different kings. . . . I always wanted to live in Africa, I felt that I would be happy, and so I am."[86]

Evidently Sheppard was well liked by the Africans. Lapsley wrote that his co-worker was a "great favorite" and that the Congolese referred to him as "'Shoppit Monine,' the great Sheppard."[87] In numerous photographs of the Presbyterian Congo mission, Sheppard is shown in close contact with the Africans, and usually in the midst of great activity.[88]

Lapsley and Sheppard worked well as a team. Sheppard, with a gift for learning the African languages, skill as a hunter, and physical strength, was the primary contact with the Africans and directed the practical needs of the mission. Lapsley, on the other hand, managed the finances and dealt with the white colonial officials. Racial proscriptions broke down, and they worked together as equals. Together they toured the Kasai, introducing themselves, preaching, teaching, providing medical aid, and ransoming slaves. These ex-slaves became the first mission converts. Other Africans came to the mission as a refuge from local wars, or to get medical care.[89]

The biggest personal concern of the two missionaries was staying healthy. Sheppard ultimately suffered twenty-two bouts of the "African fever" (either yellow fever or malaria), but his strength helped him survive. The weaker Lapsley, however, could not adapt to the tropical climate and finally succumbed in March, 1892. Sheppard keenly felt the death of his friend, since he was now entirely alone among the Africans.[90] Whether they liked it or not, the white southern Presbyterians were left in 1892 with a black man heading their missionary effort in Africa.

Alone, Sheppard continued the mission work. The Bakete, the first group with which the missionaries had had contact, were friendly and helpful, but they were satisfied with their own religion and saw no reason to switch to an alien one. Therefore, Sheppard decided to concentrate on the Bakuba, even though no foreigner had ever visited their kingdom. Bakubaland was a highly organized state with a law forbidding any of its people to direct outsiders into its territory. By this means the Bakuba had resisted European penetration.[91]

Even though Sheppard learned the language and was treated considerately by the border town chief, he could not gain directions for entering the capital. By an ingenious plan, however, Sheppard gained access into the interior of Bakubaland. He persuaded the chief to allow his guide to go to the next town to purchase relatively scarce eggs. The guide would mark the trail and secretly guide Sheppard on to the next town. By repeating this process, Sheppard was able to move from town to town toward the Bakuba capital. In the effort to exhaust local supplies of eggs, Sheppard performed wonders at egg-eating, downing thirty at one meal. His ability to get so far into the forbidden land and his fluency in the language, as well as his reputation for eating eggs, caused the Bakuba king to have Sheppard brought into the capital. Sheppard so impressed the king that he was welcomed as the reincarnation of an ancestor.[92]

Though the Bakuba liked Sheppard, his conversion efforts were fruitless. The Bakuba were not interested in abandoning their religion for another. After four months in Bakubaland the missionary returned to Luebo, where his mission grew by attracting social outcasts and ransoming more slaves. But the large-scale conversions of which he dreamed eluded Sheppard. Moreover, the loneliness of being the only American in his vicinity began to affect him, so he decided to visit the United States. After Sheppard left in 1893, three white couples were persuaded to go to the Presbyterian Congo mission, but two of the missionaries soon died and three more left because of illness, so that by 1896 only one white missionary was left. The Church had difficulty inspiring white missionaries to go to Africa, and in keeping those who did go. Combined with the expense and the relative lack of converts, the deaths of so many missionaries prompted Presbyterian leaders to consider ending their Congo mission.[93]

Probably because he realized the danger of his mission being abolished, Sheppard decided to use his 1893 visit to America as a recruiting drive for more black missionaries. At a time when their white missionaries were dying or leaving, the southern Presbyterians could scarcely refuse black volunteers.

With as much energy as if he were fighting for his life, Sheppard traveled through the South speaking about his Congo mission. Evidently he was successful in arousing interest. Sheppard's fame on arriving in America was increased by his having been made a Fellow in the Royal Geographical Society, an English tribute to his explorations into Bakubaland.[94] The *Missionary Review of the World* reported that he spoke "to crowded houses, capturing all by his eloquence, fund of humor, and histrionic qualities."[95] A Presbyterian pamphlet gave a similar account: "Dr. Sheppard told the story of his experience in numerous churches and before church assemblies so vividly and so appealingly that the whole Church took the Congo Mission to its heart."[96]

Undoubtedly the most important aspect of Sheppard's speeches was the impact upon southern blacks. The Presbyterian mission journal reported the remarkable "interest awakened" among blacks by Sheppard, and quoted a white Virginia church official:

> The people of his own race listened with deepest interest to his accounts of Africa, and the sad condition of her millions of people. A strong desire was kindled in their hearts to do something to aid in the great work of their redemption. They formed a society, which they called "The Missionary Society" . . . They are Baptists, but knowing no Baptist missionary society on the Congo, or in all Africa, they preferred for their first aid to be given to Mr. Sheppard in his work.[97]

It is significant that, while there was a substantial number of white Baptist missionaries in the Congo, the blacks preferred to contribute to the cause of a black missionary they had met personally.

Sheppard had written to the *Indianapolis Freeman*, one of the most influential black newspapers in the nation, about "my central African home," saying, "We have found the natives kind and obliging with a few exceptions."[98] Even Sheppard's parents, who were proud of their son for "carrying light into the dark places of the earth," publicized his reports from Africa.[99] In November 1893, he gave a speech to the student body of Hampton Institute which was printed in the *Southern Workman*. Much of the speech was humorous, with stories of Sheppard's prodigious egg-eating exploits and of the Africans' great interest in dogfights.[100]

Many Afro-Americans showed interest in hearing Sheppard's speeches and contributed money for his support, but stronger evidence of his influence was the number of black people who volunteered to join his Congo mission. The first person to commit herself was a twenty-six-year-old Alabamian, Lucy Gantt. She was a graduate of Talladega College, an American Missionary Association school, and had toured England with the Fisk Jubilee Singers. She then became a teacher and met Sheppard while he was a student at Stillman College. They corresponded while he was in Africa and, after she was inspired to become a missionary, Sheppard asked her to marry him. Their wedding in early 1894 was described as the "social event of the season among colored circles," a further indication of Sheppard's status among Afro-Americans.[101]

Three other missionary volunteers joined Sheppard, including a newly ordained Stillman graduate, Henry P. Hawkins, and two more Talladega graduates, Lillian Thomas and Maria Fearing. Of these,

Miss Fearing was most notable because of her extraordinary interest in Africa. She had been born a slave in 1838, and after managing to get an education volunteered for mission work at the age of fifty-six. Because of her age the Presbyterian mission officials refused to support her, whereupon she sold her house and paid her own way to the Congo.[102]

This group of four new missionaries accompanied Sheppard to Luebo in 1894. A year later they were joined by another black missionary, Joseph E. Phipps from Chicago's Dwight L. Moody Bible Institute. Although he resided in Virginia, Phipps had been born and raised in St. Kitts, West Indies, and claimed that his grandfather was Congolese. Thus, his feeling of duty to the land of his ancestors was even more specific than the usual black identity with Africa. The Presbyterian mission committee reported, "He impressed the Committee as a man of humble, earnest, and simple piety, and one who will probably be fitted to reach his own people more readily and effectually than even one of our Southern born and educated colored people."[103] Such a statement demonstrates that the white church leaders saw an advantage in black American identity with Africans. However, the Presbyterian mission board still wished to have white missionaries, and they began to turn down applications by other Afro-Americans for assignment in the Congo.[104]

Sheppard and his fellow black missionaries led the Luebo mission until 1897, when the Presbyterian leaders prevailed upon two white missionaries to join them. William M. Morrison, who took over the leadership at Luebo, seemed unprejudiced toward his black co-workers, and he aided race relations by his approach to missionary work. He advised his mission to treat the Africans "as kindly and courteously as white people," and explained, "We are their servants and not their masters. Under their black skins they have feelings and sensibilities similar to ours, which ought to be respected. If we laugh at their customs, appearance, or fetishes, we destroy their confidence in us and repel them."[105] Such an attitude could not fail to impress the black missionaries.

Another reason for the good race relations at the Luebo mission was the respect shown to the blacks. During an era when few whites acknowledged any titles of respect to black people, the Presbyterian officials consistently referred to their black missionaries as Reverend," "Mr.," "Mrs.," or "Miss." The black personnel received pay equal to that of white missionaries, and they had an influential voice in mission affairs.[106]

But probably the major reason for good relations in the integrated

mission was the attitude of the black missionaries. Sheppard grace-
fully transferred his leadership role to Morrison, and he worked
hard to cultivate good feelings with the whites. He wrote to a white
Presbyterian, "I am proud of our Southern Church, which is doing
so much for the evangelization of the negro in America and Africa.
I owe all that I am, or ever expect to be, to that Church. When you
turn your back upon us, to whom shall we go? No, stand by us, and
we will prove your trust!"[107] Sheppard and his colleagues might be
open to charges of "Uncle-Tom-ism," but as missionaries entirely
dependent on white church support they had little choice but
accomodation if they wished to continue their work. The Americans
of both races recognized that they had more in common with each
other than with either the Belgians or the Congolese. Consequently
the status of the black missionaries was probably far better than
it would have been among whites in the United States.[108]

The mission work at Luebo continued to go well. In 1896 Sheppard
reported, "We are happy and feel at home; [we] seldom speak of
returning to America." He said that he felt more satisfied with his
work in Africa than he would have anywhere else, and he hoped to
be able to stay many more years in the Congo. By 1898 Sheppard
had established a new branch mission on the Bakuba frontier, and
two years later the two mission stations had a total of three hundred
and fifty converts. Even though Lucy Sheppard's first two children
died in infancy, she continued to serve as a teacher and nurse at
the mission. However, with the birth of a third child, and after almost
succumbing to disease herself, Mrs. Sheppard decided in 1898 to
take the child back to America to be cared for by relatives.[109]

The new century brought personal unhappiness for Sheppard. As
colonial control expanded over the Kasai year by year, the black
missionaries had less independence of action. Sheppard was increasingly critical of the atrocities perpetrated on the Congolese
by the concessionaire Kasai Company, so much so that an international scandal broke out and he was brought to trial for libel in
1909. Although Sheppard was acquitted, strained relations with the
colonial government continued. He cultivated good relations with
the white missionaries, but one suspects that Sheppard preferred
exercising his own authority independent of close supervision. His
happiest letters were written between 1894 and 1897, when he headed
a predominantly black mission. The establishment of his own branch
mission soon after Morrison's arrival suggests Sheppard's independence more than it does racial conflict. In many ways, Morrison
and Sheppard were similar personalities, and they got along well

together. But the discouraging loss of his independent black world in the Kasai, plus the strain of the trial, caused Sheppard to retire in 1910. He returned to America with a trunkful of photographs and artifacts made by his beloved Bakuba.[110]

William Henry Sheppard was not a successful missionary in terms of the number of converts he won into the Presbyterian Church. Perhaps he respected Africans too much to interfere grossly in their way of life. Certainly he condemned aspects of their culture, but never to the extent that was typical of most nineteenth-century missionaries. Sheppard rejected the view that soul-saving excluded earthly considerations, and he worked hard to aid those Congolese in material ways. Whether giving medical aid, ransoming slaves, or protesting colonial exploitation, Sheppard tried to improve African standards of living. While he did not express a Pan-African ideology, he did feel a closeness to the Kasai peoples that was felt by few white Americans. Sheppard, because of his influence on black Americans and his efforts on behalf of Africans, deserves to be ranked among the most important of early Afro-American missionaries.

White churches had considerable influence on black American interest in African missions. Not only did the general European-American mission sentiment of the nineteenth century help to inspire religious involvement in Africa, but black missionaries sponsored by white churches did much to spread information on the continent among Afro-Americans.

White churches wanted to establish missions in Africa primarily because they saw such ventures as part of a world-wide effort to spread Christianity and their own denominations. But other factors directed mission sentiment particularly toward the "dark continent." Recent exploration had opened Western eyes to the previously unknown interior, and much publicity was generated as a result. In addition, American attention was attracted to prospects for black colonization, and later to outlets for expanding American markets. Denominational expansion, however, remained the primary motive.

Given the interest of white missionary societies in Africa, the question they faced was how best to accomplish the evangelical work there. Africa's supposed climatic unsuitability for whites led to the use of Afro-Americans as missionaries. Though some white churches were attracted to black missionaries as part of their colonization interests, or felt that black Americans could form a sense of identity with Africans, others utilized blacks only when they could not find enough white volunteers. The generally lower costs involved in supporting a black person, plus reluctance to sacrifice more white lives to an inhospitable tropical climate, meant that some white churches continued to use black missionaries into the twentieth century.

Despite the fact that many of the Afro-American missionaries worked long and loyally for their white sponsors, most of the sponsoring churches had only mixed results with their black representatives. About 40 percent of the black missionaries had fairly good relations with their churches and probably did average longer periods in Africa than white missionaries. But a majority of the Afro-Americans lasted only a few years. Some died of tropical diseases, and most others left the field for health reasons. A significant minority broke with their sponsors over personal and policy matters. Independent-minded missionaries like Edward Blyden, for example, alienated Presbyterian leaders. Racial conflicts between its white and black missionaries abounded within the northern-based American Board of Commissioners for Foreign Missions.

Even though they worked for white churches, most of the black missionaries directed their publicity and influence primarily to black audiences in America. They did not limit themselves to one denomination, and their influence on Afro-Americans was therefore more widespread. Many of the missionaries, for example William Sheppard and Thomas Johnson, became personally inspired to go to Africa and only then turned to a white church as a means of financing their plans. Sheppard and Johnson in particular prove that mission sentiment was not a one-way street from white to black, because they had a significant impact on increasing interest in Africa among whites.

Still, the major influence of white-sponsored black missionaries was upon Afro-Americans. Some of them, like Edward Blyden and Alexander Crummell, reached a status beyond religious reputation that established them as race leaders generally. Others, like William Colley and Thomas Johnson, were major instigators of mission organizations among independent black denominations. Even when they were not formally connected with a black church, missionaries like William Sheppard and Alexander Camphor worked to spread a more complete understanding of Africa to the black churches.

It was the witness of these individuals, along with white encouragement, that gave rise to African mission sentiment in the independent black churches. The mission ideology heavily influenced black American attitudes toward Africa, and contributed to a full-fledged Afro-American mission movement by the end of the century.

2

The Rise of the African Mission Movement in the Independent Black Churches

To understand the mission movement, the influence of the independent black-led churches must be examined. Although nearly every scholar who has written black history has noted the importance of the church as a social institution among black people, the Afro-American churches have remained a relatively ignored aspect of American social history.[1] Afro-American religion emerged as an interaction between traditional African religions and the Christianity of European Americans. According to the black sociologist, W. E. B. Du Bois, religion was "the most characteristic expression of African character" retained by black Americans.[2] African-style shamen transformed their traditional functions into acceptable ones on the slave plantations, becoming preachers, judges, doctors, and story-tellers. These transformations had to take place within the restricted limits allowed by the slave system, and increasing contacts with the religion of the dominant white society began to change African styles of worship. In addition, whites often wanted to convert the slaves to Christianity, not only because of their belief that their religion was superior, but also because of their fears that "pagan" African religions were subversive. Conversion to Christianity would, they hoped, be a means of keeping slaves pacified.

But the slaves were not powerless. Whites tried to mold blacks into a form suitable for enslavement, but blacks adopted social facets that best fitted their familiar ways within the constraints of the slave system. Religion was no exception, and Christianity suited the slaves well. Its pacifistic inclination to accept the status quo as

31

a temporary preparation for greater joys in the afterlife, combined with its emphasis on the dignity of the poor and downtrodden who would be rewarded in heaven for their earthly suffering, made Christianity appealing to the slaves. Conversion was an instrument of the oppressive class system, but it also served the blacks as protection against dehumanization. Blacks identified with the enslaved Hebrews of ancient times and with the suffering of Jesus. They were able to develop a pride in their own spiritual quality and a sense of autonomy and self-respect. This self-image not only protected them from psychological despair, but gave them the sense that they were God's new chosen people, selected for some great destiny.[3]

The earliest black Christian churches independent of white control were formed among free blacks in the North, who because they were a smaller minority had more quickly absorbed the white religion. But the vast majority of the black population in the United States was located in the slave regions of the South. Because black-led institutions were usually prohibited from operating in the South, an "invisible institution" of slaves developed to fill the religious needs of those in bondage. At the end of the Civil War, however, emancipation allowed the coming of the independent black church organizations from the North. These formal institutions merged with southern black congregations, and the "invisible institution" became the backbone of the formalized black churches.[4]

The growth of independent black churches after the Civil War was astounding. In 1860 the proportion of blacks who were members of churches was 11 percent, less than half the rate for the white population. By 1916 the black membership had grown to 43 percent, which was larger than the white rate.[5] Reflecting the denominational preferences of southern whites, the Baptists and Methodists grew fastest, with smaller numbers of Presbyterians, Roman Catholics, and Episcopalians. By 1894 the three largest Afro-American religious bodies were the National Baptist Convention with 1,349,189 members, the African Methodist Episcopal (A.M.E.) Church with 452,725 members, and the African Methodist Episcopal Zion (A.M.E.Z.) Church with 349,788 members.[6] Even this high enrolled membership rate, totaling over two million out of a black population of about seven and a half million by 1890, does not suggest the pervasiveness of the church in black society, for besides enrolled members there were large numbers of children and adults who unofficially took part in many of the activities of the church.[7]

Writing in 1903, Du Bois pointed out that the black church was the vital social center of a black community:

> Various organizations meet here—the church proper, the Sunday school, two or three insurance societies, women's societies, secret societies, and mass meetings of various kinds. Entertainments, suppers, and lectures are held beside the five or six regular weekly religious services. Considerable sums of money are collected and expended here, employment is found for the idle, strangers are introduced, news is disseminated and charity distributed. At the same time this social, intellectual, and economic center is a religious centre of great power.[8]

The black church was an even more important social center than white churches of that era, because whites had a whole range of socioeconomic and political institutions which they controlled. After the end of Reconstruction, and with the steady removal of blacks from political positions of power, the church remained the one significant institution controlled by blacks.[9]

During the era of segregation, when other types of social centers were open only to whites, a black person was almost forced into the church if she or he wanted social contacts. Since most black communities could not afford to support a newspaper, the church also served as the mechanism for distributing news.[10] Oral presentation was an important source of news in a population that was only 20 percent literate in 1870. That black literacy increased to over 55 percent by 1900 (while school enrollment rates for blacks were always below 30 percent) also suggests that the black church had an important educational role.[11] Sunday schools often operated to teach blacks to read, and church sermons encouraged members to learn to read the Bible for themselves.[12]

The major influence of black churches was through the clergymen. In the late nineteenth century, one of the few outlets for leadership open to blacks was through the ministry. After 1877 the influence of black political officials on the lives of most Afro-Americans was insignificant, in contrast to the steadily increasing authority of black clergymen. The ministers were the largest, best-trained, and most articulate professional class of Afro-Americans; they molded attitudes in the thought of the black masses more than any other group.[13]

Sociological theorists have suggested that interpersonal contact is more effective than written communication in influencing people's attitudes. That is, media exert influence by what they say; people exert control not only by what they say but by a host of other means, drawing on their prestige and support from others.[14] The black clergyman is a perfect example of this type of influence, because interpersonal contact was his main activity. He also exercised power over the attitudes and behavior of his followers through the threat of expulsion from the church, a threat not to be taken lightly when the church was the major community center.[15] Thus, somewhat like the church-centered society of colonial New England, attitudes of late-nineteenth-century black Americans were largely influenced by what was said and done in their churches.

The commitment of the black church to Africa was foreshadowed early in the century by the evangelism of several black leaders. The first Afro-American to lead a mission effort was Paul Cuffe, a wealthy Massachusetts sea captain. A Quaker, Cuffe had engaged in activities to improve the welfare of black people. He was also interested in back-to-Africa schemes, and in 1811 he visited Sierra Leone in one of his own ships, to investigate the possibilities of colonization. Four years later he personally organized and financed the emigration of thirty-eight black Americans to Sierra Leone. Cuffe sponsored this emigration not only for black American independence, but also as a means of evangelizing Africa. In fact, he seemed more interested in the "redemption of the Dark Continent" than in emancipation of slaves in the United States.[16]

Cuffe's efforts showed white colonizationists, who sometimes had very different motives, that successful emigration could be carried out. In 1816 the American Colonization Society was founded, and individual black clergymen decided to use the white organization as a means of financing their evangelical efforts. Lott Cary, a Baptist from Virginia who had bought his freedom, was the first of these clergymen to volunteer as a missionary. Cary helped to establish an African Missionary Society among black people in Richmond, and convinced the Colonization Society and the white Baptists to contribute toward his support. In 1820 he and another black Baptist preacher, Colin Teague, sailed for Sierra Leone, Cary soon moved to Liberia, where he became an agent for the Colonization Society and in 1828 was appointed acting governor of the colony. From indigenous Africans, however, Cary found more hostility toward Christianity than interest in it, so he concentrated his religious efforts on the Americo-Liberian settlers. In 1828 he died in a gunpowder explosion while making cartridges to use against hostile Africans. Despite his own rather antàgonistic reaction to Africans, Cary inspired a strong missionary interest among black Baptists. According to an influential 1887 historical book written by another black Baptist, Cary was "a legacy" of devotion: "a man with no circumstances to inspire him, bearing in his heart a tender love for the Africans who knew not Christ . . . who, while free in body, were chained in sin."[17]

An example of early independent black missionary work was that of Daniel Coker, one of the founders of the A.M.E. Church. In 1816 the denomination chose this Baltimore preacher as its first bishop, but Coker soon resigned his leadership role in order to devote himself to African missions. In 1820 he became one of the original A.C.S. colonists to Liberia, and followed his religious calling there and in Sierra Leone for many years afterward. Despite his status in the A.M.E. Church, Coker was not officially sponsored by that denomination. The new bishop, Richard Allen, was so antagonistic toward colonization that he discouraged his church's expansion into Liberia. Even though several other A.M.E. preachers later emigrated, if they wanted to do mission work they were forced to affiliate with white churches. After 1859 the A.M.E Church made some semiofficial agreements whereby certain Americo-Liberians could coordinate A.M.E. congregations among the settlers, but even this connection was allowed to lapse.[18] A major reason why black church leaders were opposed to involvement in African missions before the 1870s was the association of the mission movement with the unpopular American Colonization Society. There were also other factors which help to explain why the promising beginnings by Cuffe, Cary, Teague, and Coker did not advance for half a century.

One factor was the lack of Afro-Americans who were willing to be missionaries. For a person to volunteer to become a missionary, he or she had to agree to forego many of the material comforts of life. Having been denied economic prosperity for so long, either as slaves or landless tenants, most Afro-Americans were not prepared to give up the opportunity for financial success. Life as a missionary might have appeared depressingly similar to the deprivation which most black people were struggling to leave behind. Thus, it is not surprising that missionary volunteers were rare and that white teachers at black schools during the first decade after emancipation could not find students who "would listen with patience to anything" about African mission work.[19] Even when young black volunteers could be found, their families were often opposed to the decision.[20]

Another factor producing opposition to missions was a general lack of concern among American blacks for Africa, a view resulting from black identity as Americans. Many blacks saw themselves as totally assimilated United States citizens. This opinion was certainly not a majority view among black people, and it may have been restricted primarily to the educated elite who were indoctrinated with white ideals and who prided themselves on their "civilized" refinement. Those blacks who did feel an identity with Western values were "assimilationists" whose goals were complete acceptance by whites, or at least a self-image of "one hundred percent Americanism." At a time when there was considerable prejudice against immigrants who were not merging into the American melting pot, and when Africa was stereotyped as debased and savage, black struggles for acceptance allowed little room for a plural identity with Africa. A statement by a black South Carolina preacher, in the *A.M.E. Church Review*, typified this assimilationist philosophy. Explaining why black Americans should not feel a special attachment to Africa, he wrote: "The American Negro is no more African to-day than descendants of the Pilgrim fathers are Europeans; not as much, for . . . the Negro brought no civilization, hence took that which he found. He lost his heathenism and accepted Christianity, and in many cases became so intermingled until he has lost his color."[21] Besides advocating the argument that black Americans had lost all their African culture, he noted that Afro-American missionaries were no more suited for the tropical climate than whites and that their mortality rates were just as high. Besides, he felt, white churches were in better financial condition to send "Christian civilization" to Africa than were the black denominations.[22]

Many black leaders, religious as well as secular, felt that a plural identification with Africa weakened their struggle to gain acceptance within America. A.M.E. Bishop Benjamin Arnett spoke for many of the black elite when he told the 1893 Chicago Congress on Africa that "we should fight this [civil rights] battle as negroes, and not as Afric-Americans."[23] The strength of this assimilationist feeling can best be seen in the complaints of those who favored involvement in Africa. For example, the 1884 A.M.E. General Conference Budget report claimed that there had been "a woeful lack of interest in mission work" by church members and leaders who "thought Africa too far removed . . . too sunken in sin, too steeped in superstition and idolatry for us."[24] In other words, Africa was considered so corrupt that improvement was hopeless. An A.M.E. minister who defended missions and emigration noted, "Thousands of Negroes seem to abhor the very name of Africa." The reason for this avoid-ance, he wrote, was because they had the "hope (which can only end in despair) that the caucasian in America will at last embrace them in their arms, and take them into full partnership in industrial, commercial, social, and political lines." This hope of full acceptance may have been part of a "colonial" pattern that applies cross-culturally to the first generation of people educated in the values of a dominant society. In Africa, Asia, and Latin America there was a tendency toward an uncritical acceptance of Western values (with a negation of aboriginal identity) among the first generation of the Western-educated elite. Later, after the discrepancy was recognized between legitimate expectations of the educated "natives" and the actuality of continued second-class treatment, later generations became more critical of Western culture and more interested in preserving their own distinct identities.[25]

This colonial pattern seems to apply to some of the educated post–Civil War generation of black Americans, who were indoc-trinated into a belief in the superiority of white values and who felt they might have an opportunity to become part of that value system. Accordingly, they reacted against elements of African culture and identity that had survived in the slave community. This antipathy contributed to an ambivalence about Africa among nineteenth-century American blacks. Pan-Africanists like Edward Blyden blamed this antipathy on the influence of whites, who had written derogatory books about Africa: "From these books we learn that the Negro at home [in Africa] was a degraded being—a heathen and worse than a heathen—a fool. . . . Therefore we turned our backs upon our brethren in the interior as those from whom we could learn nothing to elevate, to enlighten, or to refine."[26]

On the other hand, there were at least a few objections by blacks to the missionary movement on the grounds that it could harm the Africans. A.M.E. Bishop Payne warned against "African Methodist Imperialism" by black American missionaries, who might end up treating Africans no better than European imperialists did.[27] A Sierra Leone professor, J. Augustus Cole, writing in the *A.M.E. Church Review*, even questioned the acceptance of Christianity itself. This acceptance, he felt, was "a very sad mistake, which will always hinder" black peole, because in adopting "the white man's religion" they had retained "the white man's vices as well as his virtues." Consequently, he argued, it would be a mistake to aid in spreading this "imitation" to Africans. "Wherever Christianity goes," Cole wrote, "licentiousness and ungodliness accompany it . . . which in their nature, are as heathenish as those [practices] already amongst the heathen tribes." Ironically, he stated, the introduction of white influences by missionaries in Africa had "introduced the worst kind of immorality." Not only did Cole oppose missions, but he felt that the A.M.E. Church should redirect its efforts toward eliminating "all idolatrous imitations, which we have acquired from the white man."[28]

The most effective opposition to the mission movement was simply to ignore it. Supported by voluntary contributions, missionary institutions could not exist if too many people ignored them. Mission sentiment inherently involved a sense of having something that the rest of mankind needed. Obviously, those blacks like Professor Cole who were uncomfortable with their church's adoption of "the white man's religion" would not support its expansion into Africa. Also, some black people who complained about segregation were reluctant to spread segregated institutions, white or black.[29] For those disillusioned with Jim Crow America, its institutions were something to be delivered from, rather than spread to others. Such sentiments were not conducive to mission sentiment, which necessitated a strong faith in the superiority of one's own culture.

The most important factor limiting mission work among the independent black churches, however, was the lack of money. The small denominations simply did not have resources sufficient to support missionaries. This was true of all the black churches before the Civil War, because they were limited to the small free black population of the North. Even after their membership base was greatly increased through their expansion into the South, the churches' first priority in the 1860s and 1870s had to be the consolidation of their new southern dioceses.[30]

Among those black organizations which did try to sponsor missions, finances remained a major stumbling block throughout the century. Thomas Johnson's black Baptist group reported in 1884 that interest in African missions was strong, "but the poverty of the people, who had so recently been slaves . . . has been the hindering cause" in mission organization.[31] Johnson could only place missionaries in Africa with the financial assistance of white Baptists. The A.M.E. Zion Church felt ill-prepared to finance large-scale missions, but members consoled themselves that God would reserve Africa until later when they could better afford the task.[32]

Even the A.M.E. Church, the best-organized black church with the most financial resources, was limited by its lack of money for missions. The denomination could not even keep its church publishing house out of debt until after 1876. Bishop Payne, realizing that previous missionaries had resigned because of lack of support, felt that too quick an expansion into Africa would financially over-extend the church.[33] As late as the early 1890s, some church leaders criticized A.M.E. expansion into Africa, and one bishop even suggested that all missionaries abroad should be recalled. This lack of financial backing affected the A.M.E. missionaries already in Africa, one of whom complained that they "almost invariably are left to eke out the most shameful existence. Not a few have been left [in Africa] to die paupers."[34] Thus, it was mostly an inadequate financial base which prevented an earlier flowering of African missions by the black American churches.

Despite financial and ideological limitations, sentiment favoring the evangelization of Africa did begin to grow among the black denominations after the late 1870s. The initial factor was the revival of back-to-Africa emigration, a nonreligious movement that pulled the church leadership into involvement. For example, in 1876 an A.M.E.Z. minister, Andrew Cartwright, single-handedly expanded his church to Liberia. Cartwright had been born a slave in eastern North Carolina about 1835, but had escaped to New England before the Civil War. While in the North he became a preacher, and in 1863 followed advancing Union armies into Virginia where he organized the first A.M.E.Z. church in the South. He returned to his native state, but by the end of Reconstruction Cartwright had become disillusioned about his future in America. He served as an agent for the American Colonization Society, and in 1876 accepted their aid to emigrate. He wished to continue his preaching and to spread the A.M.E.Z. Church in Africa, as he had done two decades earlier in the South. Therefore, even though he had no financial support or authority from denominational leaders, he organized A.M.E.Z. congregations among the Americo-Liberians. It was not until seven years later that his church officially agreed to support his missionary endeavors, by which it was drawn into Africa.[35]

Both the black Baptists and the A.M.E Church began mission work in Liberia as a result of South Carolina emigrants. Only months after the white minority in South Carolina had used violence and political pressure to overthrow the Reconstruction state government, emigration sentiment among blacks reached a high point. On July 26, 1877, a mass meeting was held in Charleston to celebrate Liberian Independence Day, and Liberian J. C. Hazeley was on hand to speak vigorously in favor of emigration. Soon, black Charlestonians

established the Liberian Exodus Joint Stock Steamship Company—the
first emigration organization formed by black southerners. By
diligent efforts the troup raised enough money to charter a ship,
the *Azor*, which left for Liberia in April 1878 with over 200 emigrants. The main speaker at the dedication of the ship emphasized
that the purpose of the group was not only to emigrate but also
"to take back the culture, education and religion acquired here [in
America] . . . until the blaze of Gospel truth should glitter over the
whole broad African continent."[36]

Among the *Azor* emigrants were two ministers, Harrison N. Bouey,
a Baptist, and Samuel F. Flegler, of the A.M.E. Church. Reverend
Bouey was sponsored by the black South Carolina Baptist Convention; he pastored in Monrovia and did some mission work among
the Gola people in western Liberia. After organizing the Liberian
Baptist Convention, Bouey returned to America in 1881.[37] Flegler
led an A.M.E. Congregation that left from Charleston, and their
settlement at Brewerville in Liberia marked the formal beginning of
A.M.E. churches in Africa. Even though Flegler returned to America
in 1881, his congregation continued to thrive under another emigrant,
Clement Irons. The mission was at first sponsored solely by the
Morris Brown A.M.E. Church in Charleston, but was later recognized
by the national church conference.[38] Therefore, among all three
independent black denominations, their initial formal involvement
in Africa was due to individual emigrants and local congregations
which pushed the church leaders into action.

Besides pressures from their own members, black churches were
affected by mission sentiment in white churches. During an era of
exploration, in which much of Africa was newly "opened" to Western
eyes, it was natural that much attention would be focused on the
continent. Interest in missions soon spread from Europe to America,
where black ministers were inclined to follow white advice on
doctrinal matters in order to keep up with contemporary religious
dogma.[39] Recommendations like those given by the white Southern
Baptist Convention in 1877, that black churches would be "blessed
and developed" by sending missionaries to Africa, did not go
unheeded. The convention report assured blacks that "the cultivation
of a benevolent missionary spirit is one of the surest methods of
securing spiritual prosperity in the home churches."[40]

Though there were some exceptions, by the late nineteenth
century there was a perceptible decline among white church leaders
who favored the use of Afro-American missionaries. Probably the
major reason for this decline was the gradual improvement of

Western medicine, which enabled more white missionaries to survive in the tropical climate. With white and black missionaries serving together, racial conflicts increased. And the original reason for utilizing black missionaries—their supposed greater adaptability to the climate—was shown to be false. The white churches, urged by these considerations, soon dropped their encouragements to Afro-Americans. With the exception of the Presbyterian Congo mission, most white churches moved toward a "whites only" policy.

The Southern Baptist Convention, for example, which had strongly supported Afro-American missionaries at its Yoruba stations, ended its advocacy after 1880. A white missionary wrote to the mission Board in 1881, "I wish to divert the minds of the Board from depending upon colored laborers from the South too much . . . It will not do well to let the colored force predominate."[41] When the last black missionary died at Abeokuta in 1881, one of the white missionaries, in reporting his death, wrote that they would "miss him sadly," but added that the Board should only send white missionaries in the future.[42] By 1882, the Southern Baptists were specifically calling for white missionaries only. Any remaining mission needs could be satisfied by employing trained African converts, who by this time were in ready supply, and who were less expensive to support and better adapted to the climate than were black Americans. The Southern Baptist Convention did not accept any more black volunteers from the United States for the remainder of the nineteenth century.[43]

There were also conflicts of white mission boards with black missionaries who acted independent of and had different opinions from their sponsors. This was especially true of the American Board missions in south central Africa, and the Presbyterian mission in Liberia. The northern Presbyterians had established Lincoln University in the 1850s specifically to train Afro-Americans as missionaries, but they began a gradual retreat from this policy after the schism with Edward Blyden. Several of Lincoln's graduates had died in Liberia, and by the 1890s the mission board replied to black applicants that they were accepting only whites as missionaries.[44]

Several Afro-American missionaries complained of inadequate financial support, especially when white co-workers were paid higher wages. Even so cooperative a person as the United Brethren missionary Joseph Gomer was upset over cuts in his salary and mission support funds, and his great anxiety about financial matters may have contributed to his death (at least, that was the feeling of other black missionaries).[45] Without adequate support from white churches, some Afro-Americans decided it would be better to depend on black denominations.

During an era when the United States was becoming increasingly segregated, integrated missions seemed an anomaly. White mission boards feared that black Americans would spread racial ill feelings to the Africans. That fear was felt even more strongly by European colonial governments, which viewed Afro-American missionaries as potential troublemakers. As imperial control tightened over the continent, more restrictions were placed upon black missionaries. Even those churches which backed their black representatives, as the southern Presbyterians did William Sheppard, experienced much opposition from Europeans. By the 1890s most colonial governments were encouraging American churches to send only white missionaries.[46]

Because of these factors relating to health, racial conflicts, and objections by European colonial governments, white church use of Afro-Americans did not keep pace with the rise of the mission movement. In fact, overall white church attention to Africa was less than it was to other areas of the world. By the first decade of the twentieth century U.S. missionaries to India alone numbered over five hundred, with another five hundred in China. Yet there were only a little over a hundred American missionaries in all of West Africa.[47] This decrease of white church interest in using Afro-American missionaries came about during the same time that black churches were becoming more interested in Africa.

The black churches, like their white counterparts, were affected by the expansionist tendencies of Christian dogma. To explain the motivation of black church mission sentiment, one often has to look no further than biblical injunctions to spread the gospel. Black Americans who were seriously committed to their religion felt a calling, which any true believer should feel, toward the unconverted. For example, A.M.E. Bishop Abraham Grant, who led the West African A.M.E. Conferences in 1899, felt that the most notable reason for missionary work was simply that it was "obeying the command of Christ."[48] Those who had no doubts about Christianity were sure that they had heavenly connections which the rest of the world needed. This attitude was expressed clearly in a song "Come Over and Help Us" in the 1899 *A.M.E. Hymnal*:

> Shall we, whose souls are lighted
> With wisdom from on high,
> Shall we to men benighted
> The lamp of life deny?[49]

Another mission hymn promised that when every nation accepted Christianity, all wars and grief would be ended, and "joy and peace" would reign.[50]

Mission work was seen by the churches as a requirement for institutional survival. Evangelists claimed that denominations which had given most attention to mission work were the most successful, while those that did not remained stagnant and would eventually disappear.[51] Such a prophesy was particularly applicable to the black churches, which had experienced most of their previous growth by expansion into the American South.

There was also a desire among Afro-Americans to build up strong institutions for their race. Leaders of black churches desired to raise their religious institutions to the level of counterpart white churches. This feeling applied to the black mission organizations, which A.M.E. leaders wished to be equal to the standards of the "best organized [white] bodies" in the nation.[52] Bishop Henry M. Turner criticized his church for not doing as much in Africa as white churches. He wrote in the denomination's newspaper that a church without missions was not worthy of respect, and could not be counted among the "great churches of the world." Not only would a strong mission crusade encourage pride of accomplishment, Bishop Turner argued, its absence would lower the reputation of the whole black race.[53] This appeal to compete on a level with whites was effective among black leaders who were trying so hard to overcome a second-class status in America.

By the late nineteenth century, the independent black churches had developed institutionally to the point that they *could* begin to think about competing with white churches in African mission work. Before this time their small size and even smaller financial base had prevented much emphasis on foreign work. Even after church expansion into the South, the major emphasis of the 1860s and 1870s was on the organization and consolidation of new congregations.[54] But by the late 1870s their southern fields were established and they had a much larger membership base to draw upon. In many ways the spread of the black churches into the South planted a more expansionist missionary sentiment in those denominations. Church leaders like A.M.E.Z. Reverend Andrew Cartwright and A.M.E. Reverend Henry Turner, who did so much to spread their churches in the South before 1870 and into Africa after that time, provided the continuity of personality and ideology between the two movements.[55]

A combination of increased Western interest in Africa, an ex-

pansionist Christian ideology, emigration sentiment, the decline of
white church use of Afro-American missionaries, and especially
the consolidation of well-developed large black denominations led
to the beginnings of a strong independent black mission movement.
The sentiment that began in earnest by the late 1870s steadily
increased through the end of the century, and the majority of
black missionaries during the late nineteenth century were sponsored
by black denominations. Between 1877 and 1900 the A.M.E. Church,
the A.M.E.Z. Church, and the National Baptist Convention overtook
the white churches in their support of African mission work. They
sponsored at least seventy-six missionaries in Africa, as well as
thirty African students who were being trained in the United States
to become missionaries.[56] This involvement is best understood by
analyzing the institutional histories of the black Methodist and
Baptist denominations.

3

Mission Organization in Independent Afro-American Methodist Churches

By the 1870s the best-organized black national denomination in the United States was the African Methodist Episcopal Church. Reflecting the legacy of its early missionary Daniel Coker, as early as 1844 the A.M.E. organized a Home and Foreign Missionary Society. Twenty years later a missionary secretary was appointed, and in 1874 a women's missionary society was formed. Most of the attention of these mission organizations was restricted at first to expansion of the church into the South, but by 1876 the church had completed this expansion; its membership surpassed two hundred thousand, in contrast to only twenty thousand members before the Civil War.[1] This resounding success in home missions led to greater interest in foreign mission work, especially after the establishment of an A.M.E. congregation in Liberia by the 1878 *Azor* emigrants from South Carolina.[2]

In 1878 the church bishops appointed James Townsend as the new mission secretary. In contrast to previous secretaries who had not given much attention to their duties, Townsend brought considerable organizational skills to his office. A Union army veteran and Oberlin College graduate, he was a respected school principal in Evansville, Indiana.[3] As a successful middle-class leader, Townsend had no sympathy for emigration schemes. But he did commit his talents to African missions, working hard within the denomination to arouse mission interest and to centralize fund-raising efforts.[4]

By 1880, Townsend's organizational efforts were paying off. An A.M.E. bishop remembered that year as a noticeable turning point

in the rise of missionary interest in Africa, "which was apparently
deepening each year throughout the A.M.E. Church." He spoke of
"numerous letters from both young men and women announcing
themselves ready to become missionaries if only a little support
could be provided. This is the true missionary spirit, and it is
growing in our Church."[5] Secretary Townsend felt that the belief
among some bishops and a majority of the membership that African
missions were a waste of money was gradually declining. By 1883
he had intensified publicity about missions by publishing annual
reports, and by visiting and writing to local church conferences.
He convinced the bishops to set aside all Easter Day collections
for missions, set up a "certificate" plan for additional contributions,
and placed over 6000 mission collection boxes in A.M.E. churches.[6]
These financial efforts resulted in an increase in mission collections
which totaled $116,023.70 for the sixteen years following 1880, four
times the amount collected in the previous sixteen years.[7]

Interest in Africa continued to grow among the church leaders
through the 1880s. The bishops' address to the 1884 General Conference demonstrated this new missionary zeal:

> The time was fully come for us to enter more largely upon the
> work of extending our church into foreign fields. . . . The
> forces which stand opposed to the army of the living God are
> not content with arraying themselves against civilization in
> Europe and America, but seek to prevent the entrance of that
> light-giving Word where nations sit in darkness and in the
> region of the shadow of death. . . . Let us seek to plant firmly
> the banner of the African Methodist Episcopal Church upon
> the ramparts of the forts of the [pagan] enemy on the shores
> and in the heart of Africa, following the openings that commerce
> has made.

Interest in Africa was also promoted among the membership by
articles in the *A.M.E. Church Review*. A symposium entitled "What
Should be the Policy of the Colored American toward Africa?"
appeared in the July 1885 issue, and two articles summarizing recent
African geographical discoveries were published in the next issue.[8]

In 1885 the A.M.E. Church decided to expand its African work
beyond the black American emigrants in Liberia. In that year a
congregation of westernized "creoles" in Freetown, Sierra Leone,
who had seceded from a British mission, requested affiliation with
the A.M.E. Church. Unable to turn down such an attractive offer
for quick expansion to an already established Christian group, at its
1886 General Conference the church sent John Richard Frederick as

their missionary to Sierra Leone. Little is known about Frederick, except that he was an A.M.E. leader in Rhode Island. Soon after his arrival in Africa he became involved with educational and social welfare projects as well as church work. He came under the influence of Edward Blyden, who was then living in Sierra Leone, and extended his attention to the indigenous Africans. Frederick thus became the first A.M.E. missionary in Africa to work among non-Christians, and he got along very well with Africans. Some interior groups requested that he open additional mission stations in their villages even before he had asked them, and he began training Africans as missionaries. He respected the indigenous ways of life and, along with Blyden and James "Holy" Johnson, he founded the Dress Reform Society to encourage westernized Africans to abandon European garb in favor of traditional African clothing.[9]

In 1889 Frederick was joined by another New Englander, Sarah E. Gorham, the first female A.M.E. missionary in Africa. Miss Gorham had been a social worker in Boston, where she was also active in A.M.E. church work. About 1880 she briefly visited some relatives who had emigrated to Liberia, and thereby became interested in African missions. Although she originally planned to become a missionary in Liberia, when she visited Reverend Frederick she was so impressed with his work that she decided to go instead to Sierra Leone. After working in Freetown, she established a mission school in the interior. Her efforts were impeded by illnesses, however, and in 1894 she died of malaria.[10]

The connection between the A.M.E. Church and Sierra Leone prompted even more attention to Africa by the church leaders, and there was even discussion about sending a bishop to Africa. At the 1888 General Conference, Bishop Jabez P. Campbell, an emigrationist who was also a vice president of the American Colonization Society, deplored the fact that financial limitations had kept A.M.E. African work restricted. But, he said, the missionary spirit "is on us now. I have been ready to go to Africa for full forty years, and that too, at my own expense. The temptation is strong now, and if none of the younger men who have been elected bishops will go, then the old man will go."[11] Another bishop who was becoming interested in Africa was Benjamin Arnett, who went to the South Carolina A.M.E. Conference in 1889 to hear Edward Blyden speak. Arnett spoke in praise of Blyden's having come directly "from the fatherland," and added, "I am not ashamed of that fatherland nor of the men that hail from it." An editorial in the church newspaper stated, "We believe with Dr. Blyden that our church, that our people in this

country have a mission to Africa."[12] Blyden's several articles on
Africa in the *A.M.E. Church Review* were making his nationalist
ideas even more familiar to the church.[13] All of this publicity had
an effect on both the church members and leaders, and even Bishop
Daniel Payne, who had previously been opposed to African expansion, now called for A.M.E. missionaries to "unfurl the bloodstained
banner of the cross upon the dark continent. Let them never call a
halt till they have constructed a stronghold in the very heart of
Africa. . . . No amount of time and money spent in such work can
be wasted."[14] Thus, by the end of the 1880s mission sentiment had
diffused through the church leadership, and more attention was
being paid to Africa than ever before.

Amid the general popularity of African missions, Bishop Henry
McNeal Turner stood far above the rest of the church leadership
in commitment to Africa. Throughout his life, Turner seemed to be
always on the center stage of history, and always involved in con-
troversy. Although he was born to free parents in 1834, he suffered
the inevitable discrimination affecting a black person growing up in
South Carolina. One occasion that particularly embittered young
Turner against racism was when he was forced to terminate his
schooling because of laws against the education of blacks. According
to his biographer, this disappointment "had much to do with the
contempt which he showed in after years for those who opposed
the progress of his race."[15]

Despite setbacks, however, Turner was intelligent enough to make
the best of a bad situation. By age nineteen he was licensed to
preach by the southern white Methodist Chruch, and subsequently
traveled around the South preaching and gaining experience. In
1858, while in St. Louis, Missouri, Turner came into contact with
the A.M.E. Church and immediately joined the independent black
sect. After preaching in Baltimore and attending Trinity College
there, he was chosen to pastor Israel Metropolitan Church—the
largest black church in Washington, D.C. While in the nation's
capital, Turner became politically active and invited Radical Repub-
licans Benjamin Wade and Thaddeus Stevens to speak in his church.
Probably because of his political connections, in 1863 Turner was
appointed by President Abraham Lincoln as the first black chaplain
in the United States Army.[16]

After the Civil War Turner moved to Georgia as an official of
the Freedmen's Bureau and led black activity in the Republican
Party there. Although he was a delegate to the Georgia Constitutional
Convention of 1867 and was elected to the state legislature, the

next year white supremacists disqualified all blacks from serving in the government. Denied a leadership role in politics, Turner turned his emphasis back to his former occupation as a religious leader. By prodigious energy, he was able to build the A.M.E. Church in Georgia into a strong black institution, and within a decade of his arrival in the state he had personally brought in forty thousand new members and trained 226 preachers.[17] His success led to his election as an A.M.E. bishop in 1880. As racial violence and discrimination increased, however, Turner became disillusioned with the United States and turned toward African emigration and missions as the only hope for black people.[18]

Henry Turner brought to his church office an abrasive personality, and he was not charitable to those with whom he differed. He lashed out against churchmen who did not actively support the missionary movement, calling them "enemies to God."[19] He was especially critical of Benjamin T. Tanner, editor of the *A.M.E. Christian Recorder*, charging that no man was more responsible for the prevailing missionary apathy in the church. Turner wrote to Tanner in 1881, "I had rather be dead than not possess that [mission] interest. How any negro can profess Christianity and be dead to the moral wants of his kinsmen in Africa, is to me a mystery." Tanner responded that if the good bishop liked Africa so much he should immediately go there. Turner shot back that if the Church would provide him with a financial base, he and others would be glad to go to Africa as missionaries.[20] Such was the turbulence of his entire career.

Although his social and political ideas differed from many of the old-guard church leadership, Turner's organizing ability and forcefulness made him quite popular among the lower clergy and membership. A young A.M.E. minister wrote, "No man in the A.M.E. Church has so great influence over the masses of our church membership and race as Bishop Turner"[21] Even Turner's enemies respected him and recognized his powerful influence. The *Indianapolis Freeman* grudgingly admitted, "The good bishop has certainly stamped himself one of the foremost Negroes in his day and generation. He clearly is the champion of a cause and has the courage of his convictions. . . . Bishop Turner is not to be set down as a crank."[22]

Turner was a master at playing politics within the church hierarchy. People to him were colleagues to be used to accomplish noble purposes, rather than friends to be confided in. His biographer states that Turner was continually busy: "He worked until he slept; then he slept until he worked."[23] Despite his unpolished and blunt manners, Henry Turner was known as "one of the most influential men in the United States. . . . When speaking, he is very impressive, and carries an audience with him as easily as the wind sweeps the chaff before it."[24]

As Turner became more disillusioned with the chances of black people in America, he began to propagandize within the church in favor of African missions. He did not limit his interests to missionary work, however. Turner advocated any number of plans for Afro-American involvement in Africa, from intercontinental commerce and emigration to agitation against European imperialism.[25] For example, in 1880 he wrote to his son that black Americans should shake off their apathy about Africa and put forth "efforts for the moral and intellectual development of that darkened continent." Turner envisioned these efforts as including many alternatives; he counseled his son, "If you want your name woven into song and history when you are dead, become an African explorer, geologist, mineralogist, or something that will enlighten the world upon her resources."[26] Turner saw no other place in the world besides Africa where talented young blacks could better themselves economically, establish their own government, and "at the same time build up a center of Christian civilization that will help redeem the land of our ancestry."[27] Turner clearly expected the westernization of Africa to be accomplished under black American leadership.

A.M.E. Mission Secretary James Townsend retired in 1888, and was replaced by William B. Derrick. Neither man cared for emigration, but Derrick was powerless to prevent Bishop Turner's equation of missions with emigration. Turner was establishing himself as the real leader of missionary concerns in the denomination, especially by 1891 when he became the first A.M.E. bishop to visit Africa. Turner increased his influence by writing detailed letters about this trip, which were published in the *A.M.E. Church Review*.[28] On arriving in Freetown, Sierra Leone, on November 8, Turner reported that he was "crazy with delight" over finally getting to Africa. He was so impressed with the cleanliness and progressive appearance of Freetown that he had to admit his surprise at the "decency" of the Africans: "I had to say, thank God for this sight!"[29]

Turner was moved to tears by the enthusiastic response of "those people—I mean our people—at the presence of a Bishop." Within two days he had organized and led the first Annual Conference of the A.M.E. Churches in Sierra Leone. Turner's sermons attracted large crowds of creoles and indigenous Africans. A number of traditional leaders told him they were ready to throw out white missionaries if the A.M.E. Church would only send black missionaries. With this type of response, Turner grandly predicted that "The A.M.E. Church can be the Continental Church of Africa."[30]

On November 23, Turner traveled south to Liberia, the object of his emigrationist dreams. He brought with him a new missionary volunteer for Liberia, T. R. Geda, as a symbol of greater A.M.E. commitment to the African republic. After a week's trip into the interior to visit indigenous African kingdoms, Turner returned to Monrovia to organize the Liberian Annual A.M.E. Conference, consisting of twenty-three preachers and two hundred members. His trip unified scattered A.M.E. congregations, which had been limited mainly to the Americo-Liberians, and created more interest in converting non-Christian Africans.[31]

In 1893, after Turner had been formally appointed as Bishop of Africa, he returned to Liberia with three new missionaries. Two of the volunteers, Mr. and Mrs. Alfred Lee Ridgel, first resided in Sierra Leone, but they moved to Liberia a year later after the death of the third missionary, G. G. Vreeland. Ridgel became the leader of the A.M.E. Church in Liberia, maintaining his headquarters in the capital city of Monrovia, where his wife operated a school. An admirer of Bishop Turner, Ridgel followed the same type of busy schedule espoused by his mentor. He often visited the scattered congregations to keep up morale and increase membership. At the same time he was writing a book, *Africa and African Methodism*, the publication of which in 1896 had a marked impact on the church in America. Ridgel's influence in Africa, however, was cut short by his death in 1896 in a boating accident.[32]

After Alfred Ridgel's death, the direction of A.M.E. work in Africa temporarily floundered. In Sierra Leone John R. Frederick had become disillusioned over inadequate church support of his missions. When pressure was put on him to transfer to another location, he resigned from the church. However, he remained in the British colony for the rest of his life, doing mission work under the sponsorship of the British Wesleyan Methodist Church, and keeping in close touch with his friend Edward Blyden. Frederick disliked the light-skinned Bishop Turner, and he accused Turner of being prejudiced against him because of his dark skin. Such a charge would be difficult to accept concerning the nationalist Turner; the bishop effectively pointed out that of the six missionaries he had taken to West Africa, three were mulatto and three were black.[33]

In 1897 Bishop Turner sent a replacement to head the Sierra Leone work, Reverend Floyd G. Snelson of Georgia. An Atlanta University graduate, Snelson reorganized the A.M.E. mission into three stations. By the end of the century he was sponsoring eighteen African missionaries in Sierra Leone, with a membership of one thousand six hundred people.[34]

Meanwhile, in Liberia the direction of A.M.E. churches passed to William H. Heard. Although Heard was an A.M.E. clergyman and a follower of Bishop Turner's emigration and mission efforts, he was in Liberia as the diplomatic representative of the United States government. Appointed by President Grover Cleveland on Turner's recommendation, Heard was both politically experienced, having served in the Reconstruction South Carolina legislature and seriously interested in Africa.[35] After his arrival in Liberia, Minister Heard considered his position as diplomat to be only part of his duties; he also worked diligently to superintend the A.M.E. missions in Liberia and Sierra Leone.[36] By the end of the century the A.M.E Church had twenty-five ministers and 1500 members in Liberia.[37]

Satisfied to oversee the mission department from his home in Atlanta, Bishop Turner redoubled his efforts to increase mission and emigration sentiment. He encouraged missionary volunteers to publicize their efforts on speaking tours, before they left for Africa and while on furlough, and in letters to the *Voice of Missions*. This newspaper, which Turner founded in 1893 and edited until 1900, was the first missionary periodical sponsored by an Afro-American denomination. It was a primary factor in the spread of A.M.E. interest in Africa and gave new vitality to the cause of missions in the 1890s.[38] In 1893 Turner also organized the Woman's Home and Foreign Missionary Society, to raise funds for African work in the Church. The first superintendent of the society traveled through nine states arousing interest in missions among the women of the church.[39] In the same year, Turner also spoke to the Congress on Africa at the Chicago World's Fair. While there, he was excited by the presence of an exhibit of tribal dancers from Dahomey, and wrote in his newspaper, "These are my folks. We all came from that stock. I shall now work for the cause of missions, as I never have before."[40]

Bishop Turner filled the *Voice of Missions* with articles about Africa, and Edward Blyden pronounced it "one of the most trustworthy records of the habits and customs and the tone of thought of the American Negro."[41] Turner even wrote a missionary song for the *A.M.E. Hymnal*, in which Africa was described as a "bright

and fair" country: "Afric's shores I long to see. . . . I must hasten
to be there."[42]

The importance of Turner's influence within the A.M.E. Church
can be judged from a tribute to him in the General Conference
Minutes of 1896:

> The feeling for Africa's redemption throughout Christiandom
> is unprecedented, and especially within our communion. The
> increased interest among us can be truthfully attributed to the
> Bishop of Africa [Henry Turner, who] . . . laid his life upon
> the altar for the salvation of Africa, morally, intellectually,
> commercially and religiously.[43]

Another bishop even suggested that Turner should be made king
of Africa.[44] Perhaps the most heartfelt tribute to Turner's influence
was expressed by H. B. Parks, who said that Turner was "the spiritual
father from whom has sprung a prolific progeny of missionary children. He has kindled the fire of missionary enthusiasm in unnumbered
souls."[45] Henry Turner was clearly an important leader in A.M.E.
Church history.[46]

During the 1890s, Bishop Turner's efforts in behalf of African
interests began to bear fruit. By 1893, for example, a course on
Africa was being taught at the A.M.E.-sponsored Wilberforce
University in Ohio. The next year Charles Spencer Smith, the teacher
of the course, visited Africa to observe mission work and to look
for opportunities for talented young black Americans. Smith published his ideas in a book printed by the church press in 1895.[47]

After mission sentiment had become a priority of the A.M.E.
Church in the 1880s, interest in Africa seemed to filter downward
to the membership from a core of leaders rather than a reverse
swell from below. This influence of church leaders in awakening
mission interest among the church membership is demonstrated by
the many letters to the editor of the *Voice of Missions*. For example,
in 1896 a member from Arkansas wrote to Turner praising a sermon
given in his church by A.M.E. Mission Secretary Derrick: "His words
on Africa enthused my soul from its greatest depths, and I myself
am Africa struck. . . . Today my heart yearns for Africa, my dear
nativity, and I ask God each day to bless the missionaries of Africa."[48] Bishop Turner rightly recognized the crucial position of
the church ministers and leaders in either making or breaking the
missionary movement, so he concentrated on the yearly conferences
when the leaders were together. In 1896, when a new Mission
Secretary was chosen, Turner made sure that it was one of his

followers. The new Secretary, H. B. Parks, revealed the debt he owed to the bishop by proposing that a new A.M.E. mission society be called "The Henry M. Turner Crusaders of the Twentieth Century."[49]

Although they shared a deep interest in missions, Parks differed in some respects from Turner. As revealed in his 1899 book, *Africa, the Problem of the New Century*, Parks lacked the spontaneous originality of thought that Turner possessed. He was more of a practical "organization man," and by 1899 he could see more clearly than could Turner the health and financial advantages of using indigenous African Christians as missionaries rather than black Americans.[50] He therefore strongly encouraged support for African students in the United States, and worked diligently to spread the gospel through them. Perhaps he was reflecting the contemporary emphasis by white churches on training Africans to be missionaries to their own people, or perhaps he was cool toward black American emigration to Africa. In any case, his emphasis on the use of native Africans was enhanced by the A.M.E.'s affiliation with a group of independent South African Methodists in 1896.

By the 1890s South Africa was distinct from any other part of the continent. Partly because of the temperate climate, to which the European could more easily adapt than a tropical one, the southern portion of the continent was overrun by white settlers and missionaries. The resulting combination of revolutionary socio-economic changes brought about by the European settlers and the more extensive ideological attack spearheaded by greater numbers of missionaries led to a weakening of native cultures in South Africa that was unmatched elsewhere on the continent.

With indigenous religions in decline, Christianity made rapid progress in South Africa. Nearly half of all black African Christians were located in South Africa.[51] These converts became the nucleus of a new class of Africans, which by the 1890s had not only been Christian for two or three generations, but was educated and westernized as well.[52] A far cry from the stereotype of the uncivilized pagan, these were the South Africans with whom the Afro-American churches associated.

The rise of the South African separatist church movement was structurally similar to the origin of the A.M.E. Church in the United States. Both separatist groups were Methodist, and both set up their own churches in reaction against racial discrimination. Until 1886 both white and black members of the English Wesleyan Methodist Church in South Africa had met together in their religious services.

But after that year the color line was drawn. Black congregations were segregated and their ministers were required to have a white chairman to oversee them and a white secretary to administer their church business. The situation grew intolerable to the Africans and in 1892 a secession movement organized the Ethiopian Church.[53]

The Ethiopian Church emphasized the principle of African control (using the name "Ethiopian" as a symbol for independence from European rule, since Ethiopia was an independent state), but retained a European-style church organization and theology.[54] The Ethiopian Church was more similar in origin, organization and theology to the A.M.E. Church than was any other independent black religious group in Africa.[55]

It was not until 1895, however, that the South African Ethiopian Church leadership more or less accidentally learned of the A.M.E Church through Charlotte Manye. This Basuto-Xhosa woman had joined a singing group which toured England and America in 1894, but the financial collapse of this group left her stranded in the United States. Somehow she enlisted the aid of the A.M.E. Church Mission Department and was admitted to Wilberforce University in Ohio. After beginning classes at Wilberforce in January 1895, she lived in the home of A.M.E. Bishop Benjamin W. Arnett and sent information on the denomination to her uncle, M. M. Mokone.[56]

Mokone, leader of the Ethiopian Church, first wrote to Bishop Turner in May 1895, requesting more information on the A.M.E. Church and on educational opportunities in America. Turner responded enthusiastically, sending church literature and suggesting that the Ethiopian Church affiliate with the A.M.E. denomination.[57] The South African church leaders thereupon began a correspondence with Turner, which the Bishop promptly published in his *Voice of Missions*.[58] Within a year the Ethiopian Church leaders decided to unite with "our countrymen" in the A.M.E. Church. Reverend James M. Dwane, a Xhosa, was elected as agent to visit the United States and complete the union.[59]

Dwane arrived in the United States in June 1896 and was officially received into the A.M.E. Church by Bishop Turner and Missionary Secretary H. B. Parks. Turner appointed Dwane as "General Superintendent" of the A.M.E. Church in South Africa, and led him on a speaking tour in the South. Dwane expressed the wishes of his colleagues when he said, "We have long desired to join hands with our brethren across the seas—we are but seeking our own."[60] The A.M.E. ministers were obviously impressed with Dwane's sophistication and attitudes. Turner reported that "everywhere Dwane went in this country the people rose by thousands to their feet to rejoice over him."[61] After a successful tour, Dwane returned to South Africa in September 1896.[62]

The crowning moment of the first decade of involvement of the A.M.E. Church in South Africa came in 1898 with a visit by Bishop Turner. This was Turner's third trip to Africa, but it was his first contact outside of West Africa.[63] His visit lasted over a month and was marked by his usual flurry of activity. The Africans responded enthusiastically, and Turner spoke to overflowing crowds. On more than one occasion he was required to leave the church where he was preaching and move outside, to allow all to hear.[64]

Turner was deeply impressed with the South Africans, and he characteristically publicized his trip in detailed letters published in the *Voice of Missions*. He felt especially honored by the presence at his speeches of African royalty. The African ministers, Turner said, "were highly eloquent and displayed a common sense that almost dumbfounded us." He characterized the church leaders as men of "exalted intellectuality . . . and possessing a Christian character as clear as a sunbeam." The bishop concluded that South Africa "is a grand field with vast possibilities for our church. . . . We have never come away from a place so reluctantly."[65] He showed great respect for the South African church leadership by breaking tradition to ordain sixty-five Africans as A.M.E. ministers. He also appointed Reverend Dwane as assistant Bishop, bought a site for an A.M.E. school, organized the Transvaal and South African Annual Conferences, and helped increase the A.M.E. membership in South Africa to over ten thousand.[66]

After observing racism among white missionaries, Turner could well understand why the Africans had seceded and joined the A.M.E. Church "of their own kith and kin." The Africans had discovered, he wrote, "that churches of their own and ministers of their own race, with the required learning and ability, would be of far more benefit in a progressive measure, than worshipping among the whites."[67] Turner's sentiments were the same as those of independent black clergy in the American South after the Civil War, where the situation had been almost exactly the same. Turner's visit in 1898 left the South African A.M.E. Church much stronger than it had been before. Its influence extended to other religious bodies, for a marked impetus had been given to African church separatism.

On the heels of Turner's visit James Dwane helped expand the A.M.E. Church into Rhodesia and the Zambezi area, and in 1898 he organized an effort to collect funds for Emperor Menelik of

Ethiopia, who had recently repelled an Italian invasion.[68] Dwane visited the United States again in September 1898, where, according to the A.M.E. Church historian, "Favors and Receptions were lavished upon him on every hand, thousands rejoicing to see and shake hands with a real, pure African."[69]

Unfortunately for church unity, Dwane pressured too forcefully for more financial contributions from the A.M.E. Church and lobbied to have his status changed to full bishop. Some of the conservative church leaders had been reluctant to approve of Turner's strong move into South Africa anyway, with the attendant financial responsibilities, so they objected to Dwane's demands. When this occurred, Dwane returned to South Africa and led a secession movement by some of the churches. Turner was "amazed and dumbfounded" at Dwane's secession, but he appealed to the loyal ministers to let the discontented members peacefully retire so as not to cause more strife. He predicted that, despite the temporary setback, the A.M.E. Church would continue to grow in South Africa—which it did, soon after differences were patched up in 1901. The A.M.E. Church in South Africa then began another period of growth, reaching a membership of over eighteen thousand by 1914.[70]

By the late 1890s interest in missions was well established within the membership of the A.M.E. church. The bishops instituted the practice of making a special annual collection for missions every Easter Sunday, and while this collection only netted $3,926.57 in 1893, it had almost doubled within four years. The contributions continued to climb to a height of $8,802.61 by the end of the century.[71] The largest contributions consistently came from Georgia (reflecting Henry Turner's influence), Pennsylvania, Maryland–District of Columbia, and Ohio.[72]

The spread of the African missions interest by the end of the century is well illustrated by the action of Bishop Abraham Grant, a church leader who had shown little interest in Africa before that time. In 1899 Grant became the second A.M.E. Bishop to visit Africa and, while he opposed Turner's emigration plans, joined Turner in emphasizing the need for missionaries and for educating African students in the United States. Before he left for Sierra Leone, Grant wrote to the *Voice of Missions*:

> I am going to help in the religious redemption of my fatherland . . . to help spread the Gospel in the dark continent. . . . Africa offers a big field for the development and spread of our Church and I believe in future years the greater part of our

> membership will be found in Africa. . . . We can best assist
> it by sending to Africa educated preachers, teachers, doctors,
> nurses and laborers, and by bringing natives here and educating
> them.[73]

By the end of the century the missionary movement among black
Americans was most established in the A.M.E. Church. There were
between 1880 and 1900 at least sixty A.M.E. missionaries in Africa:
twenty-four serving in Sierra Leone and thirty-six in Liberia (even
though many of these were restricted to the black American emigrant
population). The denomination was also affiliated with a strong black
church of over ten thousand members in South Africa. In addition,
the A.M.E. Church had supported at least sixteen African students
in black American schools.[74] This commitment to the evangelization
of Africa is not only a tribute to the effectiveness of A.M.E. organization, but reflects the dedication of church leaders like Henry
McNeal Turner.

The second largest independent black Methodist denomination in
the United States was the African Methodist Episcopal Zion Church.
Despite its similarity in name to the A.M.E. Church, the Zion Church
had a separate institutional history. The first A.M.E.Z. Church was
organized in New York City in 1796, as a result of attempts by
white Methodists to segregate their black members. The church did
not experience great growth until James W. Hood extended the sect
into the South after the Civil War, and North Carolina became the
new center for the denomination.[75]

The first serious indication of A.M.E.Z. interest in African
missions was the creation in 1880 of the General Home and Foreign
Mission Board and the Ladies' Mission Society. The church-spon-
sored Livingstone College, in Salisbury, North Carolina, was encouraged to train missionaries for Africa. Reverend Mark Bell,
who had promoted mission organization, was elected Foreign
Missions Secretary.[76]

The 1884 General Conference showed an increased interest in
Africa, centered around the visit of Andrew Cartwright, the
A.M.E.Z. minister living in Liberia. The Ladies' Foreign Mission
Society had raised over a thousand dollars in the preceding four
years, and the Conference Report noted the spread of mission
interest among the bishops. The church leaders worked to see that
mission sentiment was "being diffused among the ministry and
membership."[77]

The highlight of the Conference was Reverend Cartwright's description of his Liberian congregations at Brewerville and Cape Palmas. The Conference was so inspired by Cartwright's work that they set up a salary (only $100 less than a bishop's annual salary) for him to serve as their missionary, and empowered him to appoint preachers and hold Annual Conferences in Liberia.[78]

But the intensity of interest among A.M.E.Z. leaders in Africa did not last long, and within a few years Cartwright's salary was reduced by half, to only four hundred dollars annually. The missionary had to beg repeatedly to receive any money at all, and in 1892 he pointed out that only twice in the preceding eight years had his pay exceeded two hundred dollars. The church's lack of response toward missions was partly due to Cartwright's lack of progress in Liberia. He was a poor administrator, and had not expanded the mission. Bishop Hood had become skeptical of Cartwright, and stated that even the small appropriations to him were "far in excess of any advantage which seems to accrue therefrom."[79]

The A.M.E. Zion mission in Liberia is noteworthy because it represented the first official independent Afro-American church commitment to converting indigenous Africans. Even though his wife had a mission school of sixty pupils in 1890, by 1896 Cartwright's mission at Brewerville could report only fifty-two members—and most of those were Americo-Liberians. Andrew Cartwright served in Liberia until his death in 1903, but his mission never grew much beyond an individual effort.[80]

The 1892 A.M.E.Z. General Conference Report gloomily observed that mission interest was not strong among the membership. Mrs. Mary J. Jones, President of the A.M.E.Z. Ladies Mission Society, resigned in disgust in 1895 after 90 percent of the local women's mission groups had dissolved, and less than one-tenth of the money expected had been raised.[81] It was not until 1896 that the denominational apathy was broken. This new interest was partly due to A.M.E. Bishop Turner, who spoke to the 1896 A.M.E.Z. General Conference on "The Resources of Africa."[82]

Within the denomination the strongest voice in support of African missions was Bishop Alexander Walters. Born a slave in Kentucky, Walters was co-founder of the Afro-American Council, a black protest organization of the 1890s.[83] In 1897 Walters complimented Turner for doing "more than any other man, to arouse interest in the development of Africa."[84]

By the late 1890s the denomination was becoming more confident of its ability to administer African missionary work, a development which was reflected in the church newspaper, *Star of Zion*. The first mission propaganda included in the paper was in 1896, which stated that missionary preparation "is a momentous subject which the greater A.M.E. Zion Church cannot give too much consideration. Africa is one of the greatest countries of the world." The editor concluded that the church should "intelligently, honorably and steadily join financially and evangelically in the great crusade against mental and spiritual darkness."[85]

Denominational rivalry also played a role in promoting mission interest. For example, in 1897 the *Star of Zion* suggested that the A.M.E.Z. Church must become active in Africa before the A.M.E. Church had established itself over the whole continent. A.M.E. Bishop Turner and his followers were making every effort, according to *Star of Zion* Editor J. C. Dancy, "to occupy the vantage ground [in Africa] before Zion has an opportunity to show herself there. We do not blame them. Bethel and Zion are watching each other now as never before, and this will make both more aggressive."[86] The rivalry expressed was usually friendly, and was coupled with appeals for missionary contributions.[87]

The most tangible evidence of the rise of mission sentiment in the A.M.E.Z. Church was the decision in 1896 to appoint a Bishop for Africa. John Bryan Small, the man chosen for the position, was well qualified because of his mission interest and his personal experience in Africa. Small, born in 1845 in the British West Indies, joined the British army as a clerk at age seventeen. Stationed in West Africa for three years, he traveled all along the coast from Sierra Leone to Nigeria. However, he resigned the army in protest against British policies toward the Ashanti Kingdom. In 1871 he came to the United States and joined the A.M.E.Z. Church to pursue a career as a preacher.[88]

Within a year after his election, Bishop Small was on his way to Africa. The *Star of Zion*, which felt the A.M.E.Z. Church could no longer ignore the "awful cry" of the unconverted Africans, declared that Small had left America "to risk his life among savage, ignorant, and superstitious races . . . [who] must have the light of the cross."[89] Small's wife wrote in pity for the Africans, for having to endure "the cruelties and sufferings of the heathen world," and she spoke of the poor missionaries having to live "in a strange land, among a strange people."[90]

For his own part, Bishop Small seemed to enjoy his time in Africa. After being welcomed to Sierra Leone by A.M.E. missionaries there, he traveled on to Liberia. Small was not impressed with Andrew Cartwright, and he found the A.M.E.Z. Liberian mission in "poor condition." Under Bishop Small's direction, there were no more missionaries appointed to Liberia until after Cartwright's death in 1903.[91]

Small placed emphasis upon the area of Africa which he knew best, the Gold Coast (present-day Ghana). This area of coastal West Africa, a British colony since 1874 but occupied by European traders since the late fifteenth century, had developed by the 1890s a class of Westernized Africans similar to those in Sierra Leone and South Africa. Small had a fairly favorable view of Africans, and noted that despite having suffered at the hands of Europeans, many Gold Coast people were developing high intelligence. This literate leadership class would, he felt, be the best basis for A.M.E.Z. Church expansion. He wrote to *Star of Zion* complimenting the westernized elite, and stated, "Persons are greatly mistaken when they think everybody [in Africa] is uncivilized and unlearned."[92]

Perhaps reacting to the poor showing by Cartwright in Liberia, Small decided not to bring more black American missionaries to Africa. Instead, he concentrated upon bringing young Africans to America to be trained as missionaries at the Church's Livingstone College. Beginning with William Hockman in 1897, Small enrolled four students from the Gold Coast by the end of the century. One of these students, James E. K. Aggrey, was destined to become famous in the twentieth century as an educator and nationalist.[93]

Meanwhile, Bishop Small attracted a number of African ministers from the British Methodist Church. In 1898 Reverend Thomas B. Freeman, Jr. led many of his Gold Coast constituents in a secession movement from the white churches. In affiliating with the A.M.E.Z. Church, Freeman expressed his own black consciousness when he stated that the A.M.E.Z. Church, "composed of Africans and entirely governed and worked by Africans," would be able to "take a much greater interest in their missions in the Motherland than can be possible with missionary Boards and missionaries of an alien race."[94] *The Gold Coast Aborigines*, the first really militant black newspaper in the colony, expressed similar sentiments about the A.M.E.Z. Church, noting with favor, "It is, indeed, an entirely negro church. . . . It is the sentiment of the church, that however great may be the friendship, intellect or interest of any white man . . . he cannot successfully reach the emotional feelings of the masses of our people!"[95]

By the end of the century the A.M.E.Z. Church had established itself in the Gold Coast, with two churches, one school, seventy-one full members, and forty-five students.[96] The establishment of the denomination within four years in a part of Africa never before contacted by black Americans was due to the personal background and missionary skill of Bishop John Bryan Small.

Although the A.M.E. Church and the A.M.E. Zion Church were the largest black Methodist churches, there were other independent Afro-American denominations. These denominations, however, were simply too small and lacking in funds to support mission work in Africa.

The most notable small independent sect was a splinter group from the southern white Methodist Church. The Colored Methodist Episcopal Church (today known as the *Christian* M.E. Church) was organized in 1870, but its continued close relationship with southern whites caused its growth to proceed slowly.[97] The potential for an interest in missions was reflected as early as 1874, when the General Conference Report advocated active foreign mission work: "Nothing is more distinctive of a living, vital, and active Christianity than a healthy and successful missionary plan. The death of the missionary spirit in the Church is the prediction of the early death of the Church itself."[98] Despite this expansionist ideology, nothing was done during succeeding meetings, and the C.M.E. Church closed out the century without any missionary program.[99] There was simply no point in arousing mission interest if the church did not have the potential to support at least one missionary, and the small independent black denominations had trouble enough supporting themselves.

Within the larger A.M.E. and the A.M.E. Zion Churches, there had developed by the late nineteenth century a widespread interest in Africa. Although much of this sentiment was initially sparked by emigrationist and other nonreligious concerns, by the 1880s more and more of the denominational leaders felt ready to sponsor expansion into Africa. Once they had taken the mission interest to heart, the bishops and clergy worked to increase interest in Africa among the membership. At this time missionary sentiment was clearly being diffused from the top down. The Afro-American Methodists concentrated on adding African members from already-converted areas of the continent, whether it was the A.M.E. expansion into Liberia, Sierra Leone, and South Africa, or the A.M.E. Zion expansion into the Gold Coast. Such a technique of spreading to Christianized black people, who were reacting against white racial discrimination, replicated their expansion into the American South in the 1860s. In a sense, the movement toward Africa was merely another step in the direction of uniting all black people. To the extent that the evangelization of Africa carried the concerns of many Afro-Americans beyond the borders of the United States, it contributed significantly to the rise of Pan-African identity.

4

Mission Organization in Independent Afro-American Baptist Churches

Rising interest in an African missions movement occurred not only among black Methodists, but also in the other large independent Afro-American denomination: the Baptists. Both the Methodists and the Baptists early devoted much attention to the conversion of slaves, had racially mixed congregations, and preached in a plain simple style which uneducated blacks and whites could understand. Consequently, both denominations attracted large numbers of blacks, but more Afro-Americans converted to the Baptist creed than to any other. This growth was facilitated by the ease of black ministerial ordination and by the independence of local congregations. Local autonomy meant black control, especially after the end of slavery. Another factor suggested by anthropologists is that the Baptist form of total immersion baptism attracted slaves who remembered their West African River Cult religions.[1]

The first independent black Baptist church was formed in Boston in 1805, and was joined by independent churches in other northern cities. After the Civil War, state black Baptist conventions were formed in the South and black Baptists registered the largest growth rate in American churches of the late nineteenth century. By 1894 the membership of black Baptist churches had grown to nearly 1,350,000, three times the size of the A.M.E., the next largest black denomination. Yet the potential strength of the Baptists was diluted because of their highly decentralized organization, which promoted schisms and disunity.[2]

The lack of organized support did not prevent individual black

64

Baptists from offering themselves for mission work in Africa. The early Baptist missionaries to Liberia, Lott Cary and Colin Teague, were followed by several others sponsored in part by a northern black organization, the American Baptist Missionary Convention. These missionary efforts were largely confined to the Americo-Liberian settlers on the coast, due largely to financial difficulties of the sponsoring black churches.[3]

When Thomas Johnson volunteered to serve as a missionary in the Cameroons under sponsorship of the British Baptist Missionary Society, he was following in the footsteps of other Afro-American Baptists. Johnson was not content to serve merely as a representative for a white denomination, however. When he returned to the United States in 1880, he began a massive campaign to interest black Baptists in African missions. On a lecture tour among Missouri freedmen he reported that there was widespread curiosity about Africa, and that thousands of people wanted to emigrate, "prevented only by the lack of means." He went on to say: "The freedmen in the far Southern States are equally alive to the importance of the evangelisation [*sic*] of Africa. The work is growing in all parts. . . . At meeting after meeting I would see strong men and women weeping, as I would tell the story of what I saw in Africa . . . of the lamentable condition of our own brethren in the land of our fathers."[4] He also sponsored a mission meeting of the Wood River Baptist Association, a black group in Illinois. This association made Johnson its mission agent and called for the evangelization of Africa, "teeming with millions in grossest darkness of heathenism."[5] In 1881 he persuaded the black Baptist General Association of the Western States and Territories to set up an African missions fund.[6]

The next year Johnson went to England, where he lectured and wrote in order to raise money for missions. His most effective endeavor in behalf of his cause was his autobiography, which went through six editions between 1882 and 1892.[7] By 1884 Johnson had returned to America and resumed his mission campaign. The Annual Report for the year, issued by the black Baptist General Association of Western States and Territories, reported that Johnson had "awakened a deep interest amongst his brethren, and moved them to more determined effort to give the Gospel to the perishing millions of our race in Africa."[8]

He continued to work for mission interest, traveling through the South in 1887 to raise money for two black missionaries sent to the Congo by the General Association of Western States and Territories and the American Baptist Missionary Union, a rare attempt by both

white and black Baptists to co-sponsor missionaries. In the name of
the new Congo missionaries, Dr. Theophilus E. S. Scholes and John
E. Ricketts, Johnson appealed for black Americans "to hold the
ropes while they go down into the depths of heathenism to win
precious souls for Christ."[9] Johnson lived the rest of his life in
Chicago, and remained committed to African missions. The *Indianapolis Freeman* reported that he was very popular among black
people, and lauded his explorations and mission work in the Cameroons.[10] Johnson was clearly the foremost of those who popularized
missions among blacks in the Midwest.

Among Afro-Americans of the South where Baptist strength was
concentrated, mission interest first appeared on the state level by
the end of Reconstruction. The first missionaries to be sponsored
by them were sent by state conventions. For example, in 1879 the
black South Carolina Baptist Convention sent Reverend Harrison
N. Bouey, one of the *Azor* emigrants, as its representative to Liberia.
When he returned to the United States in 1881, Bouey served as
an agent of the Liberian Baptist Convention. Like most other former
missionaries, he labored arduously to increase interest in African
missions; in 1887 he worked for the Alabama Convention Foreign
Mission Board, and later for the National Baptist Mission Board.
Shortly after 1902 he returned to Liberia as a missionary, and
remained there for the rest of his life. During the late nineteenth
century, Bouey's influence among Afro-American Baptists was
considerable.[11]

The most active black state Baptist convention was in Virginia.
In 1879 it sent Solomon Crosby, a graduate of the Richmond Theological Seminary, to Lagos, Nigeria. Although Crosby was supported
by the Virginia Colored Baptist Convention, he occupied an unused
chapel built by the white Southern Baptist Convention mission in
Lagos. The whites were agreeable to the arrangement as "a mutual
accommodation to . . . keep our stations manned." Although Crosby
was enjoying his work, in 1881 he died of "tropical fever" after
several illnesses. The next year the black Virginia Baptists sent
another Afro-American missionary, J. O. Hayes, to Liberia. In
contrast to Crosby, Hayes lived a long life and remained at his
Liberian mission work until after 1900.[12]

For the remainder of the century African sentiment was strongest
among Virginia Baptists, who raised most of the money contributions
and "have ever been foremost in mission work."[13] The extent of this
interest was due mostly to the influence of William W. Colley.

After he volunteered as a missionary for the Southern Baptist Convention mission in Yorubaland in 1875, Colley had kept in close touch with black Baptist churchmen. He wrote that black churches should sponsor their own missionaries, because Africa "is *their* field of labor. . . . sending the 'Bread of Life' to the heathen of Africa."[14] When he returned to the United States in 1879, the black Virginians appointed Colley to travel throughout the South to raise the mission spirit.

Colley succeeded in raising mission enthusiasm among Afro-American Baptists to such an extent that in 1880 he was able to call a missionary convention in Montgomery, Alabama. Over one hundred delegates from throughout the South formed The Baptist Foreign Mission Convention of the U.S.A. Colley was elected Secretary of the Convention and presided over a collection of $478 for mission work. By the second meeting, held in Knoxville, Tennessee, in 1881, the delegates raised $1,911. J. O. Hayes, the Virginia-sponsored missionary in Liberia, was transferred to the control of the Convention.[15] The great increase in fund-raising, plus the decision to sponsor Hayes, indicates the rapid growth of missionary sentiment among Afro-American Baptists.

The 1882 Convention report concluded that "all the delegates were inspired with new zeal to do more than they had ever done for missions." The Baptist Foreign Mission Convention took its biggest step the next year, however, when it decided to support six new missionaries to Liberia. Heading this new mission was none other than William Colley. Accompanying Colley were his wife, Reverend and Mrs. J. H. Presley, and two young seminary graduates, John J. Coles and Hense McKinney. Coles, like Colley, was from Virginia and was a graduate of Richmond Theological Seminary. McKinney, a twenty-three-year-old Mississippian, graduated from the Natchez Baptist Seminary.[16]

The Afro-American Baptist missionaries established the Bendoo mission among the Vai people of western Liberia in 1884. Colley wrote that he had gone "far out into the wilds among the heathen" for the purpose of "redeeming Africa from heathen chaos." The missionaries established three stations and soon attracted seventy-five members, largely due to promises to help end the Vai tribal wars that were currently being waged.[17]

When the group of missionaries first arrived in Africa, John J. Coles and Hense McKinney entered Liberia College in order to learn Arabic under the direction of Edward Blyden, but after a few months they joined their co-workers in the Vai country. The twenty-eight-year-old Coles became the most effective missionary in the group, because his mastery of the Vai language allowed him to preach to the people without an interpreter.[18] His skilled literary and oratorical abilities also contributed to his influence among black Baptists in America.

Despite its hopeful beginnings, the Bendoo mission was not adequately supported by the Foreign Mission Convention. Colley was forced to appeal to the white American Colonization Society to pay the missionaries' transportation costs to Liberia.[19] Another problem of the missionaries was trying to remain healthy. Only a few months after their arrival Mrs. Presley died of fever, and her husband as well as William Colley were sick most of the time. In 1885 the black Baptists of Texas sent Lewis G. Jordan to join the group, but he shortly returned to America broken in health. J. H. Presley, also weakened by fever and demoralized by his wife's death, accompanied Jordan back to the United States.[20]

A year later the prospects of the mission brightened, largely due to publicizing efforts by Coles. In 1886 he published the story of the Bendoo mission in a book entitled *Africa in Brief*. Then he left Liberia, accompanied by Colley, for a promotional visit to America. While in the United States Coles lectured extensively throughout the South. His trip to America seemed to spark a new interest in missions among Afro-Americans, with some of the most prominent black Baptist leaders calling for black Americans to "give Africa the gospel."[21] Coles pled for the raising of five thousand dollars for the Liberia Mission, and this goal was reached in 1889.[22] On the tour Coles also met and married Lucy Henry of Memphis, who, along with four other missionary volunteers, Coles took to Liberia.[23]

Yet the mission again fell on hard times. Hense McKinney, one of the founding missionaries, died in 1887, and two of the missionaries brought by Coles left Africa after only a few months. When the mission became involved in local tribal conflicts, the Baptists had to flee to the coast for safety. The missionaries returned to America in 1893. Coles, only thirty-six years old, was so weakened by illness that he died shortly after his return. Lucy Coles remained active in the mission effort, serving as Secretary of the National Baptist Foreign Mission Board for two years, but the closing of the Bendoo mission marked the end of mission work among the Vai people. Black American Baptists would not again sponsor missionaries in Liberia until the twentieth century.[24]

The Bendoo mission was the earliest comprehensive effort by an independent Afro-American denomination to support a whole corps of missionaries to non-Westernized Africans. Its failure, though partly owing to insufficient financial support by the church, was mainly due to disease among the missionaries. These illnesses seriously weakened the claims of Afro-American mission promoters that black Americans were immune to the unhealthy effects of a tropical climate.

By 1894 mission work by black southern Baptists was at a virtual standstill, and reorganization was hampered by Baptist disunity. In 1895, however, the various black Baptist groups united in the National Baptist Convention. Lewis G. Jordan, who had briefly served in the Bendoo mission, was elected to head the reorganized Foreign Mission Board of the new N.B.C.

Jordan, a native of Mississippi, moved in boldly to shake off the lethargy that overshadowed the Baptist mission effort in 1896. He recounted:

> When we assumed charge of the work we found a depleted treasury, the missionaries off of the field, the whole work under a cloud, the confidence of the denomination in the Foreign Mission work sadly shaken. . . . Our Foreign Mission Board was looked upon as a begging machine, that might be helped or not. The work of giving the Gospel to the lost was not regarded as a duty laid upon Christians by their Lord.[25]

By scheduling speaking tours, establishing an efficient organization, writing *Up the Ladder in Foreign Missions*, and establishing the denominational magazine *Mission Herald*, Jordan was able to restore confidence in African Baptist missions and thus increase commitment to mission work by black Americans.[26]

Possibly because Jordan remembered his own health problems in Liberia, he directed the Baptist mission effort to another area of Africa. It was probably a combination of accident and institutional rivalry that led to the establishment of the new center of Baptist mission activity in South Africa. In 1894, during the period when there was no effective mission organization among Afro-American Baptists, R. A. Jackson, a black Baptist minister from Mississippi, had financed his own way to South Africa. Why he chose that destination is unknown, but he shortly organized an independent Baptist church in Capetown.[27] Jackson was soon joined by Joseph I. Buchanan, a black sailor from Baltimore, who evidently had not decided on mission work until arriving in Capetown as a part of a ship's crew. But, according to Jordan, "on reaching his fatherland, seeing the needs of the heathen, he felt that here was where God wanted him."[28]

No doubt part of the incentive to open a formal mission in Cape-town was also due to contemporary A.M.E. Church expansion in Africa, especially since Bishop Turner publicly chided the Baptists for not being more active in African missions.[29] Faced with A.M.E. rivalry, and presented with two established missionaries who wished to unite with them, the National Baptist Convention could hardly turn down the opportunity to expand into South Africa.

After the Convention agreed to sponsor Jackson's Capetown mission in 1896, the mission began to grow. Within two years there was a membership of over four hundred, and the church spread to Queenstown. During his trip to South Africa, Bishop Turner noted that Jackson was "known and highly spoken of by the natives everywhere." Turner encouraged the Baptists to do even more in South Africa.[30]

Jackson himself worked hard to increase black American interest in Africa. In one of his appeals for financial support, he wrote to the *Richmond Planet* that black American unconcern for missions would keep the souls of Africans in "the abyss of heathendom. . . . Shall not their blood be upon us, and upon our children? God forbid."[31] He evidently got along well with the South Africans, and soon ordained two of them as ministers.[32] By 1896 Joseph Buchanan had moved into the South African interior, where he led revivals and baptized large numbers of Africans.[33]

Despite this progress, however, Afro-American Baptists remained disunited. Some of the church's more activist mission supporters, especially in Virginia and North Carolina, felt that their organization should be doing even more in Africa. They were angered by the insistence of National Baptist leaders upon separate black organi-zation by their refusal to cooperate with the white American Baptist Missionary Union, and by the transfer of N.B.C. mission head-quarters out of Virginia. These activists set up a new organization in 1897, named after Lott Cary, the pioneer black Baptist missionary in Liberia. This development signified an increasing interest in Africa by the late 1890s, but it also typified the factionalism that hindered Baptist efforts. Despite its intense interest in Africa, and its willing-ness to cooperate with white Baptists, the Lott Cary Foreign Mission Society was not able to place its own missionary in Africa until after 1900.[34]

Meanwhile, Baptist interest in South African missions was in-creased by the visit to America of Joseph Booth, a white Scottish Baptist missionary in Nyasaland, who sought out black American Baptist leaders and convinced them that he was "a real friend of

Africa." Booth's impact was increased because he brought with him a young African named John Chilembwe, who generated much publicity.[35] Another African visitor who aroused much interest was John Tule, R. A. Jackson's brightest convert. "This was the first African baptized by one of our workers we had ever seen," said Secretary Jordan, and this tangible evidence of mission progress pleased the church leaders. The N.B.C. was so impressed with Tule that they elected him as an official missionary. Tule returned to South Africa in 1897, along with Miss Mamie Branton (who later became his wife) and Mr. and Mrs. G. F. A. Johns of Baltimore. These four new missionaries increased black Baptist progress in South Africa, even though Mr. and Mrs. Johns both died of disease within one year.[36]

The largest increase in Baptist membership occurred by a process strikingly similar to the A.M.E. experience with the Ethiopian Church. A group of seventeen African preachers and their congregations had seceded from British-sponsored Baptist missions, after racially discriminatory policies were enacted. The new group, calling itself the African Native Church, was persuaded by Jackson in 1899 to unite its entire 1,200 membership with the National Baptist Convention.[37]

The African Native Church was formally accepted in 1899 by Charles S. Morris, the N.B.C. Financial Secretary. Morris had accompanied the Nyasaland student, John Chilembwe, on his return journey from America. Secretary Morris was in many ways a Baptist counterpart of Bishop Henry Turner, since he united a strong interest in African missions with advocacy of black American emigration to Africa. Morris sympathized with the African secession from the white church, "as a protest against the prejudice that was exhibited in it. . . . They were treated in such a way in that Church that they could not stay in it. I mention these things to show that there is reason for this Ethiopian movement. It is not simply a blind rebellion on the part of the natives."[38] Regarding this trip, his first to Africa, Morris wrote to his friend Bishop Turner: "I simply can't find words to express the deep, abiding joy I have in going about all over this continent, although entirely alone, and preaching the gospel to my dear gifted, but ignorant and neglected brethren." He followed this statement with a strong attack on American racism, and an appeal for emigration.[39]

The interest of the National Baptist leaders in South Africa brought an increasing awareness of Africa in general. In his 1899 address, the N.B.C. President stressed African missions as "the all-important

question of the hour. . . . No man can be true to Christ and refuse
to support the cause of missions."[40] Because of these sentiments,
the National Baptists were interested in additional affiliations with
Africans not only in South Africa, but in Nigeria as well.

The formation of an independent black denomination in Nigeria
was the result of pressures that had been building in the British
colony for a number of years. British missionaries who had been in
the area for almost half a century had made many conversions and
had even trained a number of African clergy. By 1890, however,
these African Christians, led by some transplanted Sierra Leonians,
had begun to resent white paternalism and authoritarianism toward
the black clergy. The breaking point came in 1890 when the Church
Missionary Society, the leading British Anglican organization in
Nigeria, demoted Bishop Samuel Crowther, the only African who
held that rank. In the uproar that followed Crowther's removal,
traditional African leaders of southern Nigeria united with African
Christians to force out all white missionaries. Edward Blyden visited
from Liberia, and urged the Nigerians to secede from the European
missions and establish an independent church similar to Afro-
American churches.[41]

The leader of the protest was Reverend James Johnson, a Sierra
Leonian of Yoruba descent who had been transferred from Sierra
Leone by the Anglican Church because colonial officials became
nervous over his black nationalist ideas. In Lagos, however, Johnson
soon built an even larger following attracted by his twin ideals
of Christianity and nationalism. He felt that it would be necessary
for Christianity to overcome traditional African religions in order
for nationalism to grow, but that Christianity could not succeed in
Africa unless white missionaries were removed.[42]

In response to these ideas, developed by nationalists like Blyden
and Johnson, Mojola Agbebi founded the United Native African
Church. Though of Baptist background himself, Agbebi wanted a
nondenominational church because he felt that denominational
rivalries weakened African unity. He asked the A.M.E. Church in
Sierra Leone and Liberia to ordain his ministers, but the A.M.E.
missionaries agreed to help only if Agbebi expelled all church
members who were practicing polygamy. Since Agbebi sought to
instill a respect for traditional African culture, he refused. He moved
back to his Baptist connections and appointed as clergy Mr. and
Mrs. John E. Ricketts, the former American Baptist missionaries
sent to the Congo by Thomas Johnson. Under their direction,
polygamy was not disturbed, and by the beginning of the twentieth

century Agbebi had affiliated with the National Baptist Convention.[43]

By 1900 the National Baptists were able to report nineteen ordained missionaries in western and southern Africa, as well as nine African students being supported in the United States.[44] Under the guidance of leaders like Thomas Johnson and William Colley, who had previously served as missionaries of white organizations, the black Baptist mission work began. The effect of writings and lecture tours by missionaries from the field, like John J. Coles, Lewis Jordan, and R. A. Jackson, was crucial in keeping interest alive and attracting more missionary volunteers. The denominational rivalry with and example of the A.M.E. Church in the 1890s also provided much incentive for black Baptist leaders such as Charles Morris to expand their mission work in Africa. In 1900, National Baptist Mission Secretary Jordan was able to conclude, "Today the foreign mission work of the denomination is in a more healthy condition than at any other time in its history."[45] By the turn of the century the African missions movement among Afro-American Baptists, as among the Methodists, had become well established.

William Henry Sheppard and Lucy Gantt Sheppard, Presbyterian missionaries in the Congo, with their children, ca. 1900. Courtesy of the Historical Foundation of the Presbyterian and Reformed Churches.

Presbyterian Congo mission at Ibanj, with the Reverend William Henry Sheppard (*center, in white clothing*), ca. 1895. Courtesy of the Historical Foundation of the Presbyterian and Reformed Churches.

The Reverend William Henry Sheppard, with BaKuba men, ca. 1895. Courtesy of the Historical Foundation of the Presbyterian and Reformed Churches.

The Reverend Alexander. Crummell, Episcopal missionary in Liberia. From the *Indianapolis Freeman*, November 30, 1895.

A.M.E. Bishop Henry M. Turner (*left*) and Missions Secretary H. B. Parks (*center back*) welcoming South African Ethiopian Church representative James M. Dwane (*center front*) into the A.M.E. Church, while the Reverend J. S. Flipper (*right*) looks on, 1896. Courtesy of the Department of Missions, African Methodist Episcopal Church.

Sarah Gorham, A.M.E. missionary to Sierra Leone, ca. 1890. Courtesy of the Department of Missions, African Methodist Episcopal Church.

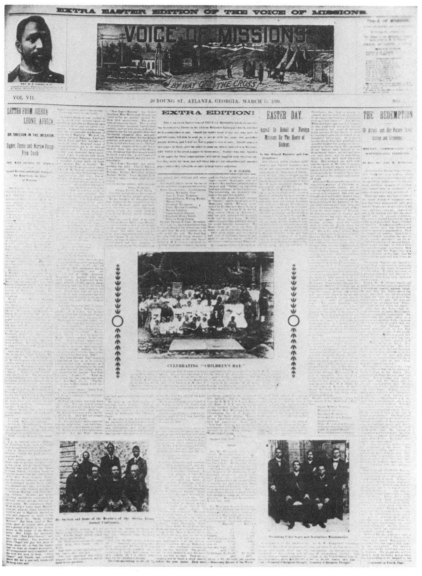

Henry M. Turner's *Voice of Missions*, A.M.E. Church newspaper, March 15, 1899.

The Reverend R. A. Jackson, Baptist missionary in South Africa, ca. 1895.
Courtesy of the Foreign Mission Board, National Baptist Convention, U.S.A.

A "witch doctor" in Liberia, ca. 1900. Photograph taken by Alexander P. Camphor, Methodist missionary, and published in his book *Missionary Story Sketches: Folklore from Africa* (1909), p. 48.

Islamic scholars in Liberia, ca. 1900. Photograph taken by Alexander P. Camphor, Methodist missionary, and published in his book *Missionary Story Sketches: Folklore from Africa* (1909), p. 36.

James E. K. Aggrey, Gold Coast student brought to Livingstone College by the A.M.E. Zion Church, 1898. From David Kimble, *A Political History of Ghana: The Rise of Gold Coast Nationalism, 1850–1928* (1963). Courtesy of the Oxford University Press.

81

Four of the Liberian Bassa students at Lincoln University; below, as they appeared on their arrival in 1873, above, in 1881. *Left to right:* Alonzo Miller, Robert Deputie, John Knox, Samuel Sevier. Courtesy of the Special Collections, Langston Hughes Memorial Library, Lincoln University, Pennsylvania.

Part Two
Redemption of a Continent: Black American Mission Thought on Africa

5

Motivation of Black American Missionaries in Africa

Black Americans who went to Africa as missionaries were in a crucial position to influence ideas about the continent, largely because so few black Americans had been to Africa and publicized their reactions in the United States. The well-educated missionaries, inspired with religious zeal, had the ability and the motivation to communicate their opinions effectively. They wanted to let their churches know that they were doing effective service in the work for which they were sent. Since they depended entirely on voluntary contributions for their support, it was to their financial advantage to publicize their work. Consequently, on furloughs to the United States or after their retirement, the clergymen often spoke or wrote about their experiences in Africa. Church presses, the largest black-controlled publishers, turned out numerous missionary memoirs, and the pulpit provided a convenient medium for those who made their living as professional speakers.

At least 113 black American missionaries served in Africa between 1877 and 1900. The majority, sixty-eight, were in Liberia—some of these had gone there as emigrants. This contingent was followed in size by twenty in the Congo, thirteen in Sierra Leone, six in South Africa, three in Nigeria, three in Mozambique, and one each in the Cameroons, Angola, and Rhodesia. Of this total, fifty were sponsored by white churches and sixty-five represented black denominations. The black church agents were all concentrated in the Europeanized areas of the continent, like Liberia, Sierra Leone, and South Africa.[1] Proximity to westernized populations was a crucial factor in determining the locations of these mission efforts.

There was much diversity among those early evangelists. They included mulattoes and blacks from free and slave backgrounds and from rural and urban areas. They came from various regions, with a majority (of the half whose backgrounds are known) from heavily black-populated states like Virginia, Arkansas, Mississippi, South Carolina, and Georgia. Although these differences existed, some generalizations can be made about the Afro-American missionaries whose family backgrounds are known. Most notable is the fact that they had fairly comfortable childhoods in families that were relatively well-to-do. Although their families were usually not wealthy, they were not afflicted by the grinding poverty that was typical of most black people of that time. The Episcopal missionary Alexander Crummell, for example, was raised by "kind and indulgent parents" who were relatively prosperous leaders in the black community of New York City.[2] The parents of the Presbyterian William H. Sheppard were moderately well-to-do; his father was a barber and his mother managed the hot springs baths at a resort for wealthy whites. Both of these jobs were high status ones (for blacks), which placed the Sheppards in close personal contact with upper-class whites.[3] American Board missionary Benjamin Ousley was born a slave, but after the Civil War his father operated a successful country store and farm in Reconstruction Mississippi. Even though his father's store was forced to close during the 1873 depression, Ousley had a comfortable childhood.[4] Fannie Worthington, who accompanied her husband, A.M.E. missionary Alfred Ridgel, to Africa, grew up in a prosperous black family which could afford to send her to elite schools in St. Louis and Washington, D.C. Her father had been a prominent state legislator in Arkansas during Reconstruction.[5] Ruby Williams, one of the missionaries sent to Liberia by the northern white Methodist church, was, according to her minister, "a devout Christian of a noble character . . . of one of the first families our city affords."[6] Their higher class status, with no "starvation-around-the-corner" psychological orientation, probably allowed these individuals to think in terms of ideological goals rather than merely basic materialistic survival.

A second generalization which can be made about the missionaries is that they came from families which were very religious and devoted to their churches. Several of them mentioned in later years the strong religious emphasis in their families, and some of them were children of ministers.[7] The emphasis on religion was usually accompanied by a strong emphasis on education. Perhaps the most striking feature of the letters written by these missionaries is the high quality of grammar, spelling, and prose. Considering that most Afro-Americans during that time were not even literate, the missionaries' educational level is exceptional. Almost all of them displayed solid educational backgrounds, and nearly half are known to have attended such institutions as Fisk University, Howard University, Atlanta University, Lincoln University, New Orleans University, Philander Smith College, Hampton Institute, and various theological seminaries. Undoubtedly there were other missionaries with higher education about whom information has been lost. The two largest occupational groups among those who had employment before they became missionaries were ministers and teachers. Such occupational choices reflect the dual emphasis on religion and education which they received in their youth.[8]

At the schools they attended, the missionaries received a strong dose of educational and religious propaganda. For some of them it was their school experience which set them on the course of becoming missionaries. Several of the philanthropic white-sponsored institutions encouraged mission commitment; the role of white teachers at these institutions is an example of direct influence of whites on Afro-American mission sentiment. At Fisk University, for example, where Benjamin Ousley was a student in 1878, two Fisk graduates left for a Sierra Leone mission. Ousley's white teachers encouraged him to commit himself as well. He recalled his reactions to a mission sermon at Fisk, in which "the wretched and degraded state of the heathen brought them before me as [if] it had been a vision. In contemplation of their wretchedness, I was not able to restrain my tears and a great burden seemed to weigh upon my heart."[9]

Another student, Henrietta Bailey (who later married Benjamin Ousley), also received her mission inspiration at Fisk. Her family opposed her decision to go to Africa; so, she wrote, she 'tried to banish the idea. Yet I could not, for it was brought up to my mind at every [Fisk] missionary meeting."[10] The importance of persuasion by the faculty of Fisk University, to a degree of commitment even beyond the family's wishes, is underscored by one of Bailey's and Ousley's white professors who wrote to the American Board recommending them as missionaries: "It is our highest ambition to fit many others for foreign as well as home [mission] work."[11]

Methodist-sponsored Philander Smith College, in Arkansas, sent three of its graduates as missionaries to Liberia in 1898. In writing a letter of recommendation for one of these graduates, a professor noted that F. M. Allen was intelligent, religious, and businesslike: "We are glad that he is turning his attention towards Africa."[12] With such reinforcement from their teachers, it is not surprising that some of the more religiously oriented students responded by becoming missionaries.

A Methodist who owed even greater inspiration to his white teachers was Alexander Camphor. After his parents' death while he was a small child, Camphor was adopted by a white Methodist preacher. He was sent to Methodist Freedman's Aid schools during Reconstruction, and then to New Orleans University. During those years he came under the influence of Methodist leaders like Joseph Hartzell and Wilbur Thirkield, northern liberals who had committed themselves to black education. They shielded young Camphor from the worst aspects of racism, and made him confident and race-proud by encouraging him to rise to his highest capabilities. At the university, the white faculty encouraged him to read books on Africa, and he organized the "Friends of Africa" society there. Camphor, with his strong developing interest in African missions, was considered a model student and graduated at the head of his class in 1889. Shortly thereafter, the university invited him to join the faculty, which provided a strong role model for other black students who held mission sentiments.[13]

Probably the missionary who most expressed his gratitude for the inspiration he received from his white teachers was William H. Sheppard. His parents had encouraged him to interact closely with upper-class whites, and as a child they placed him in the home of a white dentist. There he worked as an apprentice servant, in exchange for a basic education in reading, writing, arithmetic, and the social graces. At age twelve Sheppard was sent to Hampton Institute, where the white president of the school, General Samuel Armstrong, became his ideal. In later years Sheppard remembered Armstrong fondly as "a tender-hearted father" who was the "ideal of manhood." While at Hampton, Sheppard taught Sunday School to a poor black congregation, and from that time he determined "to carry the gospel to the poor, destitute and forgotten people." Sheppard later traced his original interest in Africa to white influences in his childhood and at Hampton, but no doubt the strong sense of religious and social duty impressed upon him by his parents (as well as their unusual admiration for cultured upper-class whites) helped to form his inclinations. African missions were a topic of concern at Hampton: in 1882 Edward W. Blyden spoke to the student body, and a Hampton graduate was serving as a missionary in

Sierra Leone. This graduate, Ackrell E. White, wrote reports back to his school emphasizing that it was the duty of black people to "redeem Africa," and encouraging the Afro-American to follow Blyden's advice about considering "Africa as his country and his home."[14] Such sentiments were entirely in accord with the mission emphasis of schools like Hampton.

As a result of their rather well-to-do family background, their educational advantages, and the inspiration many of them received from schools and teachers, the missionaries developed serious religious interests and a strong sense of duty to others. Many of them were teachers, and the black churches had a strong tradition of social service activities. A.M.E. missionary Sarah Gorham, for example, was not only active with humanitarian work in her church, she was also employed as a social worker by the Boston Associated Charities.[15] The strong sense of duty to undertake mission work overrode considerations of personal comfort. Mrs. Kelley M. Kemp, an American Missionary Association/United Brethren missionary to Sierra Leone, was afflicted with a terminal illness. Nevertheless, she still wished to go to Africa as a missionary, writing: "I can teach the women to read the Bible and sew. The doctor says I cannot live many years. The road to heaven is as near from Africa as it is from here. Yes—I will go." With this dedicated attitude, she did effective work in Africa for four years before she died.[16] Methodist Alexander Camphor and his wife went to Liberia determined to "forsake all" out of their strong sense of duty "to the unreached millions of Liberia's aboriginal peoples in their vast and uninvaded wilderness."[17] After F. M. Allen had been accepted as a Methodist missionary to Liberia, he wrote that he was becoming so absorbed in the prospects that "I cannot imagine what else I could do and be satisfied. . . . My highest ambition is to live a Christian and for humanity. That's why I have undertaken such a work . . . in that dark land."[18] Allen was a printer, and his excitement about establishing a mission newspaper is evident in his letters, which he signed, "Yours for the advancement of printing in Africa."[19] Two of Allen's colleagues gave up good teaching posts because of their commitment to missions.[20]

With the exception of those missionaries who went to Africa as emigrants, few of the evangelists cited dissatisfaction with their life in the United States as a reason for going. On the contrary, most of them were educated up-and-coming young members of the black elite who seemed to be giving up more than they gained by becoming

missionaries. They were more concerned about forsaking the comforts and pleasures of their American homes than escaping to utopia
in Africa. Several embarked as missionaries against the wishes of
their friends and families. For example, American Board missionary
Samuel Miller wrote that all his family and friends were "firmly
opposed to such an idea as going to Africa . . . [but] I am willing
to leave all friends and country for God." Likewise, James H.
Presley, a volunteer to the Baptist Bendoo mission in Liberia, vividly
expressed his reluctance to leave America in an 1883 series of poems:

> Can we leave our native country,
>   Leave the land we love so well?
> Land of joy, peace and pleasure,
>   Can we say to you farewell?
>
> Dearest mother—blessed country,
>   We thy children love thee well;
> Can we leave thy happy borders,
>   Far in heathen lands to dwell?[21]

By picturing the United States as his happy native country, in
contrast to "heathen" Africa, Presley demonstrated a strong American identity. His sense of suffering and duty, and his consciousness
of the things he was giving up, were common among the missionaries.

The missionaries' inspiration came primarily from their ideological
commitment to Christianity. All of them were very serious about
their religion, and their sense of Christian duty was real. They
believed that their religion had had a wonderful effect on their own
lives, and they desired to help everyone gain this enlightenment.
They took literally the Christian commandment to spread the gospel.
A.M.E. Reverend Alfred Ridgel, for example, received his inspiration
primarily from the Bible. He often quoted the Psalms verse that
prophesied "Ethiopia shall stretch out her hands to God" as evidence
of Africa's glorious future. When he became discouraged because of
separation from his loved ones and lack of support from his church,
he wrote: "Often I think of leaving the field and returning to my
friends and relatives where life would afford more ease and comfort;
but in the midst of these meditations, the voice of the man of sorrows
[Jesus] comes down the ages: 'Stand to your post. Hold the fort for
I am coming.'"[22] This Biblical inspiration was strong enough to
carry him over periods of discouragement, and he worked diligently
to spread the A.M.E. Church even when he felt he was not receiving
enough support.

Likewise, American Board missionary Nancy Jones received her inspiration from Biblical concepts of duty. She had decided to become a missionary at age twelve, and had become more anxious to satisfy this "pressing duty" each year. She believed that God "directs my mind and heart to Africa, the land of my Forefathers, to those who are living in darkness and sin. . . . I cannot enter into my Father's Kingdom unless I do just what he commands me to do. . . . I seem to hear the words 'Go ye into all the world.'"[23]

While Africa was often specifically mentioned in their justifications, many of the missionaries felt a general duty to save the unconverted. Samuel Miller wrote to the American Board that it was every Christian's duty "to make God's name known in all the earth."[24] Alexander Camphor believed that all Christians "owe a debt to the heathen world which they are in duty bound to pay, or else their integrity as Christians must be seriously impaired and their loyalty prove merely an empty pretension." He was inspired by a hymn he had learned in the Methodist Church:

> The heathen perish day by day,
> Thousand on thousand pass away!
> O Christians, to their rescue fly,
> Preach Jesus to them ere they die.[25]

For one who sincerely believed that an unending hell awaited all those who had not accepted Christianity, the act of carrying the message to the unconverted was an act of mercy.

Some of the missionary volunteers were recruited after listening to the testimonies of other missionaries or mission advocates. William Sheppard, for example, attracted four other Afro-American Presbyterian volunteers during his 1893 trip to the United States. Mary McLeod Bethune later remembered that when she was twelve years old she heard a missionary sermon given by the Methodist preacher J. W. E. Bowen, and from that point she resolved to become a missionary to Africa.[26] The first time Amanda Smith thought of going to Africa was during a Methodist camp meeting in 1872, when she heard some white missionaries to Asia and South America. She wrote that the meeting fascinated and inspired her. When a friend told her about another missionary in Africa, she later said, "Oh! what a deep impression it made on my mind and heart."[27] In 1878 she went to England as a traveling evangelist, and an English friend who was volunteering to become a missionary to India asked Smith to go with her. At first Smith refused, having no previous interest in India, but then she prayed to God that "if He wanted me to go to

India, to make it very clear and plain to me, and I would obey Him, and leave all and go." She felt that God commanded her to go, so she went "without the least shadow of a doubt in my mind." Later, she felt that God had sent her to India to better prepare her for mission work in Africa.[28]

Joseph C. Sherrill, a black Methodist minister in Little Rock, Arkansas, had such strong and effective missionary sentiment that he attracted more volunteers for the Methodist Liberia mission than could be accepted. He and his wife volunteered to lead the group, and his excitement is clear from his letters, which he always signed "Yours for Africa." Some of the other volunteers had to be eliminated because of poor health or because their relatives objected, but of the final choices Sherrill wrote, "A company of better prepared people could not be chosen. They are all willing to sacrifice all American pleasures and consecrate their lives to the missionary work of Africa in behalf of the old M.E. Church. They are doubtless in determination, firm in their decision."[29] Their primary motivation seemed to be their seriousness about their religion, and the feeling that educated "civilized" blacks had a duty to aid the "uncivilized" members of their race in Africa. It is not difficult to understand why young idealistic blacks volunteered to become missionaries. They had, through their education, been exposed to the nineteenth-century idea of duty, and were simply seeking consistency between their ideology and their actions.

While personal backgrounds and ideological beliefs influenced Afro-American missionary commitment, self-interest was also a contributing factor. The occupational choice to become a missionary did not bring material wealth, but it was highly valued for a complex set of reasons relating to social status. By the nineteenth century there were only a limited number of "respectable" occupations open to black people. As more Afro-Americans became educated and "refined," their rise to an elite status engendered expectations of social acceptance. By the last two decades of the century, however, a discrepancy existed between these expectations and the reduced chances for advancement as the color line was solidified. Becoming a respected missionary was one way for an American black to raise his or her social status.

The most evident example of an attempt to raise their status by becoming missionaries involved those Afro-American preachers who emigrated to Liberia. A.M.E. Zion missionary Andrew Cartwright tried to duplicate his successful religious efforts in the post–Civil

War South by going to Liberia. He felt discouraged about the future of black people in the United States, so he emigrated.[30] Likewise, Baptist missionary Harrison H. Bouey was disgusted at the curtailment of political and civil rights in the post-Reconstruction South. In the 1870s, he had served as a judge and was elected sheriff in Edgefield County, South Carolina. With the return of conservative white political domination to the state in 1877, however, he was prevented from finishing his term as sheriff. Thereafter, he became a preacher, one of the few leadership roles left to black southerners, and became interested in emigration. In this respect, Bouey was moving to a different land, independent of white control, where he felt he could better exercise his leadership abilities.[31]

One did not have to go to Liberia as an emigrant to qualify as a person interested in raising her or his status. Methodist Amanda Smith clearly had a better living standard as an evangelist. After a comfortable childhood she married, but her husband fought in the Union army and was killed during the Civil War. Her second marraige was unhappy, and she was reduced to doing domestic work while living in New York City slums. She reacted against the drudgery and hand-to-mouth existence, and she hated living in New York, so it is not too surprising that she left this unhappy situation to become an evangelist. Even when she was sometimes discouraged in Africa, she never sounded as despondent as she had in New York. She was usually comfortable, and had a wide circle of friends and much more social status and influence than before.[32]

Though it was probably not true for many of the black missionaries, some of them seemed to have a strong need for social approval from whites. This tendency applied mainly to those who served as missionaries for white churches. For example, most of Amanda Smith's friends were "refined" upper-class whites. She was race-proud, but she was also accommodating in her social attitudes and conscious that other blacks "often call me 'White folks' nigger.'" That she identified with whites might be suggested by the lines of her favorite church hymn: "There is power in Jesus' blood,/ To wash me white as snow."[33]

William Sheppard showed similar feelings. He had a life-long proclivity for working with whites, and remembered from his childhood that "the white people were always very kind to us." Whether this sentimentalizing was entirely genuine or not, Sheppard displayed an unusual bond of affection toward whites.[34] While he admired whites, however, he was somewhat discouraged about his future in America. As a young preacher he did not adapt well to the increasingly rigid segregation patterns of the deep South. Rather than protest his second-class treatment, Sheppard's reaction was to petition to become a missionary.[35]

In Africa, Sheppard could give free play to his desire for leadership. The Presbyterian mission photographs reveal that he habitually dressed in the "great white hunter" motif: an entirely white suit complete with white pith helmet. It would be going too far to argue that Sheppard wanted to make himself "white," but he clearly enjoyed the status and full range of activities open only to prominent whites in the United States. Sheppard's masterful poses demonstrate, even more than his writings, his happiness in Africa.[36]

By becoming a missionary Sheppard could gain the respect of both blacks and whites that he so dearly valued. He had considerable influence over a major operation of the Presbyterian Mission Board, had a salary equal to that of white missionaries, and was consistently addressed as "Mr." or "Reverend" in an age when few titles of respect were given to black people.[37] Since mission work was highly regarded by both white and black Americans, a missionary held a relatively prestigious position, and was able to work without much of the interference commonly caused by racial prejudice.

Thus, whether a black person went to Africa to get away from whites or to gain the respect of whites as well as blacks, mission work could fulfill this need. As refined Victorians, the missionaries strongly identified as "civilized" people. Such a characterization was not only a result of their family background and education, it was also a reaction to racist stereotypes of black "savagery." Anxiety over their status caused educated Afro-American elitists to do everything within their power to separate themselves from that categorization, and African mission work helped to fulfill this need. The best way to establish one's claim to being a "civilized person" was to follow the Christian ideals of concern for the lowly and evangelization of the faith. By placing themselves in a paternalistic situation toward Africans, black Americans could clearly demonstrate the contrasts between themselves and the "uncivilized," and thereby negate the stereotype of Afro-Americans as uncivilized savages.

Even though general mission sentiment developed out of the historical experience of Afro-American society, a psychohistorical analysis can help explain why particular individuals became missionaries. Although psychohistory has obvious limitations when applied to nonliving subjects, a brief survey of psychological theories may provide insight by clarifying the connection between historical context and individual motivation.

Psychologist Abraham Maslow has developed a hierarchy of different human needs, ranging from basic needs like physiological survival and safety-security to higher ideological needs like love, self-esteem, and self-actualization. Maslow believes that the lower needs must be satisfied before an individual can turn his attention to higher needs.[38] This pattern fits for almost all the missionaries. Having grown up in comfortable family situations where their basic needs were met, they could devote their attention to goals of self-actualization.

If Maslow's humanistic approach helps to explain why missionaries tended to come from financially secure families, a behavioral analysis can help explain the impact of mission advocates on the young volunteers. Behaviorists emphasize the importance of role models in learning: a person observes the behavior of another whom she or he admires, and models her or his own behavior accordingly. For example, almost always critical in the decision to become a minister is the influence of another member of the clergy.[39] Cognitive aspects of social learning are also crucial. Tests that have been developed to understand the relative importance of values held by an individual indicate that missionaries' most deeply held values were "religion" and "social service" to others.[40] Certainly the black missionaries held strong religious ideals and a sense of duty to others. They often mentioned the importance of admired teachers, preachers, or mission advocates, who served as role models in directing them toward mission work. That is, they were influenced not only by the arguments a speaker used to advocate missionary commitment, but also by the fact that the speaker was an admired and respected model.

Why particular individuals volunteered for mission duty, while others of similar belief did not, is perhaps answered by a Freudian psychoanalytic approach. Freud suggested three processes of personality: the *id* (to avoid pain and seek immediate pleasure), the *ego* (to pursue concrete goals realistically), and the *superego* (to actualize larger values and ideals of society). The superego inhibits the impulses of the id, and persuades the ego to seek perfectionist moral goals rather than pleasure or concrete realistic goals.[41] Psychological tests have shown that missionaries tend to have a very strong superego, as reflected by a higher need for social approval and commitment to socially valued goals.[42] The black missionaries not only followed high-status socially oriented careers, but sought social approval from both whites and blacks. Moreover, they pursued this social status even though it involved their own inconvenience. They emphasized their suffering at giving up the pleasures of home for the benefit of mankind, and in going into the "wilds" of Africa— clear evidence of superego dominance.

It is remarkable that the Afro-American missionaries' strong sense of religious duty was channeled almost exclusively into a particular concern for Africa. Only Amanda Smith had done mission work in other world areas, and except for some activity of Afro-Americans among black people of the West Indies, mission sentiment became almost synonymous with involvement in Africa. The spirit of this movement is exemplified by a popular black history text of the 1880s:

> Missionary societies exist in the colored schools, and Africa is the Continent toward which all are looking. These institutions are the great hope of Africa's evangelization by her children in America. . . . Some hearts are already burning with zeal at the thought of their brethren in Africa, and with a desire to help them. . . . A morning star of Hope for the millions in Africa who have yet learned nothing of Christianity, nor taken the first lessons of civilization, shines over the lowly cabins of their brothers in America.[43]

The black missionaries directed their particular concern toward Africa because of their strong sense of connection with the continent. They often were conscious of Africa from an early age. Several remembered stories about the continent told in their families. The Baptist John Coles, for example, remembered his mother talking about her family having been descended from the Ibo people of West Africa. Therefore, he concluded, "When I came to Africa, I came not to strangers but to my own people."[44] In Henry M. Turner's family, his grandfather was said to have been an African prince. Turner bragged about his royal ancestry, and admitted that such family traditions "doubtless had much to do in forming our African attachments."[45] Joseph E. Phipps was attracted to the Presbyterian Congo mission partly because his grandfather was Congolese,[46] and Alexander Crummell's father was from Sierra Leone.[47] Others, like Alexander Camphor and Sarah Gorham, had relatives who had emigrated to Liberia.[48] By such family traditions and connections, Africa was kept in their minds.

The Baptist minister Thomas Johnson remembered his mother telling him "that we were all free there [in Africa], but white people stole us from our country and made slaves of us." Even though his mother knew little else of Africa, what she did know imparted a favorable image of freedom and serenity. Johnson expressed a strong antislavery feeling later in his life, and this childhood association of Africa with freedom may have contributed to his interest in the fatherland. He later recalled, "For years my prayers had been that I might see Africa, the land of my fathers." The missionary spirit was particularly strong in him, and he could not rid himself of the idea of going to Africa to minister to the "thousands in Africa who were heathen." He would feel satisfied "if I could only tell them what I knew about my blessed Jesus."[49]

Johnson acknowledged an unfavorable image that most black Americans had about Africa, gained indirectly from reading or talking: "Many of my friends would tell me of what they had heard and read of Africa—the fevers, the cannibals, the reptiles, etc.—but none of these things could change my purpose."[50] It is significant that Johnson did not deny these images, but continued to feel the missionary urge despite them. Such images were implanted at an early age, if the testimony of Amanda Smith is typical:

> I remembered when I was quite young I heard my father and mother talk about Africa. I remembered, too, that I used to see a large paper. . . . It had large pictures, and Africans in their costumes and huts, and . . . some of the pictures were horrid, as I remember them now. . . .
> I seemed to see a great heathen town. There were the great boa-constrictors, and there [were] the great lions and panthers.[51]

Thus, Africa was often seen as a wild and threatening place, but it was a place that one was tied to by kinship and a common past. Also, the lower caste position of black people in the United States kept them from being accepted as "one hundred percent" Americans. The myth of African barbarism was continually held over their heads, and it was impossible for a black person to escape from an African label. This definition was imposed by a white population which was determined not to let blacks fully assimilate into American society. Some blacks reacted by trying to deny any Africanness, but others responded with an increased self-awareness of connections with Africa.

One white-imposed form of discrimination which indirectly contributed to black interest in Africa was the segregation system. In order to preserve their self-respect, black people transformed segregation into a positive philosophy for building their own movements and institutions. The late nineteenth century was an era of "self-help," "race pride," and "duty to one's race." Accordingly, as far as mission sentiment was concerned, Africa was the natural field of labor for building up the race.

The Afro-American missionaries had a consciousness of race that included black people in both America and Africa. American Board volunteer Samuel Miller, for example, stated that his reasons for wanting to go to Africa involved not only Christian commitment to spread the faith, but also his sense of duty "to do all I can for my race, here and in Africa."[52] Baptist missionary Thomas Johnson referred to Africans as "our own brethren in the land of our fathers"[53] Johnson claimed that Afro-Americans were best suited to take the gospel to Africa not only for health reasons, but also because in the great reformations of history "God has seen fit to select men to do the work, from the nation to be reformed." He saw black Americans as part of a larger black nationality which was "tied to that people [Africans] by ties of consanguinity, of suffering and wrong. We can enter into the intellectual, social and moral life as no race alien to us can do."[54]

Sometimes Africans themselves communicated this feeling of common identity to black Americans. In 1893 Mark Casely-Hayford, an educated Gold Coast disciple of Edward Blyden, wrote to the A.M.E. mission newspaper that "duty to our common race" beckoned Afro-American missionaries.[55] Likewise, Reverend James "Holy" Johnson, nationalist leader in Lagos, appealed for black missionaries from the United States to evangelize the continent along with Christianized Africans.[56] The A.M.E. Church responded in its 1896 General Conference Minutes by emphasizing that "Africa is the largest and most important of the fields that lie before us . . . on account of the relationship that exists between our race and the inhabitants of the Dark Continent." This report referred to Africans as "bone of our bone and flesh of our flesh." The "dark continent" was called upon to "arise and shine, for the light of civilization is waiting for thee."[57] H. B. Parks, the man who was elected A.M.E. Mission Secretary in that year, reiterated that Afro-Americans would make the best missionaries because they identified with "the members of its own family who are bowing to wood and stone in heathen lands."[58]

Some black religious leaders felt defensive about exclusive missionary concentration on Africa. The president of the National Baptist Convention justified this selectivity, however, by claiming that white churches were neglecting Africa, so the black churches must take up the slack.[59] Others argued along a different tack, that black missions were needed because of the misdeeds of white missionaries in Africa. One of the reasons for the founding of missionary training at Livingstone College by the A.M.E. Zion Church was church officials' distrust of white involvement in Africa.[60] The Kansas City *American Citizen* characterized the evangelization of Africa by whites as "moonshine," and little more than forcing the Africans "into submission to surrender of their territory."[61] An A.M.E. missionary in Liberia claimed that Africans preferred black missionaries because white clergymen sometimes used their positions to gain personal wealth at the Africans' expense. Such clergy, he concluded, were "a libel upon Christianity" and should be replaced by Afro-American missionaries.[62]

Their strong sense of racial duty and religious duty convinced mission advocates that Africa needed Christianity in order to progress. Black Americans saw their role as crucial because they thought they had the key to transform Africa. The major source of information about Africa, within a religious context, was the Bible. Numerous black ecclesiastical writers of the nineteenth century attempted to prove that ancient Egypt was a black kingdom, because this background could be a source of pride. Egypt was considered "the seat of ancient knowledge, the school of universal wisdom, and the mainstay of the nations of earth in her day," which negated the stereotype of African savagery.[63] But the decline of Egypt was explained in the Bible as evidence of God's displeasure with the Africans for not following the true religion.

The obvious solution to the problem of the continent's stagnation, argued Afro-American Christians, was its conversion to Christianity and redemption in God's eyes.[64] The *Star of Zion* noted that ancient Africa was the earliest civilization but "because of ignorance and vice, Africa is today in heathendom. . . . The time is coming, as the Afro-American gospel missionaries go to that dark continent, when Africa with her teeming millions will regain her former glory."[65] The *Voice of Missions* argued that missionaries could "wipe out the tears of an oppressed race . . . in Africa, where her inhabitants are groping in darkness and ignorance." It predicted a bright future for Christianized Africa, with agriculture, business, science, and literature prospering in places where only slavery and deserts then existed.[66] Another article in the A.M.E. mission newspaper, by the African Mark Casely-Hayford, claimed that conversion would do for Africa what it had done "for Europeans and other lands where the pure light of the Gospel shines. They will drive away the

remaining superstitions and idolatries and dark heathenish practices."
This conversion, he held, would make Africa "a perpetual and
courted power in the life of the world."[67] This theme of increasing
Africa's power was constantly repeated in missionary propaganda.

The missionaries all had confidence that Africans had the potential
to rise to civilization and power, once they were converted. Alexander Camphor assured his supporters that a serious effort to educate
and convert the native youths would bring about "Africa's awakening
and redemption."[68] Samuel Miller was impressed by the intelligence
of the Africans. He wrote,

> [They] possess the quality and ability, by means of mission
> work, to be elevated far above their present condition. They are
> very willing to work . . . with hearty zeal and faithfulness,
> which one would scarcely look for among a people who have
> had so little advantages as these. . . . I have found them to be
> more truthful and honest than I heard. . . . How can any
> Christian look upon their privations, physical and spiritual,
> without being deeply impressed with a desire to help them?[69]

Even when criticizing the Africans, Miller emphasized that their
faults were no worse than those of other humans. He felt it was
unfair for Africans to be branded as dishonest, and he expressed
much gratitude for being able to work among such a promising
group. Miller had a genuine desire to help the Africans, and he
felt it was the place of "civilized" Christians "to teach them the
way to go. What are we here for but to instruct?"[70] In accordance
with his philosophy, Miller emphasized the importance of school-
teaching for young Africans. Although he complained of their lack
of regular attendance, he wrote, "I find these lads so much like those
[Afro-American students] I taught, I can but love them. They make
me feel as though I were in an old Virginia school house."[71]

Another theme repeatedly emphasized by mission advocates was
that Africa's rise would benefit not only Africans, but Afro-Americans as well. This advantage was argued in an adaptation of the
theory of providential design. Bishop Henry Turner was one of the
strongest advocates of this theory, which he explained in a speech
at Fisk University in 1894. According to Turner, God had willed
that Africans be brought to America as slaves in order that "they
might come in contact with Christian civilization, and by intercourse
with the powerful white race they might fit themselves to go back
to their own land [in Africa] and make of that land what the white
man had made of Europe and of America."[72] This theory was a

clear reflection of American expansionist ideology, and it provided a sort of black "manifest destiny."

On one occasion Turner even went so far as to argue that a modified form of slavery should be reinstituted. Under this plan, Africans could be sold to civilized white and black Americans for a period of seven years, after which they would be returned to Africa "raised to a plane of civilization that would be a blessing to them."[73] Even though many Afro-American Christians accepted the theory of providential design, they retreated from Turner's extension of the argument. One of Turner's own missionaries in Liberia, Alfred L. Ridgel, answered with heavy criticism. Slavery, said Ridgel, was "the sum of all villanies. I don't believe that providence had any thing to do with the establishment and perpetuation of an institution so vile and degrading. It was born in hell."[74]

Nevertheless, much of the missionary publicity continued to repeat the idea that Africans had been placed in America with a destiny to retake the continent. A prominent A.M.E. minister, J. M. Henderson, extended the argument in opposition to European imperialism: "From the devastating flood of European civilization that in mighty waves of colonization are sweeping over Africa, God has saved a remnant of the Negro race by safely housing it in America. . . . Unto us [black Americans] Africa turns as the last human source of hope, and unto us God appears to intrust the magnificent task of redeeming a mighty portion of earth's inhabitants."[75] Henderson never explained how black Americans would be able to end European colonialism, but this philosophy did serve to give Afro-Americans a sense of world-wide importance and destiny.

Another way the mission movement could aid Afro-Americans was by increasing respect from whites. Alexander Camphor sought, by persuading the white northern Methodist Church of the importance of black Americans in the evangelization of Africa, to increase the status of Afro-Americans among whites. He wrote: "I rejoice to see the increasing interest my own race is taking in the redemption of Africa. My hope and prayer is that they may . . . thereby impress the [white] church with their zeal and love for Christ and needy humanity. . . . This field is our [Afro-Americans'] greatest work; and here we are needed to do the work that no others can do. May God lay Africa heavier than ever before upon both my church and race."[76] Other black Christians defined their goals of respect in terms of a wider audience throughout the Western world. The 1899 address of the National Baptist Convention president warned, "We can no longer hope to retain the confidence and respect of other people of the world unless we do more for the redemption of the heathen, and especially those of our fatherland."[77] A black speaker at the 1895 Atlanta Congress on Africa emphasized the potential for building "a civilization that will evoke the admiration of the entire civilized world."[78] An article in the *Voice of Missions*, entitled "Our Duty to Africa," claimed that to convert Africa would lift it "to dominion and power . . . and give us our rightful place among the first nations of earth."[79] Since God would favor Africa once it had been Christianized, the argument went, it was the destiny of black Americans to gain world respect by developing that new world power.

The desire of black Americans to gain respect was not solely a reflection of the age of nationalism and imperialism. As the status of nonwhites steadily deteriorated in the United States during the late nineteenth century, black people desperately searched for a means of progress. In leading the conversion of Africa, by a movement that was clearly popular among whites, black Christians like A.M.E. Bishop Abraham Grant hoped to "convince the world of our equality as men."[80] They directed this campaign toward white Americans in particular, because they felt that if the black missionary movement gained the respect of whites, improved race relations would surely result. Recognizing that much of the prejudice against blacks was due to the image of African savagery held by whites, Henry Turner pointed out the futility of improvement for blacks in the United States "while Africa is shrouded in heathen darkness. The elevation of the Negro in this and all other countries is indissolubly connected with the enlightenment of Africa."[81]

A.M.E. Mission Secretary H. B. Parks emphasized this self-help aspect of the movement even more than Turner. Parks wrote in 1899: "Can you see the immense credit that will reflect upon the American Negro when the world is forced to recognize the success of the movement?" Such recognition, he believed, would "do more to improve your condition at home than years of legislation. . . . Do you see that this is the road through which God would have the race ascend to its proper place of greatness? Is the race spirit strong enough in you to see it?"[82] Thus by the end of the century black clergymen were attempting to use the African missions movement as a method for raising the status and condition of black people in both Africa and America.

In utilizing the mission ideology, Afro-American Christians essentially accepted the view of Africa as savage, but they sought to undercut this image in two ways. First, they would demonstrate their own "civilized" nature by going as missionaries to convert the "heathen." Second, by converting the Africans they would redeem the continent, making of it a new civilization which would rise to world respect and place all black people on an equal level with other peoples.

To late nineteenth-century black Americans who were interested in mission work, Africa seemed the logical choice for their labors. At the root of their motivation was their serious ideological commitment to Christianity, but many other factors besides religion sent them to the fatherland. The influence of their families, schools, and churches in directing them toward missions combined with a strong racial consciousness to attract them to Africa. They believed they were helping to fulfill a larger destiny, the inauguration of a new civilization which would spark a glorious future for black people in both Africa and America.

Indeed, it was predicted that some of the "inferior" tribes would be too weak even to survive the civilizing process.[8]

The missionaries saw the westernization of the African continent as inevitable. This belief constituted a part of the Social Darwinist imperative, "Adapt or die," which was applied world-wide by westerners who supported manifest destiny. One of the black theorists who worked most intensely for the westernization of Africa was Alexander Crummell, who believed that Africans had to become civilized if they were to avoid the inevitable extermination that faced all "backward" peoples. Crummell compared Africans to American Indians and saw an inevitable conflict between savagery and civilization.[9] He described a battle which had taken place in 1882 between the Americo-Liberian settlers and indigenous Africans in much the same terms that George Armstrong Custer might have described an Indian battle: "A few brave colonists were beset by hosts of infuriate savages . . . [who] came with savage, monstrous might." The black American settlers won the struggle, "and from that day supremacy and might have ever crowned the hill of Monrovia."[10] Crummell had no concept of cultural pluralism or the advantageous diffusion of social traits from one group of people to another. He was the Puritan in the New England wilderness; for him there existed an inexorable conflict between his way of life and the way of the Africans around him—one must trample the other.

Given this attitude, it is not surprising that mission rhetoric had a martial tone. Evangelists invoked a military analogy, with "heathenism" as the enemy to be attacked. For example, an Afro-American Baptist group reported, in militaristic terms, the recent increase in mission sentiment among its members: "Africa must be conquered FOR CHRIST; and here are the trained troops under arms [missionary volunteers], and only waiting marching orders."[11] The imagery of religious imperialism pictured Africa as a territory to be "conquered" for a new Christian empire. John J. Coles, one of the black Baptist missionaries in Liberia, for example, consistently referred to Africans as "heathens," who were "servants and soldiers for hell": "This [missionary] war is a spiritual contest between truth and superstition. In it, grace is opposed by sin. . . . This people we must subdue with the everlasting Gospel."[12]

The missionaries admitted that the civilizing process might be damaging to Africans, but they never questioned its inevitability. Rather, they encouraged black Americans to support missions so as to enable Africans to lose their "heathenness" and adapt to these unavoidable changes. A.M.E. Mission Secretary Parks wrote that the African "must either fall in step and learn to march with the advancing army or must inevitably be trodden under. . . . If he resists, he will be exterminated."[13] Although the missions themselves helped bring Western influences to the continent, Parks argued that Christian commitment to Africa was necessary to cushion these influences. If missions were delayed, he wrote, it would only make adjustments by Africans more difficult. He therefore appealed to his church to take the leadership in guiding Africans into Christianity and civilization.[14]

The missionaries could invoke such antagonistic images of African cultures while still holding a racial identity with Africans because they felt that personality and culture were unrelated. Consequently, they believed that they could "free" Africans from heathenism, and the use of emancipationist terms tells much about their negative conception of indigenous culture. The Baptist missionary Thomas Johnson proclaimed that "millions are slaves to superstition and witchcraft in Africa, perishing for want of the Word of Life."[15] The 1880 constitution of the black Baptist Foreign Mission Convention of the U.S.A. declared, "The benighted condition of more than three hundred million souls in Africa, now held in chains of the grossest idolatry, cannibalism, domestic slavery, and every species of superstition, claim our most profound attention and help."[16] Similarly, the A.M.E. *Voice of Missions* called for support to missionaries "who have turned their backs upon the glories of American civilization . . . to break the bonds of superstition, chains of ignorance, to dispel the black clouds of idolatry, to overturn the temples of pernicious polygamy and Mormonism and to illuminate the inhabitants of that despised, forsaken, outraged and neglected land."[17] Methodist missionary Alexander Camphor called for Africa's "moral emancipation": "This is their only hope. It is this alone that enables mankind to cast off the chains and enter into life unmaimed and free."[18]

The missionaries' comparison of heathenism to slavery (with the use of words like chains, bonds, and emancipation) was deliberate, because they saw progress within the context of gaining freedom. An 1898 article in the *A.M.E. Church Review* interpreted black history as a progressive series of great emancipations, the first of which was a freedom from "African heathenism."[19] Black missionaries felt they were bringing freedom to Africans when they converted them to Christianity. The generation of the late nineteenth century, which was too young to have fought for their own freedom in the American Civil War, must have felt that they were reenacting the dedication of their fathers in the Union Army. They saw themselves as the new "Army of the Free," and their spirit of sacrifice matched the idealism of a military effort.

Another analogy often used in mission rhetoric was the evangelization as a rescue effort. Use of this metaphor is illustrated in a speech by the Baptist missionary John Coles pleading for support from Afro-Americans: "Let us go and redeem Africa from ignorance, superstition, nakedness, domestic slavery, human sacrifice, idols, cannibalism, and a million of other vices which now prey upon our heathen brothers. . . . Will you hold the rope while I go down into the well of heathen idolatry and spiritual death to bring up my people?"[20] Coles and other missionaries saw numerous heathen vices as a mysterious monstrous force over which the African people had little control. Consequently, mission advocates believed that Africans *wanted* to be "freed" from their heathenism, and black Americans felt that they were providing crucial aid in this rescue. Alexander Camphor was convinced that "moral and spiritual night rests like a pall upon the people and continent. Rescue must come from without. Africa, in its superstition and degradation, can not save itself."[21]

Holding the assumption that African progress could not be obtained from internal sources, the missionaries believed that Africans were pleading for assistance. Episcopal Bishop Samuel Ferguson wrote that "our brethren in darkness" were longing for "the light of civilization and Christianity."[22] Thomas Johnson wrote poetry about these Africans who were supposedly so interested in conversion, to inspire his fellow Baptists:

> "Come over and help us," is their cry,
> "Come now, oh, do not pass us by,
> We are seeking truth, we are seeking light,
> We seek deliverance from dark night.
> Can you who have the Gospel fail
> To hear our Cry, our doleful wail?"[23]

This emphasis on Africa's deep need to be rescued from heathendom helped to prevent discouragement among mission supporters, who might despair at the obstacles facing Africa's evangelization. It was logical for mission supporters to assume that God, in support of such a movement, would make Africans ready to receive the gospel.

The argument that Africans were begging for rescue from paganism was particularly developed in the A.M.E. Church. Bishop Daniel Payne wrote in the denominational history that the "savages of

Africa are calling upon all Christendom to rescue them from the pit of idolatry into which they have fallen."[24] Bishop Henry Turner was convinced that Africans were dissatisfied with their traditional cultures, and were eager to abandon their old habits and beliefs in favor of "the benefits of a civilized life and the virtues of Christianity." He noted with pleasure, on his 1891 trip to Liberia, that many Africans brought their children to be educated because they recognized that aboriginal ways would soon be gone, "and another dispensation will be ushered in."[25]

This idea of African attraction to conversion, with its theme of "freeing" Africans from heathenism, is typified by the 1899 student prize essay chosen at A.M.E. Wilberforce University. The winning essay praised the denomination's expansion among indigenous Africans, and suggested that the Africans hoped to be released from this barbarism.[26]

Mission advocates were sure that they could aid Africans because they were convinced that conversion to Christianity would place Africa on the road to civilization and power. Christianity was the best method for changing Africa, according to A.M.E. Mission Secretary Parks, because it "brings out all that makes a man nearer to perfection and nations greater and more powerful."[27] Baptist John Coles felt that missionaries would play a crucial role in Africa's rise, because they would teach "civilization" as well as religion. He predicted, "Behind the Christian missionaries must come the traders and merchants with commerce and modern improvements. Thus Africa must be lifted to a level with the present enlightened countries."[28] Methodist Alexander Camphor tried to get Africans to convert by telling them,

> [Christianity] would constitute the nucleus of an indigenous civilization which would aim to touch and improve every phase of native life, material and spiritual. Your huts would be made more permanent and sanitary; your farms more productive and varied in crops; your methods of administering to the sick and wounded more humane and scientific; your knowledge of agricultural and mechanical implements improved; simple instruction in letters imparted; moral precepts and sentiments inculcated, and the teachings of Jesus Christ as revealed in the Divine Book instilled in minds and hearts. In fact, my scheme aims to help the people in every point of their being. . . . Instead of wars . . . and poverty and darkness, there is peaceful industry, progress and prosperity. . . . Africa will be reclaimed from the barbarity and superstition that has enveloped it for ages.[29]

It is clear from these statements that the missionaries considered the conversion of Africans far more than a change in religious ideology: it was but a step in the progress toward civilization. The mission movement was committed to the concept of civilization, and missionaries worked to transform entire cultures. Christianity required a convert to "leave all for Christ," and missionaries interpreted this in a cultural sense.[30] Religion was only one aspect of a wide-range metamorphosis which they wished to produce for Africans. According to A.M.E. missionary Alfred Ridgel, "Christianity demands of the pagan a complete surrender and entire change of life, both out and in; it compels him to forsake all practices and become a new creature."[31] Even after they had converted the Africans to Christianity, the missionaries felt a duty to change Africans. Episcopalian Alexander Crummell held that the indigenous African, "albeit converted, is hardly a quarter of a man. . . . As he stands before his [Afro-American] teacher he is but a child! a crude, undeveloped and benighted child! a shadow of a man! . . . This man-child is to be reconstructed. All the childishness of inheritance is gradually to be taken out of his brain, and all the barbarism of ages is to be eliminated from his condition."[32]

The missionaries left little doubt as to the direction in which they wished to see Africans change. Crummell equated civilization with Anglo-Saxon culture, and even felt that English was the most refined language.[33] A black speaker at the 1895 Atlanta Congress on Africa hoped that, after the missionaries had prepared Africans to want such things, "the rattling steam engine and the rumbline car of commerce . . . factories and mills . . . and the tick of the telegraph shall be heard in all [Africa's] borders."[34] Africa should, according to this view, be westernized in many ways besides religion, language, and technology. A.M.E. Secretary Parks even went so far as to suggest that his goal was to get Africans to accept "all the ways and customs of the American people."[35] This desire for acculturation was so strong that one A.M.E. leader supported mission schooling for Africans "with the hope that all the recollections of their primitive life may become wholly effaced."[36]

With this strong inclination to make Africans over into Americans, the missionaries criticized many aspects of aboriginal cultures.[37] But Afro-American church people were especially critical of certain things. One of the most understandable objects of criticism was the existing slavery among Africans. Many missionaries condemned it without qualification, but Presbyterian William Sheppard did at least point out that slaves among the Bakuba were war captives and that they were "kindly treated in life." However, he noted that a slave was often killed when his or her master died so that the slave's soul could accompany the deceased master into the afterlife. Sheppard was atypical of most missionaries in that he was reluctant to condemn Bakuba culture, but he did preach against and resist this particular custom.[38]

Other objects of especially strong criticism were cannibalism and human sacrifice. Although several missionaries correctly noted that these practices were not as widespread as Western stereotypes suggested, they condemned the few verified cases. Of the "Zappo-Zaps," a cannibalist group hired by the Belgian colonial government in the Congo to terrorize Congolese into paying taxes, Sheppard wrote: "You can trust them as far as you can see them—and the farther off you see them the better you can trust them."[39] Other missionaries were so severely repulsed by the idea of cannibalism that they did not even attempt a humorous expose such as Sheppard had written. Alexander Crummell depicted the Kingdom of Dahomey, with its human sacrifice, as a despotic "carnival of devils!" and contrasted it with the "free institutions" of the United States.[40] Baptist Thomas Johnson was obsessed with cannibalism. He referred to Dahomey as "a human slaughter-house," and the only remark he made about the Ashanti Kingdom was, "How repulsive to read of the barbarous customs of offering human sacrifices." He even said of the Nigerians that it was "only about twelve or fifteen years since they were all cannibals," and thanked God that missionary influences had reduced these horrors in recent years.[41] Upon seeing human skulls on display in Old Calabar, Nigeria, Methodist Amanda Smith was shocked into imploring, "Oh, Lord, how long shall that dreadful night of heathenism last?"[42]

While Afro-Americans' reactions to such stories are easily understandable to modern observers, some black mission reactions to Africa reflect ideas of propriety that are more specific to nineteenth-century Victorian society. One complaint reflected their attitudes toward nudity. Because of the hot climate, tropical peoples generally wore few clothes and consequently had few inhibitions about bodily exposure; and missionaries were usually in a flurry to cover their converts. Upon arriving in West Africa, for example, A.M.E. Reverend Alfred Ridgel was "astonished to see how degraded these poor heathens are. You can see grown men naked, and women nearly the same way. Awful, awful, awful! The gospel is needed here."[43] Another A.M.E. missionary in Liberia wrote to the *Voice of Missions* about adolescent African boys and girls who wore practically no clothing except a two-inch strip of cloth "which they only used to hide the most delicate part of their persons. . . . In such condition as this, no matter how holy a person may be, he cannot do anything to keep his eyes from the electric power which exists between the eyes and the daily objects of this place."[44]

Another target of missionary complaint was polygamy. American Board clergyman Benjamin Ousley was disgusted by the "degrading" customs of polygamy and ritualized circumcision.[45] Baptist John Coles prayed that the "heathen will learn that one wife for one man is all God allows."[46] Methodist Amanda Smith was even more upset that prosperous African men could "buy" wives.[47] It never seemed to occur to the missionaries that such "bride-price" practices were actually a way to insure that the prospective husband had the financial ability to support his bride, and were of benefit to the bride's family. In many cases plural marriage was of more benefit to the wives than the husband, because it gave higher status to the senior wife and distributed the women's work among more in-dividuals. Often the other wives were relatives or friends of the first wife, who had persuaded her husband to take additional wives. Such benefits to women were overlooked by missionaries who were blinded by their own cultural limitations.

The Christian approach to labor roles, particularly "women's work," was also culture-bound. Many of the Afro-American mis-sionaries were particularly disturbed about African women doing agricultural labor, which they saw as "man's work."[48] Amanda Smith pitied "the poor women of Africa [who] . . . have all the hard work to do."[49] Benjamin Ousley concluded that these labor responsibilities made African women "little more than slaves." He was dumb-founded, however, to observe that the women "seem perfectly satisfied with their lot."[50] No doubt part of this adverse reaction was due to the missionaries' Victorian ideal of women as ornamental objects, but it also probably resulted from the Afro-Americans' background as slaves. In African agricultural societies, women who did the farming had considerable economic power and social status. In contrast, in the black American experience, women who worked in farming had to do so because they were slaves. Female labor was therefore an indication of low status, and to the status-conscious missionaries such practices had to be ended if Africans were to "rise" from their slave-like heathenism. Consequently, while the missionaries taught the Protestant work ethic, they also sought to define sexual labor roles.[51]

The missionaries felt that they could change African life only if they could transform indigenous belief systems. They reserved their most intense complaints for "ignorance, superstition, fetishism, and paganism."[52] American Board representative Nancy Jones wrote that she had left her "home in a civilized Christian land" to change the ways of thinking of "this dark heathen country." She observed that the Africans "are very superstitious and have no idea of the right way of living. . . . I hope to be able to help them rise from this low degraded life."[53]

One thing that particularly bothered the Christians was the indigenous belief in witchcraft. Thomas Johnson spoke of the Africans' "queer superstitions" that made them "miserable all the time; nothing but one continual dread of the witch."[54] Amanda Smith prayed for a woman who was accused of being a witch, and who had to go through a trial by drinking toxic "sassy wood."[55] William Sheppard was dumbfounded to learn that even the accused person had such faith in the method of trial by poison that he was anxious to take the poison in order to prove his innocence. This practice provoked one of Sheppard's few righteous outbursts: "Seeing these awful customs practiced by these people for ages makes you indignant and depressed and also fills you with pity. Only by preaching God's word, having faith, patience and love will we eradicate the deep-rooted evil. Everything to them is run by chance, and there are evil spirits and witches everywhere."[56]

While some of the missionaries recognized African beliefs in a Supreme Being and a spiritual afterlife,[57] they did not accept the validity of traditional religions. Baptist Thomas Johnson wrote that he was "always fearless and ready on all occasions to admonish the people" about their religion. Although the Bakwalli people, with whom he worked in the Cameroons, were cooperative with missionaries, they refused to give up their beliefs or to allow the foreigners into their fetish temples.[58] Methodist Amanda Smith described indigenous Liberians as "devil worshippers" who had "no real form of religion."[59] Alexander Camphor presented a fairly objective account of aboriginal religion, but he still felt that it represented "the darkness of fanaticism and superstition without the light of revelation!"[60]

One type of religion in Africa presented a special problem for the Christian missionaries, and that was the religion of Mohammed. Islam had diffused from North Africa with the trans-Saharan trade and had pervaded most of the West African interior during an era of religious revival in the nineteenth century. Its strength centered in the great trading cities along the northern bend of the Niger River, but Islam had enacted its own missionary movement which spread into the coastal regions as far as Liberia.[61]

Most Christian evangelists pictured Islam in the same negative light they cast on indigenous African religions. Like their white fellow Christians, the Afro-American missionaries saw Islam as a rival religion and a threat. Baptist John Coles felt that Islam was even worse, "if possible, than heathenism."[62] Similarly, a writer in the A.M.E. *Voice of Missions* concluded that while paganism "marks the lowest stratum of ignorance and superstition," Islam was even more baneful because it destroyed "the remaining vestige of humanity" in Africa.[63] H. B. Parks also took a belligerent attitude toward "Mohammedanism," calling it a "great wall of darkness against which the missionary army has been hurling itself."[64]

Other mission advocates took a less general approach to Islam and criticized it for specific reasons. Alexander Crummell noted, for example:

> There is a grand disturbing element, the malign and destructive influence of the Moslems. *They* are the grand marauders in almost every part of Africa, north, east, south, and west. Everywhere they are the great slave-traders. . . . They care more for the sword and the mastery it gives them than for any purposes of civilization. . . . They flood the continent everywhere with oceans of disaster, ruin, and bloodshed.[65]

A.M.E. Reverend Alfred Ridgel, in Liberia, denounced Muslims for several reasons. The Koran was, he said, "full of improbable, foolish tales," and Islamic tolerance of polygamy made the religion detestable to him.[66] He felt that Africa could never be civilized under the influence of Islam because it compromised too much with "paganism." Ridgel observed that Islam did not require Africans to change their whole way of life, and was pleased that Christianity did require acculturation. He was even more opposed to Islam than to traditional African tribal religions, because Muslims believed that Islam was the best religion and wanted to spread it to others. That is, Ridgel felt threatened by Islam precisely because it was similar to Christianity—in its convictions and its missionary impulse. He did not perceive this similarity, however, and saw Muslim resistance to Christianity as evidence of "the most stubborn resentment and self-satisfaction in the direful doctrine to which they cling."[67] He concluded with a call for religious warfare: "No word of censure is too severe for Mohammedanism. . . . Every Christian should be on the alert and spare no pains to urge incessant war against . . . an evil that threatens our very existence in Africa. . . . Let us pray Almighty God to forever blot Mohammedanism out of existence."[68]

While white Christians were nearly unanimous in their opposition to Islam, a minority of black Christians held a more positive view of the Muslim influence in Africa. Its most prominent advocate was Edward Blyden. He began his career as a devout Presbyterian, but even while he was missionizing, Blyden wished to impress African Muslims.[69] By the 1880s he became disillusioned with the leadership potential of the Christian Americo-Liberians, and gradually turned to educated Africans as the best potential leaders. Muslims sponsored the most comprehensive educational system in nineteenth-century West Africa, so Blyden naturally was attracted to them. After his 1886 resignation from the Presbyterian ministry, Blyden published a flood of writings favorable to Islam, chief of which was his influential book *Christianity, Islam, and the Negro Race* (1887).[70]

Blyden concluded that Islam was on the whole better suited for Africa than Christianity, and he compared it favorably with Christianity:

> I must uphold Mohammedanism not for its peculiar teachings—
> but so far as it agrees, not with European teachings, but with
> the teachings of Christ—and so far as it tends to build up my
> race in numerical strength, in self respect and physical health—
> all of which the *method* of Christians tend to undermine. . . .
> I prefer what is good for my people in the method of its propa-
> gators to what is evil in the methods of Christian teachers.[71]

Blyden felt that Islam was superior to Christianity in that it was nonracist and offered a feeling of black pride to its followers, it resisted demoralizing foreign vices like alcoholism, and it was a means of unification for most of West Africa.[72] In letters to the American Colonization Society he contrasted the peaceful spread of Islam among indigenous Africans, without wide-spread attempts to destroy African cultures, to the missionizing of Christianity in which the whole way of life of many African nations was subverted. Also, he pointed out that the Arabs were not exporting colonialism along with their religion, but "wherever Christianity has really been able to establish itself, excepting in Liberia, foreigners have taken the country, and in some places rule the natives with oppressive rigor."[73]

After the publication of his book, Blyden had considerable influence on black Christians, especially in the A.M.E. Church. His articles on Islam were published in three issues of the 1887

A.M.E. Church Review. Later attacks on Islam caused a writer in the *Voice of Missions* to defend Blyden's positive attitude toward Muslims, and to call for tolerance of other creeds which were equally blessed by God. Islam, he continued, was better for black people because it was "an impartial religion . . . a sympathetic, all-embracing reality." In contrast, the racism exhibited by whites made Christianity "a jeering, mocking system" that Afro-Americans should be ashamed of continuing to follow.[74]

The A.M.E. missionary in Sierra Leone, John R. Frederick, became one of Blyden's closest friends, and he stoutly defended the latter's *Christianity, Islam, and the Negro Race* in 1888 in the *A.M.E. Christian Recorder*. He wished that every intelligent black person could have a copy, and he complimented Blyden for his empathy with Islam. Frederick felt that Muslim anti-liquor campaigns had prevented "the greed of the white traders" from desolating Africa. Blyden, he wrote, was helping African Muslims to "understand Christianity as it is taught in the New Testament, and not as it is exemplified in the lives of its representatives from Europe. . . . The Christian negro and the Mohammedan negro have nothing to lose by fraternizing and cooperating for the great work in the regeneration of the great continent."[75] Yet even Frederick remained tied to his Christian missionary ideology, and on one occasion reported with pride the conversion of a local African king from Islam to Christianity. He looked forward to the time when all Africa would be "conquered for Jesus. The Mohammedans . . . have lost their strongest support and their stronghold is shaken. Praise the Lord!"[76]

Even Bishop Henry Turner held a more favorable attitude toward Islam than most black churchmen. In 1891 Turner was led on a tour of indigenous towns by Blyden, and the bishop revealed his admiration for the well-educated Muslim teachers when he wrote from Sierra Leone: "These black Mohammedan priests . . . with so much dignity, majesty and consciousness of their worth, are driving me into respect for them. Some come for hundreds of miles from the [interior] country—out of the bushes—better scholars than in America. What fools we are to suppose these Africans are fools!"[77] As a good Methodist abstainer, Turner was always glad to note that the Muslims preached against liquor. In many ways the moral code of Islam seemed to Turner to be similar to his own standards. "Beyond the fact that the Mohammedans allow more than one wife," he wrote, "they are as upright in conduct and civil behavior as any people in the land."[78] He saw the influence of Islam as God's plan of preparation for the redemption of Africa by Christianity. In his letter of 9 December 1891, Turner wrote: "The Mohammedan religion is the morningstar to the sun of Christianity. . . . God save the Mohammedans, is my prayer, til the Christian Church is ready to do her whole duty."[79] Thus, for Turner, Islam was not to be condemned, because he was confident that it would ultimately aid in the Christianizing of Africa.

Both Islam and Christianity, the minority opinion believed, could work for the regeneration of the continent, so they should cooperate rather than quarrel. Despite Blyden's influence, however, few Afro-American missionaries departed from the standard Christian condemnation of other religions. They did not set up any collaboration with Islam, much less with local traditional African religions. The black American missionary movement remained a distinctly Christian undertaking, comparable to that of white Americans.

The reactions of indigenous Africans to Afro-American missionaries can tell us much about the nature of the movement. There are a number of instances in which the missionaries received invitations by Africans to establish stations in their towns.[80] There are several explanations for this. Some peoples may have seen the coming of missionaries as inevitable, and wished to have black preachers as a lesser evil than whites. Or there may have been a pragmatic realization that missionaries provided an opportunity for schooling. In some instances, village leaders made their desires for education explicit, and agreed to receive the Christian message in exchange for schools.[81]

Even if Africans did not approve of all aspects of Western culture, they did recognize the great power that westerners held. After all, the industialized West presented as great a change to agricultural peoples as the agricultural revolution had brought to human history thousands of years before. Africans perceived westerners as powerful and searched for the secret of this power. Missionaries explained that Christianity was the secret of Western superiority. Since so much of the African world-view was predicated on religion, this argument had an impact on indigenous peoples. The God of the foreigners *must* be stronger than their own gods, these people reasoned, if that God allowed the westerners to dominate. This reasoning has been a major factor in the adaptation of subject peoples to invaders throughout the world, and it accounts in large measure for Third World conversions to Christianity in the past two centuries. Africans were left with a choice of avoiding the new religion or pursuing it in hopes that the power of the Western God would extend to them. Some Africans were so impressed with Western superiority that they advocated a complete departure from their traditional cultures. Others wanted a modernized society, but wished to hold on to as many aspects of their traditional ways of life as possible. This enormous variety of cultural attitudes produced diverse reactions to Christian ideology.[82]

In general, humans are slow to change their ideologies, even when presented with catastrophic changes in their day-to-day lives. Most people act within the cultural framework in which they were brought up, and this inertia provides continuity during times of change. Some people realize modifications in their lives are necessary in order to preserve as much as possible of their traditional culture, but their goal is still preservation. Accordingly, it is not surprising that Africans resisted conversion. Even among groups who co-operated with missionaries, much of their response involved only the curtailment of public rituals of their native religions, while their traditional beliefs and customs continued.[83]

Many other Africans actively resisted conversion, or remained indifferent to Christianity, a fact which the missionaries found hard to understand. For example, American Board missionary Benjamin Ousley never comprehended why Africans did not immediately see the value of Christianity, and he expressed much disgust at their skepticism. The people near his mission could not understand why they should be expected to sit through church services without being paid for their time, a logic that surprised and exasperated Ousley. Strictly opposing the idea of rewards for attendance, he insisted that people must come only out of the desire for "true light."[84] Fellow missionary Nancy Jones was perplexed at the Africans' slowness "to give up the degrading customs of heathenism," like polygamy, bride price, witchcraft, and nudity. After a year of working for conversions she was discouraged by the lack of change and wrote: "I often wonder why these people seem so slow to accept the truth that is so faithfully and plainly laid before them day by day."[85] A.M.E. missionary William Heard explained this resistance as short-sightedness and superstition.[86] Because of the lack of co-operation by adult Africans, many missionaries concentrated their efforts on the more easily influenced children. Consequently, much of their day-to-day activities concentrated on education, as well as service activities like medical assistance and providing food and shelter for the homeless. These activities, which were necessary to attract Africans, plus basic administration of the mission compound to provide for their own necessities, took much more of the missionaries' time than preaching and converting. Their writings talk much more about the Africans' ways of life and the need of the mission for more support than they do about the mundane daily schedule of the missionaries.

Even when they were attempting to preach to Africans, the black missionaries sometimes produced reactions which they did not intend. For instance, United Brethren Joseph Gomer, trying to convert a women who had recently suffered the death of two children, explained that God had taken the lives of the children because the woman had put her faith in the tribal religion. "God took them," he wrote, "to show her that he alone possesses all power." Gomer was surprised when the woman reacted by calling God "a big devil." She believed that evil spirits had killed her children, and when Gomer suggested it was the Christian God who had caused the deaths, she saw this vengeful deity as a devil.[87]

Even when Africans converted to Christianity, their reactions did not always please the missionaries. A black preacher in the Presbyterian Congo mission wrote in 1899 that his most difficult task was to make his converts feel Christian guilt. After they had agreed to accept the new religion, he wrote, they could not understand why their belief had not immediately "made them the children of God, despite all we could say along the line of total depravity of the heart."[88] This statement reveals as much about African psychological self-assurance as it does about the missionary's absorption of Christian notions about guilt and inadequacy.

In general, nonwesternized Africans reacted to black missionaries in the same way they did toward white missionaries. Some groups of Africans referred to all missionaries, including Afro-Americans, as "white men" implies that the black American clergy established no racial unity with their host people, and perhaps had trouble relating to Africans.[89] There is not much evidence in early missionary writing of negative African reactions, but a modern example may be illuminating. A group of black American Presbyterian missionaries in the Cameroons during the 1960s reported that upon their arrival, the people gave special welcome to them as long-lost relatives. However, the Africans assumed that these black people would absorb indigenous culture. When the missionaries did not adopt African customs, the villagers gradually began to consider them outsiders, or "black white" people.[90] Defining people culturally rather than racially, these Africans recognized that Afro-American missionaries came as representatives of Western culture.

Despite the missionaries' condemnation of traditional African cultures, and despite their lack of identity with indigenous lifestyles, they did emphasize the great potential for African advancement. One reason for this emphasis was that the missionaries had to show potential for change in order to keep contributions coming from their church membership. Those who had no hopes for Africa's rise, after all, would not waste their money on missions. Consequently, evangelists reported the ease with which Africans converted. Bishop Turner was a foremost promoter of this rosy picture, especially during his 1891 visit to West Africa. He wrote from the Liberian back-country:

> Africa is the grandest field on earth for the labor of civilization and the Christian Church. There is no reason under heaven why this continent should not or cannot be redeemed and brought back to God in twenty-five years. . . . The African can beat the world in learning to speak the English language . . . and in a few months at most, [can] sing and play upon the organ any gospel song in print, even before he learns to wear clothes.[91]

As can be seen from this statement, Turner had an ambivalent attitude toward African cultures. He obviously favored the westernization of Africans, but was not condemnatory of indigenous cultures, because he had faith that Africans would easily convert to "Christian civilization." He was able to admire nonwesternized Africans as "right from the bush with a mere cloth over them [but] full of the Holy Ghost."[92] The African, he theorized, "is not a pagan, but a child of superstition; he worships no wooden nor brass god, but believes more strongly in the invisible forces than we do, and so it is an easy matter to have him transfer his superstition to faith in Christ Jesus."[93]

Black missionaries not only looked forward to African religious conversion, but also to educational improvements. Several, like Thomas Johnson in the Cameroons, were "impressed with the intense desire of the people to be taught. Their great wish seemed to be, while I was there, to see their children taught how to read and write, and talk the English language. . . . It is remarkable to see how fast the children learn."[94] Methodist Amanda Smith adopted an African child, "a little raw, naked heathen" in her words, whom she taught to read. The child learned fast, and Smith concluded, "It is nonsense to say that a native African is not capable of learning." She felt that European immigrants to America were "much harder to enlighten, because they have been steeped in Romanism, and the African comes only with his superstitions, which he soon drops under civilized and Christian influences."[95] Nancy Jones, too, complimented the "natural intelligence and capacity for improvement" of the Africans.[96]

Another missionary who emphasized the Africans' potential for change was Alexander Crummell, who saw Africans as incipient capitalists. In their materialistic desires, he wrote, there was "the germ of a marked greatness in the native African in the future. . . . Greed, the acquisitive principle, is *the* grand characteristic of the native African. . . . Every head man, or chief, or king, is a merchant; and all his people, down to the very slaves, are hucksters or petty traders. Greed, inordinate, universal greed, pervades every community."[97] While Crummell was antagonistic toward native cultures, he did see the potential for Africans to become like the Afro-American settlers in Liberia. He called upon Liberians to recognize this potential and become involved in the improvement of the indigenous population:

> For here is a MAN, who, however rude and uncultivated, is sure to stand. . . . He is curious, mobile, imitative. He sees your superiority, and acknowledges it by copying your habits. . . .Why then should we doubt the full and equal ability of the native man to become all that we are, and do all that we can do? . . .
> Of their capability of reaching to any of the heights of superiority, *we* have attained, no man here can doubt, who looks at the superior men . . . native men—who have risen to a position at Sierra Leone.[98]

Crummell's culture-bound position reinforced the ethnocentric belief of Afro-Americans that they were the superior model of civilization which Africans should adopt, but at least it allowed for full acceptance of Africans once they were acculturated.

Because every missionary believed, to some degree, in the "dark continent" stereotype, the compliments about Africans were usually indirect ones. Nevertheless, some of them did occasionally speak with open favor about aboriginal cultures. Even Crummell admitted that Africa contained "populous cities, superior people, and vast kingdoms, given to enterprise, and engaged in manufacturers, agriculture, and commerce."[99] Others who were generally condemnatory sometimes complimented specific ethnic groups, especially for hospitality and industriousness.[100] Thomas Johnson, for example, saw the Bakwalli, among whom he lived, as neater, cleverer, and more moral than their neighbors in the Cameroons. He felt completely safe among the Bakwalli and appreciated their hospitality to the missionaries. He concluded that these Africans were "not a savage people, nor cruel," but "very kind-hearted."[101]

Bishop Turner was frankly impressed with some aspects of African personality and culture. The indigenous man, he wrote, "has no fear, no cowardice, no dread, but feels himself the equal of any man on earth."[102] This positive self-concept, Turner felt, could even be adopted to advantage by Afro-Americans who felt inferior. He saw Africans as moral and intelligent, and challenged stories of cannibalism which were given so much publicity in America.[103]

The missionary who made the most positive comments about indigenous ways of life, and who did most to spread an appreciation of African culture among black Americans, was William Sheppard. Upon arriving in the Congo in 1890, his first impressions of the Africans were favorable. After meeting a local king, Sheppard referred to him as "his most gracious majesty." Sheppard was also impressed by the attentiveness and "intelligent interest" displayed by the people.[104]

Sheppard did make unfavorable statements about Africans, speaking (in typical missionary terms) of "spiritual darkness" and "moral gloom." But he soon recognized significant differences among Africans and, unlike many missionaries, refused to stereotype them.[105] Even when criticizing the Africans, as he did for their heavy use of alcohol, Sheppard identified himself with them and called them "my people."[106]

His acceptance of African cultural standards is indicated by the photographs he took. Most mission pictures only showed people well-covered in Western-style dress, but Sheppard's photographs show various degrees of nudity, as the Africans actually lived their daily lives.[107] Sheppard's autobiography, which was based on the diary that he kept during his first five years in the Congo, contains much objective ethnographic description.[108] He recognized that "all the natives we have met in the Kasai are, on the whole, honest."[109]

Sheppard often lavished compliments on the Congolese. He noted that nothing was wasted by the people, that they were "economical" and "industrious."[110] He also evidenced an appreciation of cultural relativism by showing respect for African customs. For example, soon after arriving in the Congo he once carelessly threw a palm nut against a house. Unknown to Sheppard, such an act was a curse upon the home. When the village panicked, he recalled, "Immediately I went over to the excited crowd and explained my ignorance of the fact and promised to make reparation." By respecting the Africans' belief rather than dismissing it as a silly custom, Sheppard gained their confidence. On another occasion Sheppard consented at once to stop hunting near farmlands because of the Bakuba belief that his rifle fire would cause the corn to die.[111]

Furthermore, Sheppard had the strength of character to acknowledge his mistakes and to learn from the Africans. Once, to aid a village during a famine, he shot a hippopotamus for them. Disregarding their pleading advise not to do so, he swam into the lake to tie a rope around the carcass. Suddenly a crocodile appeared, and Sheppard barely escaped to shore. He begged the villagers' pardon and was ashamed of his bravery. He wrote, "Many times in Central Africa foreigners get into serious difficulties from which they cannot extricate themselves by disregarding the advice of natives."[112]

Even though he objected to some of their customs, Sheppard greatly admired the Bakuba people. He complimented their dancing, dress, personal appearance, and strict prohibitions against polygamy, adultery, and drunkenness. Their industriousness impressed him as did their custom of reserving every third day as a day of rest.[113] His admiration for the Bakuba was summarized by his statement, "I grew very fond of the Bakuba and it was reciprocated. They were the finest looking race I had seen in Africa, dignified, graceful, courageous, honest, with an open, smiling countenance and really hospitable. Their knowledge of weaving, embroidering, woodcarving and smelting was the highest in equatorial Africa."[114]

In 1893 Sheppard gave a speech to the student body of Hampton Institute, in which he emphasized the superiority of the Bakubas, and complimented their industriousness, cleanliness, and morality. He described Bakuba religion without condemnation, and was quick to point out that the Bakubas were "not idolators." The Presbyterian described his amazement on entering Ifuka, the capital city: "I had seen nothing like it in Africa. . . . [They] make one feel that he has again entered a land of civilization. . . . Perhaps they got their civilization from the Egyptians—or the Egyptians theirs from the Bakuba!"[115] Overall, Sheppard presented the Africans in a favorable light, and while not ignoring their faults he did much less moralizing than was customary for nineteenth-century missionaries.

But William Sheppard's positive attitudes remained exceptional among nineteenth-century black American missionaries. Even though several made complimentary statements, and many emphasized the *potential* for Africa's advancement, in general the evangelists had a low opinion of indigenous African cultures. They saw themselves as civilized people who were trying to bring civilization to Africans, and they did not identify with non-Western life-styles—a lack of identification which, as we have seen, was recognized by Africans themselves. The contrast between what they saw as inferior heathenism and their own superior culture understandably was a great psychological stimulus to Afro-Americans, who were accustomed to being on the losing end of contrasts with whites. The chance to see themselves as a black Elect coming to save a continent was, not surprisingly given their backgrounds, irresistible to the missionaries. Unfortunately, this elevated self-image was at the expense of understanding and appreciating African cultures. Their ethnocentrism marked the missionaries as American, under the influence of negative white-held stereotypes. No genuine Pan-Africanism could arise until black Americans had overcome such influences.

7

Missionary Attitudes toward Emigration and Imperialism

Besides expressing their attitudes about African cultures, black American missionaries voiced varied opinions on the two major "news" items relating to the continent: the emigration of Afro-Americans, and the spread of European colonial dominance over Africa. These issues were closely related, because both dealt with the westernization of indigenous peoples.

Interest in emigrating to Africa was not a new development among Afro-Americans. As early as 1815, Paul Cuffe sponsored a voyage which transported some black Americans to Sierra Leone (see chapter 2). Soon after that, the American Colonization Society was organized by whites who were interested in the future of black people, along with others whose primary motive was the removal of free blacks from the United States. Plans for the enforced deportation of all free blacks, to strengthen the slave system, were advanced by some colonizationists. In reaction, the black leadership of the North developed the philosophy that blacks had as much right to remain in America as any others. Prodded by the black reaction, many abolitionists spoke out strongly against the American Colonization Society, and its popularity among black Americans dropped considerably.[1]

By the 1850s, however, disillusionment with America had grown among many Afro-Americans. Abolitionism seemed to be declining, while the slave system was becoming more entrenched. The fugitive slave law, the Supreme Court's Dred Scott Decision, and the spread of more restrictive slave codes greatly alarmed blacks. The free black leadership began to despair of making any progress in America, and turned to other areas of the world as their only alternative. Canada, the Caribbean, Latin America, and Africa all shared the limelight as possible destinations for Afro-American emigration. Led by Martin Delany and Henry Highland Garnet, emigrationist ideas attracted a significant following.[2]

The outbreak of the Civil War in 1861 brought a radical shift in black thought. Even before the North acknowledged emancipation as a war aim, Afro-American leaders realized the increased potential for changing black people's status in America. They pressured the government to involve blacks in the Union effort and make the war an antislavery crusade. With this revolutionary turn of events, a better future for blacks in the United States seemed possible, and emigration sentiment evaporated.[3] Although struggles occurred, success seemed to follow on success as, in the next few years, slavery was abolished and three new amendments were added to the Constitution for the protection of Afro-Americans.

Black involvement in national affairs increased during Reconstruction, but by the mid-1870s experiments in racial equality were abandoned. Political and economic opression, the return to power of the southern ex-Confederates, and the removal of federal troops from the South by 1877, produced demoralization among some blacks. The 1883 Supreme Court decision against the Civil Rights Act convinced others that the gains of the past decade were falling apart.[4] Accordingly, many blacks felt so discouraged that they revived the old interest in emigration.

The American Colonization Society had been less active during the Civil War, but by 1875 the requests from blacks wanting to emigrate had picked up considerably. The year 1877 marked a crucial point in colonizationist history, because in that year the number of requests for emigration exceeded the totals of any of the prewar years.[5] It was the beginning of an era when emigration seemed to attract more Afro-Americans than at any period except the 1920s.

The difference between the late nineteenth century emigration movement and earlier trends was its relative lack of articulate leadership. In the 1850s, the debate about emigration was conducted primarily by articulate black leaders, but post-1877 emigrationists were usually lower-class uneducated blacks, people on the "mud sill" of society.[6] Most of the black leaders were so impressed by the great changes that had taken place in the previous decade that they were optimistic about continued future progress. Remembering their demoralization during the 1850s, when everything looked so bad, many black leaders did not believe that conditions would continue to get worse. Thus, most of the articulate race leaders, journalists, and authors continued to write optimistically about the future of blacks in the United States.[7] Autobiographies bristled with the theme "Up from Slavery," with hard work and racial progress as the winning combination. Although Delany and Garnet began to revive their African interests, they were too old to exert primary leadership for a new movement. The impetus would have to come from below.

The initial spark came in South Carolina in 1877, with the formation of the Liberian Exodus Joint Stock Steamship Company. This southern black group transported over two hundred emigrants to Liberia aboard the ship *Azor*.[8] As interest in emigration widened, the American Colonization Society was revived, but its limited resources could not meet the demand. From 1870 to 1890 it sponsored only 1,200 emigrants.[9] Black-led emigration movements sent several hundred additional settlers to Liberia. Others went individually, but the number of actual emigrants was only a small percentage of those who wished to go.[10]

Afro-American emigration sentiment grew because of the economic and political subjugation of lower-class blacks. But emigrationism was closely connected to missionary concerns. Numerous letters of black people who wished to emigrate gave as their motive the saving of Africans for Christ.[11] The *Azor* emigration was organized by the Morris Brown A.M.E. Church in Charleston, and its pastor complimented the settlers for taking leadership in "the evangelization of the millions of their people who now sit in darkness" in Africa. Another A.M.E. preacher said the purpose of emigration was to take to Africa "the culture, education, and religion acquired here" in America.[12]

Emigrationists were fond of applying to themselves the Biblical analogy of the ancient Hebrews being led out of Egypt. They adapted the theory of providential design to include a mass movement to the promised land. For example, one commonly expressed statement was "that God intended these United States to be to the Negro race what Egypt was to the uncultured and semi-civilized Jew—a training school."[13] In other words, destiny brought them to America to learn Christianity and civilization, and now they could take these gifts back with them to Africa. Dr. J. C. Price, president of the A.M.E. Zion Church's Livingstone College, believed that it was the duty of Afro-Americans to go to Africa and "reclaim their country, civilize the Negroes there, give them manual and intellectual education, and show them the way to build up the country."[14] Another writer, in the *A.M.E. Church Review*, was more explicit:

> If the educated and wealthy Negroes of this country would turn their attention to the development of the resources of Africa— go there, cut down the forest, build up commercial and manufacturing interests with the great civilized centres of the world, organize territories, build states, shape a government, civilize the tribes, set up an army and navy—then the world will know that the Negro is a man. . . . We must "go over and possess the land" that God has reserved for us for ages.[15]

Still other missionaries who supported emigration urged Afro-Americans to use African trade and mineral resources to accumulate wealth.[16] These ideas combined elements of Manifest Destiny and "the gospel of wealth," in the tradition of the American dream.

A number of missionaries emphasized the close connections between the evangelization of Africa and emigration to Liberia. Alexander Crummell complimented the Liberian experiment as being "in harmony with the evident mission GOD has given us for this continent; a system fitted to [become] . . . the model of numerous other civilized nations all over the continent."[17] Crummell spoke of the American black settlers as bearing "the fiery cross of Jesus, and the torch of civilization . . . so they may cross the continent . . . until the whole land shall be redeemed from grossness, and superstition, and benightedness, to culture and to grace."[18]

But this mission spirit which God had placed upon Americo-Liberians entailed an important responsibility. Reverend Crummell argued, "When the Almighty takes up a people in any of the great centres of civilization, and transplants them into a region of ignorance and benightedness, he gives such a people a commission, and imposes an obligation upon them, to undertake the elevation of the degraded people who become subject to them. . . . and to lift them up to manhood, to freedom, and moral superiority."[19] In this respect Crummell differed from those Americo-Liberian settlers who, merely wanting a place to settle, assumed no more responsibility for the African than the European immigrant felt for American Indians when he settled on the United States frontier. Crummell felt a duty toward Africans, but it was a duty based on a paternalistic relationship, with the Afro-Americans assuming the upper role. He wrote: "Our circumstances make us the guardians, the protectors, and the teachers of our heathen tribes. . . . Force, that is authority, must be used in the exercise of guardianship over heathen tribes. Mere theories of democracy are trivial. . . . You cannot apply them to a rude people, incapable of perceiving their own place in the moral scale."[20]

That Crummell had absolutely no identity with African culture is made even clearer by his attitude toward Americo-Liberian adoption of African traits. He saw Liberia as a westernized nation which must steadfastly resolve not to lose its American society "into which we were schooled [in the United States] before we came here, and which we have chosen for this nation."[21] He pleaded for the acculturation of the African into Western civilization because without that change, Crummell reasoned, the Africans "will surely drag us down to their rude condition and their deadly superstitions; and our children at some future day, will have cast aside the habiliments of civilized life, and lost the fine harmonies and grand thoughts of the English tongue."[22] In an address to new Liberian immigrants from the New World, Crummell warned them to "be tender and pitiful and earnest to the heathen around you for their souls' sake, and for Christ; but resist, steadfastly, especially for your children's sake, their vicious habits, and their corrupting influences."[23]

The most prominent mission advocate who supported emigration was Henry Turner. Besides his A.M.E. offices, Turner was also the major fund-raiser for the *Azor* emigrants. He tirelessly publicized both mission and emigration interests, especially during his 1891 trip to West Africa,[24] and for the rest of the decade while serving as editor of the A.M.E. *Voice of Missions*. The early 1890s were the high point of emigration sentiment, and these years (before Booker T. Washington's emergence) were Turner's most influential as a spokesperson for the black masses.[25]

As early as 1883 Turner stated: "There never was a time when the coloured people were more concerned about Africa, in every respect, than at present. In come portions of the country it is the topic of conversation."[26] Of the Afro-American spokesmen who asserted that blacks did not want to emigrate Turner said: "[They] are simply advertizing their ignorance. I know the sentiments of the American negro. I have barrels and boxes full of letters [of people wanting to emigrate to Liberia]."[27] Yet he sometimes admitted that his was a minority position, "as a great mass of them [black Americans] are anti-African in the emigrational sense; but it is only a question of time when they will awake from their slumber and see things in a different light."[28] Turner lashed out with ven-

geance against blacks who opposed emigration, calling them "white
men's scullions" and other demeaning names. For example, when
an anti-emigrationist contemptuously sent Turner "the liberal sum
of five cents" for the Africa fund, the good Bishop sent his "grateful
acknowledgements" saying: "There are hundreds of thousands of
asses in this country, but you are the first one who has thought
to tender a little help."[29]

Turner was ready to cooperate with any agency, as long as it
could provide the resources for getting blacks to Africa. Although
he admitted that he disliked some of its policies and regretted its
ineffectiveness, Turner served as a vice-president of the American
Colonization Society. He wrote, "Its merits exceed its demerits
as much as the light of the sun exceeds the light of the moon. . . .
Thank God for the Colonization Society! But for it, the American
Negro, in point of self government and the ability to manage a
country, would be absolutely blank."[30]

Turner also agreed to ally with whites whose motives for emigration were entirely different from his own. In 1890, some conservative
white southern leaders attempted to reduce black voter strength
by advocating federal aid to emigration. While he knew the racist
motives of the sponsors, Turner praised the idea.[31] His action was
one of those occasional instances in history in which spokespersons
of opposite extremes advocate the same means to produce entirely
different ends.

Bishop Turner's appeal, if it did not convince many of the black
elite to join him, at least influenced some. In a poll conducted by
the *Indianapolis Freeman* in 1893, a significant minority of black
leaders agreed that a limited emigration might be a good thing.
Almost all of them prefaced their remarks with the statement that
they opposed any deportation of Afro-Americans not wishing to
leave the United States, but Bishop Turner also felt that way. These
spokespersons felt that emigrants should be skilled or educated,
and have financial resources to allow them to settle comfortably
in Liberia.[32] Ironically, this type of successful Afro-American was
the least likely to be attracted to Africa.

But Bishop Turner's voice remained powerful in the churches,
and during his career he influenced other missionaries to support
emigration. For example, one A.M.E. minister in Liberia wrote
to Turner that there were two reasons for emigrating: to escape
terrible conditions in the United States, and to bring Christianity
to Africans. He predicted that emigrants could best spread the
message to the indigenous peoples, who "only need to be enlightened

and directed by the generous spirit of the gospel to render them the most happy of mankind."[33] The *Voice of Missions* emphasized that Africa needed Christian religion to regain its ancient glory, but it also needed "the best that our American civilization can give it, incarnated in intelligent, resolute, and high-minded negro colonists."[34] Turner used his influence to have A.M.E. minister William H. Heard appointed as United States diplomat to Liberia, and Heard actively supported missions and emigration during his appointment in the 1890s.[35]

The A.M.E. Church was not the only denomination which reflected emigration interest. Andrew Cartwright, A.M.E. Zion missionary in Liberia, continued serving as an agent for the American Colonization Society, as he had done in North Carolina before emigrating.[36] Baptist Thomas Johnson felt that the colonization of Liberia would be the opening for Christianity's spread throughout Africa, because Liberians were aware of "their great responsibility, to exert their influence upon the natives."[37] His Baptist co-missionary John J. Coles agreed that Liberia was doing "untold good" for the conversion of the continent.[38] An even more prominent Baptist mission spokesperson who favored emigration was Charles S. Morris, financial secretary of the National Baptist Convention. Morris became a convert to emigration in 1898, after witnessing a "blood-thirsty mob" of whites attack the black community in Wilmington, North Carolina. He strongly denounced the racism which he saw, and his hopes for the future of black people in America were dim.[39] With this viewpoint, Morris turned to emigration and went to Africa. He wrote to Turner in 1899 that the Afro-American's duty was to redeem "the vast and splendid continent of his forefathers. I came to Africa in response to that as the central conviction of my life. . . . My only regret is that God did not put it into my heart to come ten years before." After seeing the pleasant climate and economic opportunities in Africa, Morris could not understand why so many black Americans had "such an everlasting dread" of emigrating. He believed that if a million emigrants came to Africa, it would revolutionize "the conditions of the poor natives who are . . . waiting for leadership, enlightenment and Christianity. . . . You are God's appointed leaders of these waiting, restless millions."[40] Emigrationists like Morris merely adapted the mission idea of raising Africa to civilization, by utilizing black American settlers as the means. If missionaries believed that colonies like Liberia offered the best method of redeeming Africa, evangelical and emigration interests coincided.

Not all missionaries supported emigration, and part of this lack of support was because Liberia had not been notably successful in attracting indigenous Africans. Much of the antagonism between Americo-Liberians and Africans arose because the Liberians believed that they were appointed by God "to enter this goodly land chasing away its moral darkness and revealing to the millions of its aboriginal inhabitants the deep degradation in which they were living, and the awful destiny to which they tending."[41] With this vision, the Americo-Liberians could not understand that the Africans might be satisfied with their own culture and might not want to be "saved." Liberians expressed resentment that the Africans did not appreciate what they were trying to do for them. One wrote, "Our natives have the stupid idea of all Barbarians; that we have come to oust or deprive them. Whereas so far from that, we have come to deliver them from heathenism."[42] This "delivery" did not always work to the Africans' advantage. From the earliest settlements, when costal tribes realized that they would permanently lose their lands, there were resistance movements and attacks upon Liberian settlement. This process repeated itself as different societies were incorporated into Liberia, especially when land was claimed without payment or the Liberians did not carry out their treaty obligations. The Africans particularly resented Liberian restrictions on their trade. Africans could qualify for equal status only if they abandoned their own culture and accepted westernization and Christianity. Thus, few Africans gained citizenship status, even though they were taxed and subject to Liberian law. In a process that was remarkably similar to United States expansion into Indian lands, a series of frontier wars erupted as various groups tried to gain their independence.[43] Liberia's expansion was curtailed, and it did not present as successful a model as many Afro-Americans had hoped it would.

Probably the most important reason for the lack of enthusiasm for emigration was that Liberia was not doing well economically or politically by the late nineteenth century. What had been a fairly prosperous trading situation in Liberia was in decline by the 1870s, caused by the combination of a world-wide depression, greater direct European trade in Africa which bypassed Liberian middlemen, the rise of the Brazilian coffee industry and the European sugar beet industry in competition with Liberian cash crops, and a series of disastrous foreign loans owed by the Liberian government. Moreover, as European powers competed for territory in the "scramble for Africa," both Britain and France took lands which Liberia claimed. There were fears that all of Liberia would be added to the colonial empires of the Europeans. Although Liberia did manage to retain its independence, it was clear by the 1880s that its expansion into West Africa was ended. It no longer held the potential for becoming a major African empire.[44]

A.M.E. missionary Alfred Ridgel reflected a wide-spread disillusionment with Liberia in a letter to the *Indianapolis Freeman*, one of the most influential black newspapers. His testimony was especially dramatic because of his previous commitment to emigration. He wrote from Liberia: "Africa is a sickly country. One can die here without any effort whatever. Oh, the African fever is simply awful. . . . I would not advise our people to come here unless they had money. This is no place for a poor man. . . . The Negro may as well content himself in America. . . . Only a short while and all Africa, save Liberia, will be under the complete control of white men."[45] His sentiments were echoed by other missionaries,[46] and even Edward Blyden began to see indigenous Africans as having more leadership potential than the Americo-Liberians.[47]

In general, most missionaries declined to support emigration because they did not have much faith in a black-led political independence movement for Africa. In a process strikingly similar to the black response after Reconstruction, the clergymen retreated into an apolitical form of leadership. If they could not redeem Africa by political authority, their next best choice was a moral redemption through missionary expansion. Such an alternative was a familiar one for black Americans, whether it operated through the churches or through the self-help approach of Booker T. Washington. Both approaches provided a means of black community organization and leadership while working around the political status quo. In addition, emigrationists were hampered by the accusation that they were abandoning the struggle for equal rights in America. A mission supporter could maintain a close feeling with the fatherland, while still working for racial equality in the United States. Though sacrificing the idea of a political empire in Africa, the missionaries held out hope for redeeming the continent through a substitute Christian empire.

The major factor influencing Afro-Americans to turn to ideological and social means of "raising" Africa, rather than political expansion, was European imperialism. By the 1880s and 1890s, the nations of Europe had begun a competitive scramble for African territory that left few areas of the continent untouched. The black missionaries responded to this development in different ways, depending on the degree of their commitment to Africa's westernization.

Some missionaries were prepared to encourage European imperialism, even if it meant that Africans would lose their political independence and come under the control of whites. These missionaries felt that imperialism was part of God's plan to open the continent for westernization and enlightenment. They argued that Christianity had expanded in the past by force of arms, and it was justified in doing so with Africans. In any case, they saw European takeover as inevitable, as part of the world-wide advance of civilization over barbarism. Africans had the choice of adapting or being exterminated. Social Darwinist ideas emerged in the notion that out of such changes the "fittest" would survive and lead a regeneration of Africa.[48]

One advocate of this view was Alexander Crummell, who believed that no people could rise to civilization except under the direction of others who were already civilized. He described the lack of civilization as "the most pitiful, the most abject of all human conditions," and felt that Western control was necessary for progress. He was especially favorable toward British colonial expansion, and lamented the fact that all of West Africa was not under English sway, but he also praised Belgian King Leopold's expansion up the Congo. According to Crummell, the European drive to open Africa was "the highest philanthropy or the most zealous religionism."[49] "Africa needs," he wrote,

> a grand POLICE FORCE all over the continent, restraining violence, keeping open grand avenues of commerce, affording protection to missionaries and travelers, protecting weak tribes and nations from powerful marauding chiefs. . . . I rejoice in this [imperialist] movement. I have the largest expectations of good and beneficence from its operations. I have the most thorough conviction of its need, its wisdom, and its practicality.[50]

A more forceful defense of Western intrusion into Africa could not be written, and Crummell's views were fairly typical of Afro-American reactions to the "opening" of Africa during the early years of its partition.[51]

Missionaries who strongly condemned African cultures, like Baptist John J. Coles, welcomed imperialism because it promoted westernization. Coles was favorably impressed by the efforts of Belgian King Leopold and "our beloved Henry M. Stanley" to open the Congo to European influences.[52] A.M.E. missionary Alfred

Ridgel felt such a deep need to break "the strong cords of heathen-ism [by] . . . a moral, intellectual and industrial redemption" that he regarded colonialism as a "godsend." European control, he concluded, caused many Africans to become "educated in easy circumstances, [who] would have been savage heathen."[53]

This favorable attitude toward imperialism was especially evident among Afro-American missionaries in British colonies. A notable example of relations between imperialists and missionaries involved the 1898 Hut Tax Revolt in Sierra Leone. Even though the imposition of a new tax was the immediate occasion of the revolt, its under-lying cause was oppressive military interference by the British colonial officials.[54] Yet, Superintendent Floyd Snelson of the A.M.E. mission there did not attempt to understand the reasons for the revolt. He condemned the rebels as "lustful and bloodthirsty sav-ages," even though they specifically protected missionaries.[55] Another A.M.E. evangelist wrote to the *Voice of Missions* complimenting the British colonial government for doing such an effective job in imprisoning the insurgent leaders.[56] A black missionary of the American Soudan Mission, J. A. L. Price, contemptuously explained that the revolt had occurred merely because the indigenous peoples wanted "to dominate" their country without English influence, not as a result of legitimate grievance. He gave no reason to justify British interference, but assumed that the Africans should welcome Western control.[57]

Even missionaries who expressed more favorable attitudes toward traditional Africans sometimes complimented British control. A.M.E. missionary John Richard Frederick was impressed with British administration in Sierra Leone. English expansion into the interior caused him to "have nothing to fear but rather everything to hope for in the future."[58] In South Africa, Baptist Charles Morris claimed that the colonial government's treatment of blacks was "infinitely better" than in the southern United States, and that Africans had "more reason to sing 'God Save the Queen' than we have to sing . . . 'My Country Tis of Thee.'"[59]

No doubt missionaries partly supported imperialism because the missions themselves were sometimes dependent upon the colonial government for support. For example, when a local Sierra Leonian headman threatened to expel the United Brethren mission from his town, the British officials imprisoned him. The black missionary Joseph Gomer remarked that this action by the British was "a direct interposition of the hand of Providence. Our God is with us and for us."[60]

Another reason why Afro-American missions did not challenge colonialism was the realization that missionaries were sponsoring their own form of cultural imperialism. Evangelists like Nancy Jones expected Africans to abandon their traditional ways of life, to follow Afro-Americans "not only as teachers, but as leaders in every proper line of industry, education, religion, and social life."[61] The idea of exporting their own lifestyle to culturally "backward" peoples was a central aspect of late nineteenth-century imperialist thought, and many of the black missionaries took inspiration from it. A.M.E. Mission Secretary H. B. Parks, for example, favorably compared his denomination's expansion with United States imperialism in the Pacific. Africa, he wrote in 1899, "is the new colonial possession of the Missionary Department of the A.M.E. Church."[62]

Sometimes support for imperialism came from unexpected sources, as from the nationalist Edward Blyden. Blyden was an admirer of upper-class English manners and considered it one of his greatest honors to have been Liberia's ambassador to the Queen. He felt that Britain could help to accomplish his great goal of uniting West Africa into one large powerful nation. In Blyden's view, a major stumbling block to unification was tribal antagonism and warfare, and he believed that dissolving these differences under the British umbrella would be beneficial. He did not fear British power, because he assumed that whites could not live permanently in the tropical climate, so that European control would be only a short peace-bringing stage in preparation for nationhood. Blyden believed that Africans would profit by borrowing the best aspects of English government and culture, while still retaining their traditional values. He therefore encouraged the British to educate Africans and train them for self-government.[63] Blyden's assumptions may have been naively optimistic, but they were part of his vision of African nationalism.

Not all Afro-American missionaries shared these trusting attitudes about European motivations, and there was considerable dissent about Western political power in Africa. This dissent usually originated from a missionary's direct experience with colonial exploitation, and it tended to come from clergymen in the Portuguese and Belgian colonies of central and southern Africa. Sometimes it was only a qualified resistance to the colonialists, as in the case of American Board missionary Samuel Miller. In 1884, when a local chief drove out the mission, the whites asked the Portuguese Angola officials to force the Africans to reaccept them. But Miller resisted such coercion, and only agreed to return if the African leaders invited them back.[64]

Other American Board missionaries were more directly critical of the Portuguese colonial system. In Mozambique, Benjamin Ousley felt that Portuguese racism was as bad as in the southern United States, and shortly after his arrival he wrote, "We have already been made to feel that we are members of a despised and degraded race." He believed that, far from being civilized by colonialism, the Africans were worse off for their contact with Europeans. He damned the Portuguese for encouraging liquor trade, setting a bad moral example, and not protecting local tribes from Zulu military raids.[65] Nancy Jones agreed with her fellow worker about the poor quality of Portuguese government. She informed black Americans that "wherever the whiteman has sway, the native is, as a rule, treated with the same prejudice of caste so well known in other lands. The kaffir is a 'dog' and little better than a slave."[66]

Some evangelists expressed anti-imperialist sentiments which suggest that their racial identity with Africans outweighed their Western identity. This was especially true after the 1896 victory of Ethiopia over Italian imperialist invaders, a victory which was received with some pride and celebration by Afro-Americans. For example, the wife of an A.M.E. Zion bishop referred to these glad "tidings of Negro victories" as "the uprising of an oppressed race daring to assert manhood. . . . Let us hope that our ancient glory is soon to be restored."[67] An A.M.E. minister called upon his church to protect Africans from being trampled beneath the "iron wheels" of white invasion, as had been done to American Indians.[68] While most speakers at the Atlanta Congress on Africa favored imperialism, at least one protested against "the high-handed seizure of territory from weak and semi-barbarous people." European conquest, he continued, brought Africans "under a system of bondage far more appalling than the heathenism in which they were found."[69] A black missionary volunteer wrote to the *Voice of Missions* that Afro-Americans should emphasize to Africans that the continent "is their own country, no body elses; teach them military tactic; teach them how to hold their own country in spite of all opposition, and to be their own rulers."[70]

Henry Turner, whose goal was to develop black-led independent nations, saw colonialism as merely another case of whites taking control away from blacks. Unlike those who saw European involvement as the best way to elevate Africa, the bishop consistently opposed imperialism and felt that Europeans were perpetrating a giant theft, one that would be comparable to the stealing of Africans in the slave trade.[71] He said that the debauchery imported into

Africa by the white man did far greater damage to the Africans than all the exaggerated incidents of barbarism.[72] In judging imperialism, Turner was sometimes inclined to see conditions from the Africans' point of view, and he sympathized with African hatred of the Europeans: "The native kings hate them, especially for robbing them of their lands. The French are hated as the devil. . . . France is more intolerant, it seems, in her colonial possessions than is England, and far less compromising. The Germans are abominated by the Mohammedans because of the ship-loads of rotgut whiskey they land along the coast."[73] Even though he was less critical of the British colonial system, which allowed Africans a certain amount of home rule, Turner was skeptical that such concessions would last long. He simply did not trust whites when they held political power over blacks, and he recognized that racism was deeply embedded in the white mind. He was especially concerned about areas like South Africa, where there was a large white settler population.[74]

Turner's fears concerning South Africa were reinforced by Baptist missionary R. A. Jackson. Writing from Capetown, Jackson concluded that white settlers, especially the Boers, meant "certain death to natives and sudden destruction to [their] real advancement." White settlers had in many areas made "a hell on earth" for the Africans. He felt that if Afro-American settlers did not soon emigrate to take over parts of the continent, "the [white] enemy may burn the bridge here and you shall never cross at all."[75] Jackson unquestionably identified Africa as his homeland, and he resented colonialism as an encroachment into the black world.

The missionary who made the most significant protest against imperialism was William Sheppard. He exerted a major influence in exposing atrocities in the Belgian "Congo Free State." King Leopold's form of indirect rule through concessionaire companies was tragic, Sheppard felt, and pressure for profits caused many abuses of the Congolese people by the company officials. The unsettled condition of Congo society in the late 1890s naturally disrupted missionary progress, so the clergy had ample reason to complain. For example, the 1899 Report of the Presbyterian Congo mission complained about the effect of government actions in the Kasai area, saying that a large number of the people had been taken away by the State for forced labor, "and those who were permitted to remain were mightily perturbed in spirit lest a similar fate would be theirs. . . . [Consequently] the interest of the people about things spiritual was being converted into base indifference."[76]

The Protestant American missionaries, with neither national nor religious loyalties to Leopold, openly criticized the Free State government. In 1898 a government officer imposed a heavy cash tax upon the Kasai peoples, to force them to work for Europeans. By this arrangement, the Company got cheap labor and government ended up with most of the cash. In addition, the government used feared cannibalistic Zappo-Zap soldiers to collect the tax. Because he could speak the languages and was "much loved by all the tribes," Sheppard was chosen to make an investigatory tour of the Kasai. Among his findings was that the Zappo-Zaps were using their tax-collecting forays as a cover for slave raids and cannibalism. He concluded that a more exploitative system could hardly be devised.[77]

On the basis of Sheppard's findings, the Presbyterian mission called for a State Inquiry. When the Inquiry did not punish the officials responsible, and no improvement took place in the situation, Sheppard exposed the abuses.[78] This story caused the Presbyterian Mission Board to appeal to the United States Department of State to protest directly to King Leopold. The exposé became internationally famous and had a great effect on American and British mission organizations.[79]

Sheppard's thoroughness and persistence in exposing the Congo atrocities was a mark of his deep concern for Africans, and may have revealed his resentments against all forms of racism. The *Southern Workman*, in publicizing his exploits, explained Sheppard's success as a product of his "tact, heroism, and friendly relations with the natives."[80] The black missionary, fully supported by other Presbyterian missionaries, continued his campaign so relentlessly that the concessionaire Kasai Company took him to a colonial court in 1909 for libel. Sheppard's "crime" consisted of writing an article in the mission newspaper which traced the decline of the Bakuba society. Before the coming of the Europeans, he wrote, the Bakuba had farmed their own lands and were prosperous. However, with the entry of the Kasai Company the people were forced to work for the whites, making rubber. The cash wages they received, after taxes, were too meager to buy the goods that they needed but no longer had time to produce for themselves. Thus, the introduction of a cash economy, on Belgian terms, had produced a dramatic decline in their standard of living. In the trial, which was internationally publicized, Sheppard's defense not only showed his love for the Africans but his own identity with his Kasai home as well. After proving the truth of his statements, Sheppard was found not guilty.[81]

Although Sheppard was acquitted in his trial, strained relations with the colonial government continued. As whites established more intensive control over the Congo, Sheppard as a black man had less freedom to operate. Once he lost his independence and saw the continued decline of his beloved Bakuba people, Sheppard gave up the fight and returned to America. During his twenty years in Africa, however, he had done much to promote an appreciation of Africa culture and to arouse sympathy for exploited colonial subjects.

Black American missionaries held diverse opinions on the issues of emigration and imperialism, but their attitudes on both these topics depended on how strongly they felt the need for Westernization of the continent. Missionaries like Alexander Crummell, who strongly condemned traditional life-styles, supported both emigration and imperialism as the best means of "elevating" Africa by outside influences. Others, like William Sheppard, felt more respect for African culture and saw less justification for Western intrusions. Their degree of antipathy toward whites was still another factor accounting for this diversity of opinion. Although Britain came in for less criticism than other colonial powers, white settlers were seen as damaging to African interests.

The Afro-American condemnation of imperialism should not be understated, but it was weakened because of the lack of respect for traditional African cultures. The missionaries' prime goal was still the conversion of the continent. The contradictions in these views are typified by A.M.E. Bishop Benjamin Arnett, who voiced anti-imperialist appeals for "the redemption of the Dark Continent from the control of foreign nations," yet favored the westernization of Africa and its "emancipation from the intellectual darkness of the centuries." Once the people become westernized, he predicted, an African independence movement modeled on the American Revolution would emerge. Arnett felt that "the days are coming when Africa will produce a Jefferson who shall write a new Declaration of Independence." A republican form of government would be formed, and Christianity would "be the rule of life and conduct in the great republic of redeemed Africa."[82] Arnett's ideals, like those of black mission advocates generally, reflected his American background more than it did African conditions. Even when voicing emigrationist or anti-imperialist sentiments, most mission supporters looked forward to the "redemption" of the continent along distinctly Western lines.

8

Mission Relations with Westernized Africans and African Students in the United States

Since most Afro-American missionaries regarded Africa as culturally backward, it is not surprising that their goal was to transform the continent into modern westernized societies. Nor is it surprising that missionaries responded enthusiastically toward Africans who adopted European ways, as examples of the "civilized" African who could emerge from the "dark continent."

Most of the acculturated Africans with whom the missionaries came in contact were in the British colonies of Sierra Leone, Gold Coast, Nigeria, and South Africa. They were English-speaking and literate, and so could communicate easily with Afro-Americans. British philanthropists had made serious efforts to improve the conditions of Africans during the early to mid-nineteenth century, and the response of some Africans had been a complete departure from their indigenous cultures in favor of a European model, even including minor details of dress and fashion. Some of the individuals were probably of low status within their traditional societies, but others simply admired the power of the westerners. In Sierra Leone, for example, there existed a large "Creole" community, which considered itself a loyal part of the British empire. The Creoles were largely descended from enslaved Africans whom the British navy had freed and resettled in the colony. This multi-ethnic group was grateful to the English for liberating them, for protecting them from indigenous interior groups, and for educating them. The British did not raise a strong color bar against "civilized" Africans, and these subjects fancied that they were among the Queen's favorites. They modeled themselves after educated Englishmen, tending to idealize British virtues and play down British faults.

After the 1860s, however, racism began to displace the ideal of equality in English thought, and paternalism or antagonism became the norm. The westernized Africans were disillusioned by their subsequent loss of status, and were left culturally moorless when they were spurned by Englishmen. Some began to question the ideal of Europeanization, worked to reestablish an African identity, and began nationalistic resistance.[1]

While Europeanized Africans were reacting against prejudiced actions by whites, they still held their basic Western orientation. They were opposed not to westernization, but to racism. What they needed were new role models, who shared the "civilized" ideal but who also treated them as equals. It was at this time that the Afro-American missionaries arrived. A congenial relationship developed between the two groups, because the missionaries and the westernized Africans each offered the other an important ally in their goal to "redeem" Africa.

As emphatically as they denounced traditional cultures, the black missionaries praised the westernized Africans. In the first place, acculturated Africans were usually well educated. Their refinement delighted the Afro-Americans, who saw it as indicative of Africa's potential to rise. For example, Baptist Charles Morris confessed his ignorance of the continent before traveling there, and was surprised at the maturity of thought of the Anglicized blacks in South Africa: "If anyone had told me I should find such intelligent, bright faced, thoughtful people as I have seen by the hundreds in all of these cities—men of my own race . . . I would have said that it is absurd to expect to find men of such breadth, such culture, such ability in Africa. Yet here they are."[2] On his first trip to West Africa in 1891, Bishop Turner was especially impressed by a man from Lagos, who was "black as ink" and educated in ten different languages. The bishop lectured black Americans: "Talk about the African being ignorant, here is one who has no superior for book learning in our country."[3] Alfred Ridgel warned aspiring black American missionaries that they should not come to Africa until they were educated, because otherwise many "highly cultured" westernized Africans would be on a higher level of intellect than the missionaries.[4]

The black missionaries realized that their greatest chance of increasing their church's membership base was through the acculturated Africans, so they treated them respectfully. In Liberia,

Episcopal missionary Samuel Ferguson strongly criticized the Americo-Liberians for opposing the inclusion of educated Africans in the government.[5] Once an African adopted Western ways, Ferguson was firmly committed to according him or her equality. In 1886, for example, Ferguson engineered the appointment of a Christian member of the Gdebo people as an agent for the American Colonization Society. The Gdeboes, he realized, were suspicious of the coming of more American immigrants, and such an appointment would improve relations and set a role model for other acculturated Africans. He complimented this appointee as being "in the front rank of the Gdeboes that have been brought out of the darkness of heathenism," who would help to bring about "a perfect union between the aborigines and the Americo-Liberians."[6] In 1896 Ferguson became the first missionary to ordain a native African as an Episcopal pastor, a man who eventually rose to become a bishop.[7]

The tone of missionary statements concerning westernized Africans was dramatically different from their descriptions of traditional cultures. Baptist Thomas Johnson, for example, was most respectful when he met Bishop Samuel Crowther, a westernized convert in the Anglican Church. Johnson expressed "great pleasure" upon meeting Christian Africans in Sierra Leone and Nigeria, and was "delighted" to visit African-operated mission schools.[8] Likewise, in South Africa Charles Morris accepted African Christian ministers as "men of real eloquence and power." The uneducated African was "a diamond in the rough stage"; but once westernized, Morris argued, the African should be considered completely equal.[9]

Black missionaries may have been just as ethnocentric as white missionaries, but they did not share the racist sentiments that whites all too often exhibited against even "civilized" Africans. The black missionaries lifted their prejudice once an African accepted Western norms, and they were more than happy to accept her or him as equal. This treatment made the acculturated Africans respond enthusiastically to the expansion of the black American churches. In 1894, for example, a Nigerian clergyman wrote in a letter (typical of many from Africa which were published in *Voice of Missions*) that his people were anxious to welcome Afro-American missionaries, and that he wished "to enlighten my countrymen [black Americans], the descendents of Africa, on the greatness of their home land and induce them to return to a congenial clime, to their own people, their own home."[10] The newspaper of the Gold Coast westernized elite welcomed the arrival of A.M.E. Zion missionaries, saying they were "ready to educate and christianize us and make the land of our common ancestors a glorious habitation in the eyes of the world." A later article concluded that the Afro-American churchmen were "bone of our bone and flesh of our flesh, [who] would naturally take a much greater interest in their missions in the Motherland than can be possible with . . . missionaries of an alien race."[11]

Many of the westernized Africans shared black Americans' negative opinions of indigenous cultures. For example, the Sierra Leonian editor of the militant *West African Reporter* in 1882 authored a "Negro Creed" intended to instill pride in being black, in which one of the emphases was advocacy of the continent's "restoration from barbarism and superstition to civilization and Christianity."[12] James Johnson, whose infuence had much to do with the rise of nationalism in Sierra Leone and Nigeria, developed a theory that Afro-Americans were representative of the best true African potential. He shared the view that ancient Africa had declined because it rejected Christianity, and believed the way for it to rise to world power was to be "redeemed" under black American missionary leadership.[13]

The attraction of acculturated Africans for black American Christianity developed most strongly in South Africa.[14] Reverend James Dwane, one of the leaders of the independent Ethiopian Church in South Africa, described for the A.M.E. church his early "heathen" life "enveloped in ignorance and darkness." After hearing a missionary speak, Dwane remembered, he "could not get rid of the sense of guilt and liability to [God's] punishment," so he converted.[15] Another Ethiopian Church leader wrote to the *Voice of Missions* that Africans were "still under the kingdom of ignorance and heathenism," so he was gratified that civilized Afro-Americans "recognized [Africans] as their fellow country people."[16] The westernized South Africans were as concerned about negating the stereotype of "African savagery" as were black Americans. They wrote to Bishop Turner that they favored the ending of tribal identification and tradition because "it has not only caused hatred among ourselves, but debarred Christianity and unity." Turner was in complete agreement with them, saying that all Africans should unite, "regardless of tribes or locality. . . . We are all one." There were no tribal distinctions among black Americans, Turner pointed out, and so there should be none among Africans.[17]

Bishop Turner held up the civilized ideal as the means for African advancement. Encouraging enterprising blacks to emigrate, so that they could set an example for the Africans, he wrote in the *A.M.E. Church Review*: "Men of character, courage, enterprise and property, would be hailed with joy by the natives and, at the same time, be an object lesson to them, that the same possibilities are open to them also when they are sufficiently elevated to merit, and demand them. . . . It is a question of condition . . . [of being] civilized."[18] A.M.E. Mission Secretary H. B. Parks reiterated Turner's feelings, saying that the Ethiopian Church was "struggling at the edge of the great ocean of ignorance," but that it was "the only implement with which the evangelization and civilization of the Dark Continent would be logically effected."[19] Parks' statement shows that, despite an active interest in Africa, he continued to think of it as a Dark Continent. The mission impulse was to light up this darkness, and the best means of doing this, most black mission advocates thought, was through the westernized Africans.

By affiliation with established congregations of African Christians, the black American churches had the advantage of immediate institutional growth, without waiting for individual converts. This process was very similar to the expansion of the northern independent black churches into the American South after the Civil War, and its progress was attractive to blacks who were depressed by worsening race relations of the 1890s. Their affiliation with westernized African churches, in fact, developed into the most successful form of involvement of black American churches in the continent by the end of the century. Writing in 1899, Secretary Parks expressed the common view of the mission movement when he concluded that the westernized Africans were "the connecting link between the uncivilized millions in Africa and the American Negro."[20]

Another type of contact between Africans and black Americans, which was also an important "connecting link" between the two groups, occurred with the coming of African students to the United States. Since few Afro-Americans had ever seen a real person from the fatherland, the exposure of Africans through the schools and churches had much influence on changing the black community's attitudes toward Africans. These students' backgrounds, and their relations with Afro-Americans, therefore warrant particular attention. The following analysis is based upon information covering sixty-eight Africans who attended seventeen American schools between 1870 and 1900. Their geographical origins in Africa were diverse: thirty-two were from Liberia, seventeen from South Africa, eleven from Sierra Leone, four from the Gold Coast, and one each from Ethiopia, Gabon, and Nyasaland.[21]

Most of these Africans were acculturated converts who were sent by African missionaries to be trained in the United States for the purpose of becoming missionaries themselves. Some churches were beginning to feel that converted and educated Africans would be able to do more effective mission work among their own people than would outsiders. Indigenous Africans, it was believed, would remain healthy in a tropical climate and would have no language or cultural barriers with their congregations. Because of segregation, most of the African students were enrolled in all-black schools where the interaction with Afro-Americans was intense. The Africans were exposed to an even wider segment of the Afro-American masses through the black churches.

The earliest American colleges for Africans were sponsored by white churches which were interested in the Afro-American settlement of Liberia. For example, the Northern Presbyterians founded Lincoln University in Pennsylvania in 1854 to train black missionaries for Africa. In its early years, Lincoln's students were from the United States, or were the sons of Afro-American emigrants in Liberia. But in 1873 nine indigenous Africans were sent to the campus by black missionaries in Liberia. These young Africans' arrival at the struggling school proved timely. The depression of 1873 had destroyed the fund-raising drive, but the college took the newly arrived students on a publicity tour, and they proved to be such attractive attention-getters that Lincoln was able to survive the depression. After this first group of Africans proved so valuable, Lincoln continued to draw others—twenty before 1900, sixteen of whom were from Liberia. Because of its pioneering effort, Lincoln had more African students than any other American college in the nineteenth century, and continued to attract Africans, like Kwame Nkrumah and Nnamdi Azikiwe, in the twentieth century.[22]

Another white-sponsored school which attracted Africans in the 1870s and 1880s was Fisk University in Tennessee. The American Missionary Association sponsored five African students at Fisk, who were later sent to Sierra Leone as missionaries. In 1890 these alumni sent another African to Fisk for a mission education. In that year the Fisk Bulletin demonstrated great interest in African missions, remarking that the African students "forcibly illustrate the vital relation which the Christian education of Colored people of the South sustain to the civilization and evangelization of the Dark Continent."[23]

Some Africans even managed to attend white institutions. The most famous of these was Orishatukeh Faduma. Actually born in British Guiana in 1857 with the name of William J. Davis, at an early age he and his family emigrated to Sierra Leone. In 1884 he became the first black graduate of the University of London, after which he returned to Sierra Leone. Even though Faduma was westernized and well-educated, under the influence of his friends Edward Blyden and James Johnson he identified with his Yoruba ancestry and changed his name to a more traditional one. In 1891, Faduma left for the United States and was accepted into the Divinity School of Yale University. Within three years he had earned his degree, and was ordained as minister to a black Congregational Church in Troy, North Carolina. He also served as principal of the Peabody Academy there, where he remained until 1914, when he returned to Africa.[24]

Another African who attended a white school, and who also went on to become an influential black nationalist, was John Langalibalele Dube. He was educated by American missionaries at the American Board Zulu mission, and in 1887 was sent to the United States for further education. He enrolled in Ohio's Oberlin College preparatory department, remained in school for two years, then worked at various jobs before returning to Natal in 1892. After four years of preaching among his native Zulu people, Dube came to New York City for theological education at the Union Missionary Training Institute. He lived in Brooklyn until 1899, when he was ordained a Congregational minister, but he traveled widely over the nation. On one of these trips Dube visited Alabama's Tuskegee Institute and met Booker T. Washington. Their meeting resulted in an immediate friendship, and Washington's ideas on industrial education became the most important aspect of Dube's subsequent career in South Africa. The Zulu student spoke at the 1897 Tuskegee commencement, and at Virginia's Hampton Institute shortly thereafter. With Washington's assistance, Dube raised enough money to return to Natal in 1899.[25]

Faduma and Dube were clearly not typical of African students in the United States, but a few others also turned up in white schools. In 1871 a white Evangelical United Brethren missionary in Sierra Leone sent a young Sherbo student to be educated in the public high school of Dayton, Ohio. Eight years later this student graduated and, with his Afro-American bride, returned to his people as a missionary.[26] In 1892 a Liberian Bassa student was reported at the unlikely location of Lewiston, Maine, in the Nichols Latin School.[27]

Despite these instances, and the influence of universities like Lincoln and Fisk, the major contact between Africans and Afro-Americans by the 1890s was in black-sponsored schools. As with Africans in white-sponsored institutions, most of these students were sent by missionaries. Black denominations wanted educated Africans for the same reason that their white brethren did, to train them as missionaries who would help to spread their churches in Africa. The Afro-American mission movement's interest in African students provided a major contact between black Americans and Africans.

By the 1890s each of the major independent black Baptist and Methodist denominations had observed surprisingly high rates of illness and death among its missionaries. This experience in the difficulties of Afro-American adjustment to the tropical climate, plus the availability of African converts persuaded more of the black mission supporters to turn to Africans. In 1894 one such supporter predicted that the mission movement of the Afro-American churches would fail unless African students were trained in the United States and sent back to their own people as missionaries. Each such student, he wrote, "would at once become a powerful example to his people of the civilizing power and influence of the gospel." Not only were African missionaries more credible than outsiders in preaching to their own society, but their Western education made them more effective than traditional African leaders in dealing with whites.[28]

The earliest Africans sponsored by a black church were five students from the Liberian mission of the Colored Baptist Foreign Missionary Convention. These students were attending Central Tennessee College in Nashvile in 1892.[29] Five years later, missionaries in South Africa sponsored by the National Baptist Convention sent four South African students to the United States. The Baptists arranged for each of these students to attend a different black college in the South.[30]

The most famous African sponsored by the black Baptists was not sent by one of their own missionaries, but by a nonconformist Englishman, Joseph Booth, who had established a Nyasaland mission. In 1895 he visited the United States to raise money for his mission, and while in America he made contacts with militant black leaders.[31] The black president of Morgan College in Baltimore arranged for the college press to publish Booth's book, *Africa for the African*.[32] Booth advocated full independence for African colonies as soon as possible, with all European land holdings being returned to African ownership. He saw black Americans as the best leaders to help Africans prepare for decolonization and develop the continent.[33]

One of Booth's most promising students in Nyasaland was John

Chilembwe, and in 1897 Booth brought this Ajawa student to the United States.[34] Baptist Foreign Missions Secretary Louis Garnett Jordan arranged for the support of Chilembwe's education at Lynchburg's Virginia Theological Seminary.[35]

The second black church to sponsor African students was the African Methodist Episcopal Church, which began its involvement more fortuitously than did the Baptists. Its earliest sponsorship of such students was largely the result of Bishop Turner's efforts. On his trip to Liberia in 1893, Turner so inspired a fourteen-year-old African that this youth came to America and was enrolled by Turner in the Alabama Normal Institute in 1894. Within two years Turner had sent another African, a Sierra Leonian, to the black Alabama school; and by 1899 he reported three more students from Sierra Leone who had entered the theology department of Morris Brown College in Atlanta.[36]

The most significant role that African students would play in the A.M.E. Church came about as the result of an accident. In 1894 and 1895 a choir of South African mission students, on tour in the United States, ran out of money. While there is no way of knowing what happened to most of these stranded Africans, two Xhosas were enrolled in Lincoln University.[37] Another member of the group was a twenty-one-year-one Methodist Basuto named Charlotte Manye. An A.M.E. preacher took her to Bishop Benjamin Arnett, who strongly supported African missions and whose son would later be a delegate to the 1900 Pan-African conference. Arnett enrolled her in the denomination's Wilberforce University in Ohio and brought her to live with his family. While at Wilberforce, Manye wrote such encouraging letters back to her Methodist kinsmen in Africa that ten other South African students were sent to Wilberforce before 1900. An even greater effect of her letters was that the Ethiopian Church leaders got in touch with Bishop Turner and soon decided to join the A.M.E. Church. Such a large annexation was the basis for a dramatic growth of the A.M.E. Church in South Africa.[38]

The South African students at Wilberforce so captured the imagination of the church leaders that, on his 1898 visit to Africa, Bishop Turner bought land in Queenstown for an A.M.E. college in South Africa. The denomination's Mission Secretary, H. B. Parks, became convinced that the best policy would be to train Africans themselves to preach to their own people. Such a college, Parks claimed, would "do for the South African Negro, starting at the beginning, what Wilberforce and other Negro training-schools are doing, after long delay, for the American Negro."[39]

The third largest independent Afro-American denomination, the African Methodist Episcopal Zion Church, soon followed its sister churches in developing an interest in African students. Again, this interest grew out of its missionary commitment. The most influential A.M.E.Z. supporter of African students, Bishop John Bryan Small, convinced the church leaders to place primary mission emphasis on training Africans rather than black Americans. An African missionary would, he felt, be less expensive for the church to support, would already know the indigenous language and customs, and would have an emotional attachment to his people.[40]

Under Bishop Small's leadership, at least four African students came to America between 1897 and 1900. All of these students attended Livingstone College in North Carolina, which stressed an academic and theological education rather than the industrial training approach. Bishop Small returned from an 1897 trip to the Gold Coast with the first African student. Coming from a wealthy westernized family of Cape Coast merchants, this student hardly fitted the stereotype that most whites held of Africans as "uncivilized savages."[41]

The next student brought by Bishop Small, James Emman Kwegyir Aggrey, from a prominent Christian Fanti family, became one of Livingstone's most famous graduates. Aggrey had been such a good student in the British mission school that he was made a teacher by age fifteen. By the 1890s he was a respected young man among the educated westernized elite at Cape Coast. Aggrey showed sympathy for incipient African nationalism in 1898 when he served as an officer of the Gold Coast Aborigines' Rights Protection Society.[42] Possibly because of his political bent, he suddenly agreed to accompany Bishop Small to America in 1898. He adjusted so superbly to Livingstone College that after his graduation he remained there as a teacher for another two decades.[43]

The last two Africans brought by Bishop Small, in 1899, were less notable than Aggrey. They did, however, fulfill A.M.E.Z. wishes by returning to the Gold Coast as missionaries soon after their graduation.[44]

Thus, by 1900 the three major Afro-American denominations were each sponsoring African students in the United States. The reactions of black Americans who became exposed to Africans in the late nineteenth century can tell us much about the ethnic relations between the two groups.

During this era the proponents of interest in Africa were continually complaining about the prevalence of negative stereotypes about "the Dark Continent." Racist views of Africa often portrayed it as nothing but a jungle inhabited by "savage cannibals," and this view was accepted by many educated black Americans who had been indoctrinated by whites.[45]

Unfortunately, such stereotypes were reinforced by a number of Afro-American charlatans who passed themselves off as African for monetary gain. For example, in 1891 a "Zulu prince" gave a speech at the St. Louis A.M.E. Church, in which he described in great detail how Zulus ate human infants and worshipped crocodiles. Fortunately, these untrue claims were corrected, and the person was exposed as a South Carolinian who knew nothing about Africa.[46] But his ruse was not uncommon; one black Cincinnati writer lamented that people had "been humbugged so often" that their interest in Africa was becoming frustrated.[47] True promoters of Africa, like Bishop Turner, complained that "no such brutal degradations are found anywhere in Africa as some of these African imposters are palming off for the purpose of extorting money."[48]

Some of the African students were shocked by the extent to which some black Americans believed these stereotypes. A Liberian student at Lincoln University, for example, wrote a number of letters to the *Washington Bee*, complaining of the "mass of misrepresentation about Africa" which prejudiced "the American Negro public against their [African] brethren." Both white and black Americans, he claimed, shared a misconception of Africa as "a barren waste, a hot bed of fevers" with its people living "in the most abject barbarism."[49] Another Lincoln student wrote that his Afro-American classmates expected Africans to be "hideous-looking creatures" who had no intelligence.[50] And a Sierra Leonian student at Alabama Normal Institute was stunned that some Afro-Americans "even dared to demand of me whether Africans possess tails like the monkey." He stated that many black people stereotyped all Africans as heathen, and "that to be a heathen is, necessarily, to be idiotic."[51] It is not surprising that such inaccurate descriptions of Africa were promoted by white racists; after all, a major justification for slavery was that Africa was "savage." That many of these views were accepted by some blacks is an indication of the lack of firsthand information about the ancestral continent from sources other than white-written documents.

Considering such unfavorable attitudes of some Afro-Americans toward Africans, it is not surprising that there were instances of bad relations between the culturally different blacks. The experience of George Peabody, the son of a Bassa prince in Liberia, provides explicit evidence of such conflict. In 1891, after he had been at Lincoln University for four years, Peabody reported that all African students there were dissatisfied and would have liked to change to another school. He wrote, "I have been taunted, discouraged, and dogged out and almost tormented out of my life. I have suffered at Lincoln what I never suffered in heathendom. . . . Why should there be prejudice [against Africans] at Lincoln?" But besides misinformation and prejudice among Afro-Americans, Peabody's own feelings of superiority may have been partly responsible for the strain. The teaching at Lincoln, he wrote, might be good enough for those "aspiring to second class citizenship in America," but it was not good enough for the Africans. In an obvious slur directed at American ex-slaves, he said of Africans, "We are free men and not freedmen."[52] Such attitudes were not likely to win favor.

Most of the conflict between the two black groups occured at Lincoln University, but discord sometimes arose in other schools. At Livingstone College, for example, one student insisted on following his tribal customs and was not tolerated by the Afro-Americans or even by the more westernized Africans there. Another Livingstone alumni left the A.M.E.Z. Church and set up his own independent mission after returning to the Gold Coast—a move that implies a less-than-complete acceptance of the black American church.[53]

In general, however, students who were sponsored by the independent black churches had a better relationship with black Americans than did those at Lincoln. This was probably due to the positive example set by the black leadership at the independent colleges. Of the five Liberian students at Central Tennessee College, for example, four were highly complimented by their black Baptist sponsors. A former black Baptist missionary admired Monolu Massaquoi, a Vai medical student, as "gentlemanly in deportment and an excellent student." The others were also praised, except for one "undisciplined" Kru boy who had "attended a feast of the cannibals of his tribe, and tasted the flesh, which he says was good." Another of the students had trouble communicating because his knowledge of English was limited, but even he exhibited "much more decorum than some boys who have had their birth in a Christian land." All in all, this missionary evaluated the African students individually, much as he might have described American students, and held little prejudice toward them. The most hopeful sign, he said, was that "they all seem to understand that they are here to be educated for teachers of their people in Africa."[54]

The black American students at Central Tennessee College also seem to have reacted favorably to the African students. One American student wrote to the *Freeman* a letter of commendation about his Vai classmate: "As a student and Christian gentleman he is an honor to his race and a high tribute to the mental and moral capacity of the inhabitants of the dark continent." This letter appealed for contributions to aid the Vai people, who were in the midst of a famine.[55]

Probably the most notable example of good relations between an African Baptist and black Americans was the case of John Chilembwe. He characterized Afro-Americans as his "good friends" while he attended the Virginia Theological Seminary, and the Baptist Mission Secretary remarked that "few men have come to this country and made more friends than Brother Chilembwe."[56] Yet even Chilembwe may have felt somewhat nervous and aloof around black Americans. One of his classmates vividly remembered "his general unlikeness to the other students. In all, his air." This student remembered asking him about his name; Chilembwe replied, stiffly (and with exaggeration), "It means *Prince*. My father is a King."[57]

While some of the African students were aloof, or even hostile to black Americans, the evidence suggests that the majority of the Africans had very good personal relationships with their black American brethren. Even at Lincoln University, the two South African Xhosas became active and popular students. They were from Presbyterian families in South Africa, and after completing their undergraduate requirements they entered seminary school at Lincoln. By 1900 they had attracted eight other South African Presbyterians to the college.[58]

The eleven South African Methodists at Wilberforce University had even better relations with black Americans. Charlotte Manye, residing in the home of Bishop Arnett, was "regarded as a member of the family." Her good feelings toward Afro-Americans were obvious, in her encouragement of other Africans to enroll at Wilberforce and join the A.M.E. Church.[59] Some of these students were Cape Coloured, and all were highly acculturated to Western values. Writing in the A.M.E. mission newspaper, Bishop Turner complimented them for their refinement, and noted that all of the students spoke English well, were quite literate, were committed Christians, and had excellent intellectual qualities.[60] The good relations with the African students, plus the missionary concern of the A.M.E. Church were reflected in the 1899 prize essay at Wilberforce. Written by an Afro-American student, this essay praised Africans as superior to the "savagery" of lynching and racism in America.[61]

The Africans attending Livingstone College also had successful relations with Afro-Americans. The first student at the A.M.E.Z. college, William Hockman, was remembered as an excellent student and "a high quality fellow."[62] But it was J. E. K. Aggrey who had the best relationship with his black American sponsors. His educational background made him better prepared than most of the American students, so he was placed directly in the college classical department. According to his biography, Aggrey was "extremely popular" with his fellow students, and the president of Livingstone looked upon him as a model student. To support himself, Aggrey was employed at the A.M.E.Z. Church Publishing House. He also contributed articles to a white newspaper, the *Charlotte Daily Observer*. When he graduated with honor in 1902, Aggrey won a gold medal for English composition and another for "general scholarship and deportment."[63] The fact that he was asked to remain at the college as a teacher is further evidence of Aggrey's good relations with A.M.E.Z. leadership.

Why did black Americans react in such different ways toward African students? Geographical origin of the students does not seem to have been a determining factor.[64] Neither is there a consistent pattern of relations between Africans and Americans at certain schools. Lincoln University, which in general demonstrated bad relations with its African students, had very good relations with its South Africans. And Livingstone College, with perhaps the best record, had one or two instances of discord.

What does seem to be decisive in the ethnic relations of the two groups, more than any other factor, is the degree of westernization of an African. Afro-Americans reacted most favorably to those African students who had already been exposed to Anglo-Saxon education and culture. The intellect and refinement of westernized Africans surprised and impressed black Americans who had expected savages. By demonstrating a "civilized" manner, as defined by Victorian standards, these acculturated Africans negated the "savage" stereotype and allowed Afro-Americans to look upon the fatherland as something to be proud of. They may or may not have been seen as typical by black Americans, but they at least proved that Africa had the potential for westernization.

In contrast, those Africans who came from a non-Western background were less well-received by the Afro-American community. With no strong cultural bond between them, black Americans had no real incentive to identify with traditional African cultures. The Americans essentially accepted the ethnocentric notions that were current at the time.

To understand black American attitudes toward Africa, it is important to analyze the image of their homeland which these African students presented. Most of these students had been trained in Christian missions, and as successfully indoctrinated converts they had accepted the standard missionary view that Western culture held the key to Christianization. For example, a Lincoln University alumnus, who was working as a Presbyterian missionary in Liberia, revealed an essay by one of his students which expressed this notion: "Africa must be saved and . . . we look to you all who live in the West who have civilization and Christianity for the gospel light."[65]

Such idealization of the West was often accompanied by a condemnation of traditional African culture. Ironically, one of the most negative pictures of Africa was presented by George Peabody, the Liberian Bassa student who so disliked his black American classmates at Lincoln University. Although he had fond memories of his pre-Christian life, he chose rather "to suffer afflictions with the people of God, than to enjoy the flesh-pots of heathenism. . . . One day with the Lord was better than ten thousand days of pleasurable sin."[66] Peabody called for missionaries to "break down the systems of polygamy, devil worship, superstition and ignorance."[67] He showed disrespect for his tribal religion by revealing its secret religious ceremonies, and he categorized it as degraded superstition: "The only good that it does is that it punishes murder, theft, and procures peace in time of need among the tribes. Yet little are these means of justice unless . . . the soul was hopeful of a rest beyond this life."[68] Writing in the *A.M.E. Church Review*, Peabody was critical of African "gross ignorance," and said that the only hope for the continent was to "be purged by the Redeemer's blood. Then may she welcome civilization."[69]

Another African who criticized his homeland was Edward Mayfield Boyle, a Sierra Leonian student at Alabama Normal Institute. Soon after arriving in the United States in 1897, Boyle appealed for black Americans to go to Africa as missionaries. As instances of Africans' "backwardness," he cited idolatry, superstition, and nakedness: "To reclaim these people, the sons and daughters of Africa [in America] must feel it their duty to heed the call. . . . Come over and help for we are groping in darkness still."[70] Significantly, within two years Boyle was disillusioned with Afro-Americans, and he became more defensive about Africa. Even though he had himself contributed to a negative image of the continent, he reacted against the stereotypes about Africa held by many black Americans.[71]

The Zulu student John Dube gave a fairly favorable image of his people. He described them as "a superior and conquering people," "intelligent and quick-witted," and "generous." The Zulus were, he wrote, "in no respect inferior to the whites. They are as capable of as high a degree of culture as any people." Despite his desire for Christianization, he presented a fairly neutral ethnographic account of Zulu religion and social patterns. He even suggested that Zulus had been better off before being corrupted by white "evil traders" who set a bad example for those who believed "that all the wise white man says and does, must be right."[72]

Dube believed firmly in the need for more missionaries, but he was primarily concerned with the future progress of African people: "When the people are converted, they have better tastes and higher ideals. . . . It tends to transform their material as well as their spiritual life . . . and better their temporal condition." His concept of progress was admittedly ethnocentric, contrasting "heathen" degradation with the "wonderful things, such as steamships, wagons, frame houses, furniture, machinery, etc., which the civilized man can make." With conversion and skilled training, Dube argued, "Zulus could see their own sons and daughters making some of these great things, which they think only white men can do, and which have made them appear as superior." Dube's stand can hardly be called militant, yet his appeal for black advancement contributed to nationalist thought. He deplored the fact that great wealth was being extracted from the continent through gold and diamond mining, while Africans were kept at low-paying unskilled jobs. "Will not those who believe in fair play, and in the principles taught by the carpenter of Nazareth, help to give the Zulus an industrial education, which will enable them to have a share in the rich benefits?" Dube believed that the best means of advancement would be to create a class of educated black "Anglo-Saxons of Africa [who] . . . will become a mighty power for good in the Dark Continent."[73] His attitudes were elitist and westernized, but they had much in common with what Afro-American leaders were saying about black advancement in the United States.

Another ambivalent attitude toward Africa was presented by the Yale student Orishatukeh Faduma. On the one hand, Faduma favored the conversion of Africa. At the 1895 Atlanta Congress on Africa, for example, he spoke of the need to convert Africans from superstition and fear.[74] Besides supporting missions, Faduma also favored the partition of Africa among colonial powers. The founding of Belgian King Leopold's Congo Free State, he predicted, would be of great advantage to Africa.[75]

On the other hand, Faduma did not offer a blanket condemnation of African culture, and he presented a fairly complete ethnographic description of the West African Yoruba society, free of excessive moralizing. He compared the Yoruba to the ancient Greeks and characterized them as "by no means a savage, but . . . a semi-civilized people."[76] Although Faduma was in general sympathy with the missionary movement, he offered a number of criticisms of missionary paternalism. His primary criticism concerned the westernization of Africans: "The general impression is, that in order to civilize and Christianize the African, he must be foreignized. Hence, one's native name, dress, and food must be changed." Africans do not need, he said, that which would "denationalize or deindividualize them, not what will stamp them out of existence, but what will show that God has a purpose in creating race varieties."[77] While Faduma retained his belief in missions, he had an appreciation of African ways of life that reflected a philosophy of cultural relativism.

Perhaps most outspokenly pro-African of the African students was Thomas A. Johns, a Liberian at Lincoln University. A follower of Edward Blyden, Johns tried to create a more favorable impression of indigenous Africa. In a series of letters to the *Washington Bee*, he complained about Christian attempts to wipe out traditional cultures and substitute Western customs, in contrast to Islamic missionaries who respected the local values. Africans were, he asserted, honest, loyal, and benevolent, and they should be honored by black Americans rather than condemned.[78]

If not all of the African students in America presented a favorable image of traditional African culture, they nevertheless exerted a positive influence on black American interest in the fatherland. John Chilembwe provides a striking example of the influence of these students on Afro-Americans. In less than three years Chilembwe spoke in numerous black churches, in at least six states, under the sponsorship of the National Baptist Convention. The Mission Secretary declared that during these tours Chilembwe "so touched the hearts of the American Negroes everywhere that many were moved to tears of sympathy and resolved to join in the salvation of Africa."[79] One black Virginia Baptist said that "the coming of that African into my home brought me face to face, as never before, with my responsibility for the redemption of all the world and especially Africa."[80]

Face-to-face contacts with westernized Africans particularly impressed black Americans. Concerning the entry of three Sierra

Leonians into Morris Brown College, Bishop Turner wrote, "Everybody appears to be amazed at their learning, refinement, and general intelligence. So many of our people in this country believe all Africans are mere heathens, that they are paralyzed with surprise to find such boys coming."[81] The westernized Africans and the Afro-Americans shared a common ground in their interest in Christianity and "civilization," which led them to be mutually attracted to each other. These close personal relations also helped to correct black Americans' misapprehensions about Africa in general. This was particularly true at Livingstone College, where the prominence of intelligent and well-educated Africans went far to remove old notions of a savage Dark Continent. An Afro-American student who came to Livingstone in 1899 remembered that, in contrast to public schools for blacks, "Africans were not looked down upon as inferior by this campus." Instead, the student wrote, Livingstone faculty emphasized "the greatness of ancient civilizations in Africa, the people from whom we are descended." The African students were looked up to by the whole college community, and Aggrey especially was considered "a scholarly genius."[82]

There were other ways in which the Africans exerted a positive influence on black Americans. Although information on the subsequent careers of many of the African students has been lost, several stayed in the United States after their graduation. Some of those who remained became prominent in their professions, which made a favorable impression on black Americans. Orishatukeh Faduma became a minister and principal of a school in Troy, North Carolina, where he served as a respected leader until 1914.[83] Samuel S. Sevier, a Lincoln University graduate who returned to Liberia in 1882, was appointed as assistant consul to the United States diplomat in Liberia. When the diplomat (Moses Hopkins, also a Lincoln alumnus) died in 1886, Sevier became acting consul, but shortly afterwards he returned to the United States and became a teacher at Livingstone College. Sevier taught about Africa at the A.M.E.Z. school, and remained in America for the rest of his life.[84] His more famous successor at Livingstone, J. E. K. Aggrey, taught there from 1902 until 1924.[85]

Perhaps the most interesting case of an African who made a successful career in America is George Waltham Bell. Although he was born in Ethiopia, during his childhood Bell and his family were exiled to Malta because of his father's opposition to the Ethiopian king, Menelik I. Eventually George joined the British navy, but resigned some years later while his ship was docked in the United

States. He then entered Lincoln University. After his graduation in 1883, he went on to medical school in St. Louis, and eventually became a prominent doctor in Arkansas. In a notable career, Bell was elected as a State Senator in Arkansas (1890–97), led a legal defense against segregation, founded a county medical association, authored a medical text on consumption, and established the Arkansas Colored Infirmary.[86] Unique though Bell was, he and the other Africans who rose to leadership status in the South demonstrate that educated and refined Africans were not discriminated against by black Americans.

African students not only influenced the attitudes of black Americans, they also exerted an influence in Africa. Over one-third of the students served as missionaries in their homeland by the beginning of the twentieth century. Undoubtedly others also became missionaries after 1900. By providing contacts between Afro-American churches and African Christians, the students not only aided the growth of the black churches, but also served an important function in black intercontinental relations. The role of Charlotte Manye in the South African Ethiopian Church affiliation with the A.M.E. Church (discussed earlier) is the best illustration of this influence. The impact of the African students was not felt only in religion. Two Lincoln University graduates, for example, who earned advanced degrees in medicine and law, returned to Liberia to become prominent in those fields.[87]

The students' greatest impact on Africa was in the development of black nationalism. The most violent case of anticolonial resistance by a former American student involved John Chilembwe. After graduating from the Virginia Theological Seminary in 1900, he returned to Nyasaland to establish a National Baptist Convention mission. By 1915 increasing pressures from white settlers led Chilembwe to mount a bloody attack that ended in his execution. His training under Joseph Booth, and the militant atmosphere at the Virginia Seminary, undoubtedly contributed to his resistance leadership.[88]

Yale graduate Orishatukeh Faduma, who returned to Africa in 1914 with Alfred Sam's emigration movement, influenced nationalist thought in both Sierra Leone and Nigeria.[89] In another section of the continent, Wilberforce University graduates Charlotte Manye, her husband Marshall Maxeke, and James Tantsi organized the South African Wilberforce Institute, which developed into one of Africa's leading black educational institutions. They also became active in the organization of the South African National Congress, the strongest black voice in early twentieth-century South Africa.[90] And John Dube pressed so strongly for an industrial education approach that he became known as "the Booker T. Washington of Africa." In 1901 he established the Zulu Christian Industrial School, modeled after Washington's Tuskegee Institute, which became another leading black educational center in South Africa. Like Washington, Dube was a moderate capitalist, yet he became the first president of the African National Congress in 1912 and contributed important leadership until his death in 1946.[91]

Certainly the most prominent American graduate, in terms of modern Pan-African thought, was J. E. K. Aggrey. In 1924 he left Livingstone College and returned to the Gold Coast as a teacher at the famous Achimota College. Though politically moderate, Aggrey communicated a strong sense of black pride to his students. Because a number of his pupils, especially Kwame Nkrumah, were inspired by him to become leaders, Aggrey is noted as a father of African nationalism.[92] Thus, late nineteenth-century African students in the United States had an influence in both America and Africa.

One conclusion to be drawn from this case study in ethnic relations is that cultural identity and common interests were more important than race in fostering close relations. The mere fact that Africans were of the same skin color was not enough, by itself, to produce a feeling of identity with them by black Americans. A shared cultural world-view made both the Afro-Americans and the westernized Africans feel that they could gain an advantage by identifying with each other, so they moved closer together.

Although ethnic conflicts sometimes emerged, the exposure of westernized Africans, through the churches and in black intellectual circles, did much to undermine black American stereotypes of African savagery. Although black Americans may still have looked down upon traditional African cultures, they did establish contacts from the mission movement with the emerging westernized African elite. These contacts would prove to be crucial, on both sides of the Atlantic, in the emergence of twentieth-century Pan-African thought.[93]

9

The Impact of the Mission Movement on the Rise of Pan-African Sentiment

Despite its antagonistic attitudes toward indigenous African cultures, the mission movement had an important effect on the development of Pan-Africanism. The black missionaries may have gone to Africa with ethnocentric ideas that they, as "civilized" persons, were highly superior to the "heathen savages" whom they were going to save, but at least they had a concern for Africa—to "redeem" it and see it rise in world respect and power. The information about the continent that they broadcast through the most influential institution of Afro-American society, the church, did much to develop an African interest among the black masses.

The mission movement emphasized the concept, crucial to the rise of Pan-Africanism, that the future status of black Americans was inevitably tied to that of Africans. "There ought to be a pride in the land of our forefathers," suggested the *A.M.E. Church Review.* "Never will Africa's sons [in the United States] be honored . . . until Africa herself sits among the civilized powers."[1] As this statement indicates, Afro-Americans were beginning to argue that it was useless to aspire toward equality in America as long as whites held such negative opinions about Africa. Although the missionary solution was to "civilize" Africa, thus removing the cause of the offending stereotypes, at least they saw Africa as salvageable, and the interest created in the fatherland's glorious ancient past—and its potential future—helped produce an image of something other than a dark continent. What was dark, they believed, needed only to be enlightened. The continent could remain dark in the minds of Afro-Americans only as long as they knew nothing, or cared to know nothing, about it.

The next major step in the rise of Pan-African feeling was to challenge the stereotypes themselves. Again, it was the mission movement that provided the earliest steady contacts with educated westernized Africans, who were disproof of the myth of African savagery. This direct evidence of Africa's potential for "civilization" was psychologically beneficial to black Americans who had been bombarded with racist stereotypes about the inherent barbarism of Africans. Except for a handful of Liberians brought over by the American Colonization Society, most late nineteenth-century black Americans had never seen a real African. Church sponsorship of African students, both in black colleges and on speaking tours, gave many Afro-Americans direct contact with their "brethren" from across the sea.

The Christianization and westernization of Africans removed a barrier to black Americans who were loath to identify with people who were considered "uncivilized." To be black was low enough status in the Western world; to be a black "savage" was even lower. As long as Afro-Americans accepted Victorian notions of what constituted savagery, there was no advantage to be gained from identification with Africa. Black Americans had worked too hard building up a self-image as civilized people, in reaction against racist stereotypes, to risk any connections with "real savages." But unlike those blacks who shunned any involvement with the fatherland, mission advocates believed that Africa had the potential to be redeemed and to rise to civilization. The acculturated Africans were evidence of this potential, and black Americans were overjoyed to discover Africans who shared their values. As a means of challenging racism, providing for the uplifting of non-Western Africans, and bolstering black American self-confidence, westernized Africans provided the vital link between the hemispheres. They were crucial in the rise of Pan-African identity.

Westernization of some Africans was not only a convenient means of establishing contacts with black Americans; it was also a precondition for the establishment of Pan-Africanism among Africans themselves.[2] Before the coming of the Europeans, the various ethnic groups that occupied the continent did not hold a common identity as "African." For a feeling of unity to take hold, an outside threatening "other" group was necessary. Africans felt no more unity with each other than the peoples of the world today feel because of their common humanity. As with native Americans and Asians, nationalist ideas emerged first among those who were most in contact with the invaders.

Edward Blyden is a good example of the trend toward African nationalism. Few Africans of the past two centuries were more familiar with Western culture than Blyden, yet he was an intense African nationalist. He was heavily influenced by the examples of contemporary European nationalism, and in some ways his ideas were a reflection of other "pan-" movements going on at the same time.[3]

Imanuel Geiss, an historian of Africa has suggested five conditions of twentieth-century Pan-African consciousness: (1) Africans' identification as one people beyond a separate ethnic identity, (2) solidarity of all Africans and persons of African descent around the world, (3) return of diaspora blacks to the fatherland to live and work, (4) formal associations of Africans and black Americans, and (5) close intercontinental communications among an intellectually active black elite.[4]

Even though its ideas were couched in religious rather than political terms, the Afro-American mission movement exhibited elements of all these conditions, well before 1900. (1) The missionaries encouraged an African identity and were impatient with particular tribal identities and traditions. (2) They hoped to convert Africans so that all blacks would share solidarity through Christianity. (3) They made a commitment to work in Africa as missionaries, and some of them supported widespread emigration. Bishop Turner even claimed that God was improving Africa's climate in preparation for the return of black American emigrants and missionaries.[5] (4) The mission idea promoted formal associations of Africans and Afro-Americans through the independent black denominations, and the readiness of American churches to affiliate with established groups of westernized African Christians is indicative of this Pan-African orientation. (5) The contacts provided through the churches served as a communication medium among like-thinking blacks in both continents. The missionaries were exceptionally well-educated for blacks of their time, and they were an important part of the intellectual elite of Afro-American society. Western-educated Africans were also usually trained in the ministry, or at least trained by missionaries, and they too were an intellectual elite among Africans. Unfortunately, the missionaries' antagonistic attitude toward other religions hindered communication with aboriginal and Islamic religious leaders. But the closeness of acculturated Africans and black Americans established important intellectual links between the two groups. They may not have been very politically alert, but considering the powerful forces behind black disfranchisement in America and European imperialism in Africa, there may have been no other realistic way for the two groups to associate. The intercontinental communications developed through the mission movement helped pave the way for greater political effectiveness in the twentieth century.

Of the necessary conditions for the growth of Pan-African sentiment, the one that remained the longest unfulfilled and was most necessary was black Americans' willing acceptance of, and identification with, Africa and indigenous African cultures. Though most missionaries preferred to identify with westernized Africans, some aspects of black mission thought celebrated a wide Pan-African identity with Africa as a whole—even including nonwesternized peoples. In its most general form this idea expressed "my race" as including *all* Africans in the same group with Afro-Americans, with Africa as the real "home" for all black people. For example, a poem in the A.M.E. *Voice of Missions* praised Africa as a land of "Pleasures and happiness, / The land of the brave, the free," and it concluded with a verse addressed to Afro-Americans:

> Oh, why will you stay away longer,
> They are waiting for you and me;
> Waiting and longing to welcome us back,
> To our home across the sea.[6]

Not only did the missionaries realize that they and Africans shared a common ancestry, but they felt familial ties with contemporary Africans as well.[7] For example, A.M.E. missionary Alfred Ridgel identified with ancient Africa as the mother of civilization, and referred to it as his "ancestral home . . . and best of all, the land of freedom." He criticized the black American who "turns to Africa with a frown, and contemptuously exclaims, I'M NO AFRICAN! The negro seems to think that Africa is the most debased, shameful, and worthless country on earth. He seems to feel himself humiliated and outraged when associated with Africa."[8] The missionaries clearly did not think Africa worthless, and they did much to challenge such thoughts among black Americans. Bishop Turner enjoyed showing photographs of Africans to black Americans, and he was amused when they expressed surprise that the Africans looked just like themselves. Turner replied, "Of course they do. Are we not all Africans?"[9]

Sometimes missionaries associated Africa positively with Biblical events. Methodist Amanda Smith was excited to visit Egypt, because it was the birthplace of Moses and the hiding place for the infant Jesus. She noted that God had bestowed a "great honor on the black race" by using Africa as the shelter for Jesus, and upon seeing black Egyptians she wrote, "I felt proud that I belonged to that race when I saw such nobility in ebony."[10] Ancient times and the present were welded together in her Pan-African pride of race.

Perhaps the strongest statement of black American racial identity with Africans is contained in a remarkable letter to the secretary of the American Board from missionary Samuel Miller. He had left his station in Angola to protest the bad treatment of the Africans by his white co-workers. He wished to return to Africa as a solitary missionary, but he despaired of working harmoniously with whites

> unless there be a change in them in respect to their treatment of the native. I have always regarded the natives as my own race and have treated them as such and always will. . . . I think it is hard for any one other than an African or a descendant of Africa to sympathize with and feel for an African as a brother. . . . My attachment to them has become so strong that I prefer to work there [in Africa] rather than anywhere else.[11]

Samuel Miller's candidness is remarkable, as are his positive feelings of identity and sympathy with the Africans. He was so unwilling to compromise that he left his happy life in Africa rather than work with racists. Miller's continued interest in Africa is shown by a letter that he wrote to the Board more than a year after his return to Virginia, in which he inquired about the progress of the Angola mission. He had received letters from some of his Ovimbundu students, asking why he did not come back to Africa. Miller was complimentary of their writing ability and Christian sentiments, and he was pleased to keep in touch with them.[12]

Miller's closeness to the Africans is attested to by an insulting letter about him from one of the white missionaries. His rapid mastery of the Ovimbundu languages, his easier interaction with the people, and his general independence (see chapter 1), stirred resentment in the white missionaries, one of whom wrote,

> [Miller] has not the strong principles of puritan fathers instilled into him from his youth. . . . I scarce dare breathe it but I *fancy* he sometimes enjoys a social pipe [of tobacco, with the Africans]. . . . There is a familiarity in the manner of salutations

on the part of the natives in *his* case which is not seen in any
other one. . . . He insisted that laborers here should have the
same wages as in America. . . . I do not think that this lack
of judgement is altogether a *personal* defect, but rather peculiar
to the [black] race.[13]

Other black Americans also felt close to Africans. Baptist Charles
Morris appealed for the use of black missionaries on the basis that
they did not exhibit color prejudice toward the Africans. Citing
an example from South Africa (probably referring to Baptist R. A.
Jackson), Morris told the conference:

I saw an American negro, who, last year, baptized some 300
people in that country. And as I sat in his house the native
men and women came . . . and there was such a freedom and
lack of formality as would be impossible in the house of any
other missionary than a black man. . . . [At night] this missionary's little daughter slept in the middle and those two
heathen girls on either side. That would be impossible to any
other missionary than a black man. . . . The American negro
can do a work there that no other people can do.[14]

Several of the missionaries wrote of their close friendships with
indigenous Africans. For example, after two years in Mozambique,
Nancy Jones remarked that the villagers continually demonstrated
a "friendly spirit." She said, "I go among them every day and I
have learned a great deal of their home life. I am not at all lonely
. . . and I have great comfort in my work." After returning to the
United States, she expressed longing for her African friends.[15] Mrs.
Joseph Gomer was even lonelier after leaving Africa. She remained in
Sierra Leone for two years after her husband's death, but was persuaded
to return to America for health reasons. In America, however, she was
ill at ease, and talked repeatedly of her years among the West Africans.
"She had so identified herself with them," wrote a church co-worker,
"that they were her dearest friends in the world."[16]

Considering the close personal feelings that many black missionaries developed toward non-Western Africans, their ideological
condemnation of indigenous ways of life was sometimes overridden
by their personal respect for the people.[17] Occasionally one finds
statements by missionaries which compliment indigenous cultures
as equal or even superior to Western culture, although such statements are relatively rare and plainly contradictory to the major
emphasis of mission thought on non-Western life-styles. For example,
while A.M.E. Reverend Alfred Ridgel usually emphasized the need

to wipe out "heathenism," he could still praise Africans for their manliness in holding on to their traditions.[18] Pan-African sentiment, as revealed in these and other instances, was clearly present in the nineteenth-century mission movement.

The growth of Afro-Americans' respect for non-Western Africans was partly due to the influence of Edward Blyden, who retained close ties with black missionaries even after he seceded from the Presbyterian church. He advised black Americans to challenge slanted descriptions of their fatherland written by whites, because "no people can interpret Africans but Africans."[19] He worked to bring black Americans and Africans closer together by fostering respect for the valuable features of African culture: the central place of family and plural marriage as the basis for society, co-operation and mutual aid rather than individualistic competition, avoidance of divisive property rights, and less drudgerous work patterns. Seeing Africa as the cradle of civilization, Blyden believed that Africans had a more sympathetic and closer relationship than other peoples with nature and with God. He argued for the recognition that although each race was different, each could contribute distinctive qualities to world-wide human development. All of these complementary differences, he felt, contributed to God's plan.[20]

Blyden viewed African cultures as religious in their own right, and believed it was not necessary for Africans to convert to Christianity to receive God's blessing. In *Christianity, Islam, and the Negro Race*, Blyden argued that Christianity was not always the best for the African. He looked with favor on Islam,[21] and said of indigenous religions: "There is not a tribe on the continent of Africa . . . which does not stretch out its hands to the Great Creator. . . . More proofs are furnished among the natives of interior Africa of their belief in the common Fatherhood of a personal God by their hospitable and considerate treatment of foreigners and strangers than are to be seen in many a civilized and Christian community.[22] Preferring a universalistic deism to a narrow religious creed, Blyden did not forsee the inevitable takeover of the continent by Western Christianity with all its ethnocentric adornments. Despite his personal contradictions, in one belief Blyden was clear: non-westernized Africa had a future. African culture, he argued, was not only as good as, but superior to, the West.[23] In 1880 he spoke of the future:

> Africa still lies at the gateway of all the loftiest and noblest traditions of the human race. . . . Africa may yet prove to be

the spiritual conservatory of the world. . . . When the civilized nations, in consequence of their wonderful material development, shall have had their spiritual perceptions darkened and their spiritual susceptibilities blunted through the agency of a captivating and absorbing materialism, it may be, that they may have to resort to Africa to recover some of the simple elements of faith.[24]

Edward Blyden's close identification with Africans and praise of African culture made an impact upon some missionaries, and his ideas formed the basis of a reform movement in Liberia. Some of the missionaries began to challenge the old antagonistic feelings toward the Africans and call for greater opportunities for them. An A.M.E. missionary, criticizing the Americo-Liberian tendency to look down upon the indigenous people, wrote. "We must allow our [nonwesternized] brothers the same opportunity that we once asked and are now asking our white friends to allow us."[25] His recognition of Africans as "brothers," and his conclusion that prejudice against them, whether racial or cultural, was similar to discrimination against Afro-Americans, were important elements in building a true Pan-African identity.

In Sierra Leone, A.M.E. leader J. R. Frederick became a close friend and follower of Blyden, He adopted Blyden's cultural relativism, and advised his co-workers to learn the native language as quickly as possible and to "let them feel that you love them. . . . Avoid everything like interference with their long-established customs."[26] He even joined Blyden in founding the Dress Reform Society, through which acculturated Sierra Leonians attempted to recapture part of their traditional African heritage.[27]

The black American who most vigorously publicized feelings of unity with non-Western Africans during the late nineteenth century was Henry Turner.[28] While missionaries like William Sheppard were respectful of indigenous groups, they did not promote feelings of Pan-Africanism to the degree that Turner did. The A.M.E. bishop admired almost every aspect of African society, and felt an attraction to the people themselves. He refused to stereotype them, explaining that "there are as great tribal variations among the Africanites as there are national differences among the peoples of Europe and the Americas."[29]

Turner's favorable impressions were not limited to westernized Africans. From Liberia he wrote, "The man who buys the African heathen for a fool is a bigger fool." Turner was particularly impressed by the African royalty he met in the interior of Liberia. He said the meeting with King Kobbena Eljen of the Kromantic tribe was "the honor of my life." About another king, of the Kroo people, Turner noted "his intelligence and general information. He was dressed as a gentleman and very polite. His subjects, or people, treat him with great respect. . . . I have traveled scores of miles through the interior and noted the tact, taste, genius and manly bearing of the higher grade of the natives."[30]

As he grew more disgusted with Afro-American resistance to emigration, Turner became even more complimentary about Africans. By 1896 he declared, "I have a very high reverence for many of the customs and traditions of these [African] people. This polluted and bastard [Western] civilization scattered by white men is more of a curse than a blessing."[31]

Turner admired the self-confident spirit of the Africans, and sometimes contrasted them as superior to black Americans.[32] He felt that Afro-American degradation resulted mainly from subservience to white men. In direct opposition to a widespread feeling, Turner did not see slavery in America as preferable to freedom in Africa. He stated that in Africa, "the struggle for existence even as a heathen imparted a higher cast of manhood and business sagacity than slavery" in America.[33]

To incite black Americans to greater militancy in demanding their rights, Turner emphasized the theme of African manliness. In a speech to the National Negro Convention in 1893, he stated that a "naked African . . . possesses more manhood than fifty of some of our people in this country."[34] He also recognized the relativism of cultural standards, and praised the Africans for respecting their own kinds of beauty. In contrast, he criticized black Americans who, ashamed of their race, went to such extremes as using hair-straighteners and skin-bleachers.[35] Like the twentieth-century advocates of the sentiment "Black is Beautiful," Turner called for black pride. Africans were more sensible because "they all believe that they resemble God, or, are created in God's image. But the American Africans believe that they resemble the devil, and hence the contempt they have for themselves."[36] Turner not only felt a respect for indigenous cultures and a sense of identity with them, but he believed that black Americans could benefit by emulating their African kindred.

Once they had accepted the validity of African cultures, some mission supporters developed a full-fledged Pan-African feeling.

This sentiment was most radically expressed by their opposition to European imperialism. While several Afro-American missionaries protested exploitation of Africans by Europeans,[37] others further questioned the very right of whites to be in the continent. This was especially true of Bishop Turner, who openly advocated anti-colonialism in *Voice of Missions*. In 1896 he printed a letter from an African who appealed for black Americans to help achieve "the freedom of your brothers in South Africa. . . . We are sinking down every year through the bad treatment of white men."[38] During South African leader James Dwane's visit to the United States, Turner took him to speak at several black conventions. Turner reported an enthusiastic response during Dwane's speech to an A.M.E. conference in Atlanta: "He was frequently cheered during its delivery, especially when he assured the vast audience that the Africans would never allow the white man to dominate and ride rough shod over their country." Dwane predicted that Africans "would soon be able to run great civilized governments. Then they would say to the European nations, 'hands off.'"[39] Turner himself spoke in similar fashion when he visited South Africa in 1898. Addressing large crowds of Africans, he expressed a militant black nationalism that was even more Pan-Africanist than in his usual speeches. He was quoted as saying:

> The white man does not appreciate our [black] values, because he believes himself by divine right to be the dominant race. . . . The black is the race of the future, and one day the black man will wake up and shake off the white man's yoke. He is already rubbing his eyes and feeling his muscles. . . . The time has now come to replace them [whites], with their antiquated methods and superannuated principles. Our new doctrine is more suited to the African awakening, and only the sons of New Africa may be trusted to propagate it, not any aliens.[40]

Turner's speeches in South Africa repeatedly emphasized the need for close identity between Africans and Afro-Americans, for solidarity against white domination. His militant stand was not an isolated one; other black American mission advocates shared his sentiments. Perhaps no more eloquent statement could be made than a letter in the *Voice of Missions* by an unknown black man who supported missions and emigration. This correspondent wrote in 1895 complaining about European powers:

> Without legal authority, [they] take possession of [the Africans'] richest lands . . . and then send an army there to prevent

the African from claiming and trying to keep in possession the things that are already his by right of inheritance . . . and the poor Africans, like the American Indian, will have to take just what their enemies see cause to give them, or be shot down like dogs. And when I think of it, the blood in my veins boils. . . . [Afro-Americans should] prevent any further intrusion upon the rights of our African brother. . . . The Negro race will never be what it ought to be until the American and African Negroes unite and compel the civilized world to respect their rights.[41]

These thoughts, which demonstrated a true Pan-African identity, obviously went well beyond the usual mission ideology. But even if they do represent a minority viewpoint within Afro-American mission thought, they demonstrate Pan-American feelings arising out of a missionary concern for the fatherland. Furthermore, there were cases in which individuals advanced from mission commitment to Pan-African activism. For example, Theophilus E. S. Scholes, the Baptist missionary in the Congo (1882-90) and in Nigeria (1894–99), gave up his mission work in 1899 to become a free-lance writer. He published three books in the next decade on the theme that the British empire should be transformed into a commonwealth of equal states, in which Africans would have an active voice. He was a prominent spokesperson for Pan-Africanism in the early twentieth century, and had considerable influence on African nationalists through the 1930s.[42] In a way, Scholes replicated Edward Blyden's transformation from minister to nationalist, and no doubt other missionaries did this in a less noticeable manner.

The most direct evidence that the mission movement contributed to Pan-Africanism is the 1900 Pan-African Conference itself. The organizer of this conference was a black lawyer from Trinidad, but among the participants from the United States, the most active were primarily influenced by the mission movement. At the 1899 planning session for the conference, four of the African participants were Christian ministers from Lagos and South Africa, and three of the five United States planners were associated with the A.M.E. Church: Bishop Henry Turner, Bishop J. F. Holly, and Professor William Scarborough from Wilberforce University.[43] At the conference itself, fourteen of the thirty-two participants were from the United States. Although little is known about several members of this group, the most prominent were A.M.E. Zion Bishop Alexander Walters (a leader of mission sentiment in his denomination), Benjamin Arnett (son of an A.M.E. bishop who strongly supported missions and had African students stay in his home), Mr. and Mrs. J. F. Loudin (choral directors at mission-oriented Fisk University), Reverend Henry B. Brown (an admirer of Henry Turner), Henry R. Downing (a former United States consul in Angola) and W. E. B. Du Bois.[44]

Du Bois clearly was not mission-oriented, and he stands out as an exception to the other prominent American participants at the London conference. As a well-educated academician, he represented a new breed of secular black leadership. He had little patience with the religious emphasis of the black elite, and voiced no desire to "redeem" Africa. Yet, it might be ventured that even Du Bois absorbed much of his interest in Africa from mission sources. Such a suggestion is speculative, because in his own writings Du Bois was vague about the origins of his sentiments.

The young professor certainly did *not* absorb his African interest from "back-to-Africa" emigrationism: he had never supported it before 1900, and later in the 1920s he strongly opposed the emigration schemes of Marcus Garvey. He remembered a few family traditions about his African ancestry, and his doctoral dissertation on the Atlantic slave trade related academically to African history, but for the inspiration that interested him in the fatherland we must look elsewhere.[45]

In the 1890s, before Du Bois' involvement in the Pan-African Conference, he was exposed heavily to the mission interest in Africa. As a young professor at A.M.E. Wilberforce University, and later at Atlanta University in Bishop Turner's hometown, Du Bois could not escape the black churches' emphasis on Africa's evangelization. Even more important was the influence of Alexander Crummell. This clergymen so impressed the young professor that Du Bois devoted an entire chapter to him in his 1903 book *The Souls of Black Folk*.[46] Crummell opposed emigration, but strongly supported mission goals for improving the continent. He felt a potential for African and American black unity once Africa was civilized.[47]

Under Crummell's influence, Du Bois was beginning to think in terms of Pan-African unity. This is most evident in a pamphlet that he wrote in 1897 for Crummell's American Negro Academy. In this pamphlet Du Bois referred to Afro-Americans as "the advance guard" of the world's black people, whose "destiny is not absorption by the white Americans. . . . [or] a servile imitation of Anglo-Saxon culture, but a stalwart originality which shall unswervingly follow Negro ideals." He called on black people around the world to wield more influence in world history "through a Pan-Negro Movement," and he considered the advancement of Africa as a crucial part of the struggle of blacks to improve their own position in the United States.[48] That same year Du Bois lauded Africa as "the greater fatherland," in a letter exploring the possibilities of an Afro-American development program in the Congo.[49] Sentiments like these, expressed even before 1900, preceded his involvement in the twentieth-century Pan-African conferences which made him known as the "Father of Pan-Africanism." Du Bois' interest in the fatherland obviously was an extension of his intellectual interest and concern for black nationalism within the United States, but he did not invent totally new ideas. The view of Crummell that black Americans were the forerunners of a black civilization which would be spread to Africa, and the view of Blyden that distinctive black ideals would flourish under Pan-African unity, are clearly reflected in Du Bois' writings. These ideas were being discussed in the 1890s within the milieu of the mission movement. While Du Bois did not strongly support the Christianization of Africa, his interest in the fatherland nevertheless was greatly influenced by mission concerns.

To understand the development of Pan-African sentiment among twentieth-century Afro-Americans generally, its origins should be seen not just in terms of emigrationism but also in terms of the movement to evangelize Africa through Christian missions. To do otherwise is to ignore a major component of nineteenth-century Afro-American thought about Africa. The Pan-Africanists of 1900 did not begin a new direction in black thought, but elaborated attitudes already developed. The mission movement built a strong interest in Africa, and produced a minority opinion which looked favorably upon indigenous African cultures. Some black thinkers had already reached a full-fledged Pan-Africanism before 1900, even surpassing the ardor in the sentiments by Du Bois. It was this background that allowed Du Bois and his followers to bring a new flowering of Afro-American thought. Only by coming to terms with their dual heritage, from Africa as well as America, could black people lay the foundation for a new identity in the black renaissance of the twentieth century.

Conclusion

The African missions movement is an important part of Afro-American social and intellectual history, reflecting the wide range of thought among late nineteenth-century black Americans. The mission advocates shared a belief in many basic tenets of Christian ideology, but they held diverse opinions about a number of topics relating to contemporary Africa. Mission thought was full of contradictions, especially in those writers who tried to reconcile Pan-African feelings with the idea of converting Africa from "heathen savagery."

These contradictions were especially notable in the thought of Bishop Henry Turner. There was no question that Turner felt a high regard for African peoples and cultures. Yet he never deserted the missionary and westernizing goals of Christianity, which would ultimately destroy the African ways of life he so admired. Caught between an evolving philosophy of cultural relativism on the one hand and a commitment to Christian ideology on the other, his solution was to extol African culture while remaining convinced that it would have to change to adapt to westernization. His Victorian Christian progressivism thus made Turner an enigma: a black leader calling for a return to Africa—remaining a resident of America himself, in detached admiration of African culture—yet abetting an attack on that culture through mission conversion.

Bishop Turner's "African Dream" has been called simply a revised version of the American Dream.[1] Perhaps this can be illustrated by quoting Turner's poem, "Our Sentiments," which he frequently reprinted in his A.M.E. newspaper, *Voice of Missions*:

> My country, 'tis of thee,
>   Dear land of Africa
> of thee we sing;
>   Land where our fathers died,
> Land of the Negro's pride,
>   From every mountain side,
> God's truth shall ring.
>
> My native country, thee,
>   Land of the black and free,

> Thy name I love;
> To see thy rocks and rills,
> Thy woods and matchless hills,
> My heart with rapture thrills,
> Like that above.[2]

While Turner was singing praises to Africa, he was singing to the tune of what was then the national anthem of the United States. Disillusioned and bitter toward the country of his birth, and leading a movement to renounce that country in favor of the African fatherland, in his goals and viewpoint Turner nevertheless remained an American. The contradictions in his philosophy reflected the ambivalence toward Africa of many black Americans.

Interest in Africa among late nineteenth-century independent Afro-American denominations is not surprising, because the black churches were merely following their historic patterns of expansion. The Afro-American churches had never gained most of their members by converting non-Christians to Christianity, but by attracting previously converted blacks who were dissatisfied with racism in white churches. That was the process which brought about the organization of the black churches in the first place, and their major growth occurred among the Christianized freed people of the South after the Civil War. The expansion into Africa during the 1880s and 1890s was essentially a repetition, in a new area, of the expansion into the American South a few decades earlier. Despite efforts by some black missionaries to convert tribal Africans, the main success and thrust was with Anglicized Africans (especially in Liberia, Sierra Leone, the Gold Coast, and South Africa) who were already Christianized. Concentration on "natives that had been redeemed from heathenism by [white] organizations which have preceded ours"[3] was consistent with previous patterns of Afro-American church expansion.

This pattern was not quite consistent with church ideology, which emphasized conversion of "heathens," but that did not interfere with the emergence of a mature mission ideology among Afro-American Christians by the end of the century. Black churches were sponsoring missionaries in Africa and African students in the United States, while the rallying cry of "Africa for Christ" was heard throughout America. The spread of this ideology, with its often contradictory notions about Africa, is typified by the 1899 student prize essay at Wilberforce University. Carrie Lee, a young A.M.E. Church member, wrote in praise of mission expansion and characterized indigenous Africa as "a barbarous piece of humanity, speaking an odd language and as wild as the beasts that made their abode there." Missionary operations, she believed, were the Africans' only hope, and through the darkness they were calling to their "enlightened brethren" in America. She predicted a bright future for the continent: "Yes, Africa, we will aid you in your admirable efforts; we will help to rouse the genius of your slumbering people. . . . Do not despair, the American Negro hears your cry."[4]

The black response to Africa's supposed "cry for help" was a distinctly American one. Not only was it inspired by white missionary sentiment, but it had elements of self-interest for black people in the United States. By redeeming Africa, the missionaries hoped to gain the respect of whites and thus improve their own status. They went to Africa as representatives of American culture, and many of them felt they were making great sacrifices by leaving the United States. Their positive image of America contrasted with their mainly condemnatory attitude toward traditional African ways of life. Missionaries could differ over secondary issues like emigration, Islam, or imperialism but their stance depended on whether or not they thought these factors would help or hinder the westernization of the continent. In the main, the mission interest perpetuated the negative "dark continent" image of Africa. Missionaries not infrequently showed a kind of respect for Africa by expressing high hopes for its future, and could praise individual Africans who had become "civilized" in a Western sense; but they felt that they must ultimately "save" Africans from their past and present, and in the process of saving them tried to transform them into something that was alien to their African heritage.

While mission ideology espoused a conservative ethnocentric view of African cultures, it ironically also presented a program for radical change. By seeking to build up Africa to inaugurate a new black civilization, black missionaries' goal was considerably different from that of most white missionaries. Black American Christians largely shared the white stereotypes of African savagery, but they believed that conversion was the secret to releasing the continent from this degradation. Mission advocates sacrificed for this program of redemption and regeneration because they had faith in the power of religion and westernization. A.M.E. missionary Alfred Ridgel voiced the hopes of many Afro-Americans when he wrote in 1895 that "Africa will soon rise from her slumbering tomb and take her place among the nations of the world."[5] Without recognizing the duality of thought in this desire, it is impossible to understand the value system of late nineteenth-century black Americans, and the relation of that value system to the rise of Pan-African feeling in the twentieth century.

Reference Matter

Appendix A

Representative Mission Hymns Written by Black Americans

A Hymn of Sympathy and Prayer for Africa

Alexander P. Camphor

Far across the mighty ocean
    Is a land of palmy plains,
But that land is not enlightened;
    It is one where darkness reigns.
There the heathen in his blindness
    Knoweth not the blessed word,
Nor of Jesus Christ, the Savior,
    Precious Lord, our only Lord.

Africa, 'tis name, that country,
    Far away from this bright shore,
Far removed from light and knowledge,
    Far remote from Christian lore;
There, for many, many ages,
    Ling'ring still in blackest night,
Africa, dark land of hist'ry,
    Void of light, is void of light.

How can we remain contented
    In illuminated homes,
While our brother gropes in darkness,
    And in heathenism roams?
Should not his complete salvation
    Be our earnest, prayerful plea,
Till that long-neglected country
    Shall be free, yes, wholly free?

Africa, thou ebon country,
    How we long to see thee free!
E'er shall we, for thy redemption
    Work and pray, till thou shalt be
Free from every degradation,
    That has cursed thy sunny land,
This constant supplication
    Of our band, our Christian band.

Missionary Hymn for Africa

Joseph Wheeler

O, Africa, in darkness
    Thy land shall all be bright;
Thy people shall be favored
    With hallowed Gospel light.
The coming years will bring thee
    Great Blessings yet undreamed;
Thy people shall be numbered
    Among the earth's redeemed.

The ancient seers have spoken
    The word at God's command,
They told the sacred story
    Of Ethiop's outstretched hand;
They cry to God in pity,
    Send, Christians, to their need,
O, labor for the Master!
    Sow now the precious seed!

Arise, O Afric's children,
    Enter your fatherland,
Take ye the Gospel banner,
    Go forth at God's command;
Remember, Christ is with you,
    His arm will you defend,
Remember Jesus' promise:
    I'm with you to the end.

O, God of grace and mercy,
    Look from thy throne above,
On Africa whose millions
    Have never known Thy love;
Grant that the Spirit's power
    On them may now descend;
Grant Thou our prayer in mercy,
    As at Thy throne we bend.

These two hymns were awarded first prizes in hymn-writing contests sponsored by Gammon Theological Seminary in 1894 and 1895. Quoted in J. W. B. Bowen, ed., *Africa and the American Negro: Addresses and Proceedings of the Congress on Africa* (1896; Miami: Mnemosyne Publishing, 1969), pp. 236—37.

Appendix B

Contributions to the Mission Department of the A.M.E. Church, 1864–96

Years	Mission Secretary	Amount	
1864–68	John M. Brown	$ 5,425.65	
1868–72	James A. Hardy	9,317.32	
1872–76	G. W. Brodie	6,556.42	
1876–80	Richard H. Cain	5,947.80	
	Subtotal (1864–80)		$ 27,247.19
1880–84	J. M. Townsend	$34,811.83	
1884–88	J. M. Townsend	19,001.09	
1888–92	W. B. Derrick	25,675.47	
1892–96	W. B. Derrick	36,535.31	
	Subtotal (1880–96)		$116,023.70
	Total		$143,270.89

From H. B. Parks, *Africa, the Problem of the New Century* (New York: Mission Department of the A.M.E. Church, 1899), p. 16. Statistics were not printed for the years before 1864 or after 1896.

Appendix C

Contributions, by State, from the Special Easter Sunday Collection
to the Mission Department of the A.M.E. Church, 1897–99

	1897	1898	1899
Georgia	$1,149.82	$1,119.22	$1,298.40
Alabama	458.04	567.20	577.58
Maryland and D.C.	456.73	929.19	569.79
South Carolina	384.32	408.82	434.63
Florida	398.65	310.44	304.44
Texas	212.62	287.76	364.02
Missouri	335.22	297.64	305.70
Mississippi	192.02	283.04	340.23
Arkansas	153.57	228.41	345.33
Louisiana	159.52	211.82	232.85
North Carolina	133.88	166.64	164.03
Kentucky	126.78	104.42	180.28
Tennessee	62.44	125.82	121.13
Virginia	8.70	198.31	117.93
Delaware	92.15	112.52	0
Oklahoma	13.68	20.41	19.35
West Virginia	0	22.65	0
Total for the South	$4,338.41	$5,394.31	$5,375.69
Pennsylvania	$ 842.50	$1,042.09	$1,307.95
Ohio	339.83	507.13	709.95
New York	367.94	295.52	249.73
New Jersey	194.85	318.21	213.51
Illinois	112.48	156.14	120.17
Indiana	98.44	106.78	88.45
Michigan	89.89	73.29	167.08
New England	87.91	46.00	84.87
Wisconsin	3.52	3.74	0
Total for the North	$2,167.36	$2,548.90	$2,941.71
Kansas	$ 142.30	$ 183.54	$ 169.05
Colorado	79.45	100.05	137.99
Nebraska	55.10	48.00	0
Iowa	34.59	46.07	88.46
California	30.80	0	22.00
Washington	12.00	2.80	8.00

	1897	1898	1899
New Mexico	8.00	6.40	0
Montana	4.00	11.00	0
Minnesota	0	10.00	0
Wyoming	0	7.73	0
Utah	0	4.00	0
South Dakota	2.50	0	0
Total for the West	$ 368.74	$ 419.59	$ 425.50
Bermuda	$ 29.00	$ 46.47	$ 35.36
Canada	$ 7.73	$ 20.72	$ 24.35
Grand Total	$6,910.97	$8,429.99	$8,802.61

Totals computed by the author from congregational reports in the *Voice of Missions*, 1 July 1897, 1 June 1898, and 1 June 1899.

Appendix D

Black American Missionaries in Liberia, 1877–1900

Name	Home	Education	Years in Africa	Location of Mission
Presbyterian Church (North)				
James M. Priest (?–1883)			1843–83	
Darius L. Donnell		Lincoln U.	1879–?	Monrovia
Oscar H. Massey		Lincoln U.	1895–?	Monrovia
Walter F. Hawkins		Lincoln U.	1899–?	Monrovia
Protestant Episcopal Church				
Samuel David Ferguson (1842–1916)	South Carolina		1865–1916	Cape Palmas
Methodist Episcopal Church (North)				
Alexander Priestly Camphor (1865–1918)	Lousiana	New Orleans U.; Gammon Theological Sem.	1897–1918	Monrovia
Mamie Weathers (Mrs. A. P.) Camphor	Georgia		1897–?	Monrovia
J. A. Simpson	Georgia	Gammon Theological Sem.	1899–1908	Greenville
Mrs. J. A. Simpson			1899–1908	Greenville
Joseph C. Sherrill	Arkansas		1899–post–1908	Cape Palmas
Mrs. Joseph C. Sherrill	Arkansas		1899–post–1908	Cape Palmas
F. M. Allen	Arkansas	Philander Smith C.	1899–?	Monrovia
Ruby Williams (Mrs. F. M. Allen)	Arkansas	Philander Smith C.	1899–?	Monrovia
Joseph A. Davis	Arkansas	Philander Smith C.	1899–?	
Miss Amanda Davis	Arkansas	Arkansas State Normal C.	1899–?	

Name	Home	Education	Years in Africa	Location of Mission
Miss Amanda Smith (1837–?)	New York		1882–91	Monrovia

A.M.E. Zion Church

Name	Home	Education	Years in Africa	Location of Mission
Andrew Cartwright (1835–1903)	North Carolina		1876–1903	Brewerville
Anne (Mrs. A.) Cartwright				Brewerville

Baptist Foreign Mission Convention of the U.S.A.
(National Baptist Convention)

Name	Home	Education	Years in Africa	Location of Mission
Harrison N. Bouey (1849–?)	South Carolina	Baptist Theological Sem.	1879–81	Gola
J. O. Hayes			1882–? post–1900	Monrovia
William W. Colley (1849–1909)	Virginia	Richmond Theological Sem.	1883–1909	Vai
Mrs. W. W. Colley			1883–?	Vai
James H. Pressley	Virginia		1883–85	Vai
Hattie J. (Mrs. J. H.) Pressley (?–1884)	Virginia		1883–84	Vai
Hense McKinney (1860–87)	Mississippi	Natchez Baptist Sem.	1883–87	Vai
John J. Coles (1856–94)	Virginia	Richmond Theological Sem.	1883–93	Vai
Lucy A. Henry (Mrs. J. J.) Coles	Tennessee		1887–93	Vai
E. B. Topp			1886–87	Vai
Mrs. E. B. Topp			1886–87	Vai
J. J. Diggs			1886–?	Vai
Mrs. J. J. Diggs			1886–?	Vai
R. L. Stewart			1893–1900	Monrovia

A.M.E. Church

Name	Home	Education	Years in Africa	Location of Mission
Samuel F. Flegler	South Carolina		1878–ca. 1881	Monrovia
Clement Irons	South Carolina		1878–post– 1900	White Plains
S. A. Bailey			1878–post– 1900	Carysburg

Name	Home	Education	Years in Africa	Location of Mission
L. G. Davis	Texas		post-1890– post-1899	Campbell
Floyd G. Snelson	Georgia	Atlanta U.	1897–1900	Freetown
Mrs. F. G. Snelson			1897–1900	Freetown

Note: The following Sierra Leonians were also A.M.E. ministers in the 1890s: Henry M. Steady, George Dove Decker, Mrs. Fanny Decker, David B. Roach, E. T. Martyn, Mrs. Lucy D. Martyn, F. M. Stewart, J. A. John, Mr. and Mrs. J. H. W. Gooding, J. F. Gerber, William Jones, J. H. Parks, and J. P. Richards.

Appendix F

Black American Missionaries in Western, Central,
and Southern Africa, 1877–1900

Name	Home	Education	Years in Africa	Location of Mission
Southern Baptist Convention, Mission to Nigeria				
William W. Colley (1849–1909)	Virginia	Richmond Theological Sem.	1875–79	Yoruba
Solomon Cosby (?–1881)	Virginia		1878–81	Yoruba
Baptist Missionary Society of Great Britain, Mission to the Cameroons				
Thomas L. Johnson (1836–post-1892)	Virginia, Illinois		1878–79	Kpe
American Baptist Missionary Union, Livingstone Inland Mission on the Lower Congo				
Theophilus E. S. Scholes, M.D.	Jamaica		1882–90	Kongo
John E. Ricketts			1885–93	Kongo
Letitia (Mrs. J. E.) Ricketts			1890–93	Kongo
Lulu Cecelia Fleming			1887–99	Kongo
J. J. France			1887–99	Kongo
Nora A. (Mrs. S. C.) Gordon (married in 1895 to S. C. Gordon of the British Baptist Missionary Society)			1889–93, 1895–?	Kongo
William A. Hall			1889–1916	Kongo
Clara Ann Howard			1890–95	Kongo
James Christopher Dawes			1893–94	Kongo
Bessie E. Gardner			1893–95	Kongo
George Henry Jackson			1893–94	Kongo
Grace Jackson			1893–94	Kongo
Stephen E. Jackson (brother of G. H. Jackson)			1893–94	Kongo
Elizabeth Garland Hall			1894–1915	Kongo

Name	Home	Education	Years in Africa	Location of Mission
American Board of Commissioners for Foreign Missions				
Samuel Miller	Virginia	Hampton Inst.	1880–85	Ovimbundu, Angola
Benjamin F. Ousley	Mississippi	Fisk U., Oberlin C.	1884–93	Inhambane, Mozambique
Henrietta Bailey (Mrs. B. F.) Ousley	Mississippi	Fisk U.	1884–93	Inhambane, Mozambique
Miss Nancy Jones (1860–?)	Tennessee	Fisk U.	1888–97	Inhambane, Mozambique, Rhodesia
Presbyterian Church in the U.S. (South), Mission to Luebo, in the Kasai Region of the Congo				
William Henry Sheppard (1865–1927)	Virginia	Hampton Inst. Stillman C.	1890–1910	Bakete, Bakuba
Lucy Gantt (Mrs. W. H.) Sheppard (1867–1941)	Alabama	Talledga C.	1894–1910	Bakete, Bakuba
Maria Fearing (1838–?)	Alabama	Talledga C.	1894–1915	Bakete, Bakuba
Lillian Thomas		Talledga C.	1894–1918	Bakete, Bakuba
Henry P. Hawkins		Stillman C.	1894–1910	Bakete, Bakuba
Joseph E. Phipps	W. Indies	Moody Bible Inst.	1895–1908	Bakete, Bakuba
National Baptist Convention, Mission to South Africa				
R. A. Jackson	Mississippi		1894–post-1899	Capetown
Joseph I. Buchanan	Maryland		1894–post-1899	Middledrift
G. F. A. Johns (?–1898)	Maryland		1897–98	Capetown
Mrs. G. F. A. Johns (?–1898)	Maryland		1897–98	Capetown
Mamie Branton (Mrs. John) Tule			1897–?	Capetown
(married to a South African missionary educated in America)				
Charles S. Morris	Massachusetts		1899–1900	Capetown

Appendix G

African Students in the United States, 1877–1900
In order of mention, chapter 8

Name	Years in the U.S.	Country of Origin	Ethnic Group
Yale University, New Haven, Connecticut			
Orishatukeh Faduma (William Davis)[a]	1891–1914	Sierra Leone	Yoruba
Lincoln University, Lincoln, Pennsylvania			
John Knox[b]	1873–?	Liberia	Bassa
Calvin Wright[b]	1873–?	Liberia	Bassa
Samuel S. Sevier*[c]	1873–84, 1886–1918	Liberia	Bassa
Edward Wright[b]	1873–?	Liberia	Bassa
Robert Deputie*[d]	1873–82	Liberia	Bassa
Alonzo Miller*	1873–82	Liberia	Bassa
Robert King*	1873–82	Liberia	Bassa
Thomas Roberts*	1873–83	Liberia	Vai
James Wilson*[c]	1873–82	Liberia	"Congo" Recaptured African
John Dillon	1877–?	Liberia	
George Waltham Bell	ca. 1878–post-1918	Ethiopia	
Thomas Amos	1879–?	Liberia	
Thomas Campbell	1882–?	Liberia	
Thomas Sherman	1886–?	Liberia	Vai
J. W. N. Hilton*	1886–90	Liberia	
Thomas A. Johns	1886–post-1889	Liberia	
George Barh-Fofoe Peabody*	1886–91	Liberia	Bassa
Luke Anthony[e]	1886–ca. 1896	Liberia	Bassa
Samuel Ross	1887–?	Liberia	
Frank Itita Boughton	1887–92	Gabon	
Charles Dunbar[f]	1890–95	Liberia	
Ulysses Campbell	1891–?	Liberia	
Robert Beadle	1892–?	Liberia	
Thomas Katiya*	1896–1903	South Africa	Xhosa
Edward Magaya*	1896–1903	South Africa	Xhosa

Name	Years in the U.S.	Country of Origin	Ethnic Group
Thomas Lewis	1898–?	Liberia	
Ralph Beadle	1899–?	Liberia	

Fisk University, Nashville, Tennessee

Name	Years in the U.S.	Country of Origin	Ethnic Group
A. P. Miller*	post-1870–pre-1890	Sierra Leone	Mendi
Mrs. A. P. Miller*	post-1870–pre-1890	Sierra Leone	Mendi
Nathaniel Nurse*	post-1870–pre-1890	Liberia	
A. E. Jackson*	post-1870–pre-1890	Sierra Leone	Mendi
Mrs. A. E. Jackson*	post-1870–pre-1890	Sierra Leone	Mendi
Albert B. Howett	1890–?	Sierra Leone	Mendi

Nichols Latin School, Lewiston, Maine

Name	Years in the U.S.	Country of Origin	Ethnic Group
Lews P. Clinton (Somayou)	pre-1892–?	Liberia	Bassa

Dayton, Ohio High School

Name	Years in the U.S.	Country of Origin	Ethnic Group
Daniel Flickinger Wilberforce*[d]	1871–78	Sierra Leone	Sherbro

Unidentified school, Ashville, North Carolina

Name	Years in the U.S.	Country of Origin	Ethnic Group
Etna Holderness	ca. 1893–1897	Liberia	Bassa

Alabama Normal Institute, Normal, Alabama

Name	Years in the U.S.	Country of Origin	Ethnic Group
Wesley Pitman	1894–post-1897	Liberia	
Edward Mayfield Boyle	pre-1896–1899–?	Sierra Leone	

Oberlin College, Oberlin, Ohio

Name	Years in the U.S.	Country of Origin	Ethnic Group
John Langalibalele Dube*[a]	1887–91, 1897–99	Natal	Zulu

Morris Brown College, Atlanta, Georgia

Name	Years in the U.S.	Country of Origin	Ethnic Group
A. G. Decker	1899–?	Sierra Leone	
G. P. Richards	1899–?	Sierra Leone	
I. A. Johnson	1899–?	Sierra Leone	

Name	Years in the U.S.	Country of Origin	Ethnic Group
Wilberforce University, Wilberforce, Ohio			
Charlotte Makhomo Manye*[a]	1895–1901	South Africa	Basuto-Sepedi
Charles Lentallus Dube	1896–1904	South Africa	Zulu
Thomas Masiza Kakaza	1896–1902	South Africa	Abambo
Henry Colbourne Mxikinya	1896–1900	South Africa	Amahlubi
Marshall Macdonald Maxeke*[a]	1897–1903	South Africa	Xhosa
James Yapi Tantsi*[a]	1897–1905	South Africa	Tembu
Adelaide Tyandyatwa Tantse	1898–1905	South Africa	Tembu
Harsent Nggbe Tantsi	1898–?	South Africa	Tembu
Mbulaleni Kuzawayo	1899–?	South Africa	Zulu
John Manye	1899–?	South Africa	Sepedi
Michael Seganoe	1899–?	Bechuanaland	Tswana
Central Tennessee College, Nashville, Tennessee			
Momolu Massaqui (Albert Thompson)	ca. 1891–?	Liberia	Vai
Benjamin Payne	ca. 1891–?	Liberia	Bassa
Frank Payne	ca. 1891–?	Liberia	Kru
Harold Wood	ca. 1891–?	Liberia	Kru
Gilbert Haven	ca. 1891–?	Liberia	Dye
Extein Norton University			
Monte Kama	1897–?	South Africa	
Shaw University, Raleigh, North Carolina			
Alfred Impey	1897–98	South Africa	
Wayland Seminary and Benedict College, Greensboro, North Carolina			
Alfred Seeme	1898–?	South Africa	
Virginia Theological Seminary, Lynchburg, Virginia			
John Chilembwe*[a]	1897–1900	Nyasaland	Ajawa
Isiah Ighati	1898–?	South Africa	
Livingstone College, Salisbury, North Carolina			
William Hockman*	1897–1902	Gold Coast	Fanti
James E. K. Aggrey[a][g]	1898–1924	Gold Coast	Fanti
Osam-Pinanko (Frank Arthur)*	1899–1903	Gold Coast	Fanti
J. Drybold Taylor*	ca. 1899–1902	Gold Coast	Fanti

* Known to have returned to their native countries as missionaries.

[a] Returned to Africa and became an influential figure in African nationalist movements.

[b] Remained in America, and never returned to Africa.

[c] Went to Liberia as a missionary, but returned to the United States one year later and remained there until his death.

[d] Married an Afro-American who accompanied him as a missionary to Africa.

[e] Received M.D. degree from the University of Pennsylvania, and returned to Liberia as a medical doctor.

[f] Received law degree and returned to Liberia as a lawyer. He became a prominent Liberian political leader.

[g] Returned to the Gold Coast as a school teacher.

Notes

Introduction

1 Alexander Walters, *My Life and Work* (New York: Fleming H. Revell Co., 1917), p. 253.

2 Ibid., pp. 259–60.

3 Clarence Contee, "The Emergence of Du Bois as an African Nationalist," *Journal of Negro History* 54 (January 1969): 48, 52–53; Rayford Logan, "The Historical Aspects of Pan-Africanism, 1900–1945," in *Pan-Africanism Reconsidered*, ed. American Society of African Culture (Berkeley: University of California Press, 1969), pp. 37–39.

4 Edwin S. Redkey, *Black Exodus, Black Nationalist and Back-to-Africa Movements, 1890–1910* (New Haven: Yale University Press, 1969); Hollis R. Lynch, *Edward Wilmot Blyden: Pan-Negro Patriot, 1832–1912* (London: Oxford University Press, 1967); Cyril E. Griffith, *The African Dream: Martin R. Delaney and the Emergence of Pan-African Thought* (University Park: Pennsylvania State University Press, 1975); Walter L. Williams, "Black American Attitudes Toward Africa, 1877–1900," *Pan-African Journal* 4 (Spring 1971): 173–94; Walter L. Williams, "Black Journalism's Opinions about Africa during the Late Nineteenth Century," *Phylon* 34 (September 1973): 224–35; and Walter L. Williams, "Nineteenth Century Pan-Africanist: John Henry Smyth, U.S. Minister to Liberia, 1871–1885," *Journal of Negro History* 63 (January 1978): 18–25.

Chapter 1
Sources of Afro-American Mission Sentiment

1 Joel Williamson, *After Slavery: The Negro in South Carolina during Reconstruction, 1861–1877* (Chapel Hill: University of North Carolina Press, 1965), p. 201; Edward M. Brawley, ed., *The Negro Baptist Pulpit* (Philadelphia: American Baptist Publishing Society, 1890), pp. 256–62; *A.M.E. Church Hymnal* (Philadelphia: A.M.E. Book Concern, 1892); Joseph R. Washington, *Black Religion: The Negro and Christianity in the United States* (Boston: Beacon Press, 1964), p. 229.

2 Matthew 28:19–20; Mark 16:15. Quoted in National Baptist Convention, *Mission Herald* 1 (March 1896): 4; reprinted in *Mission Herald 90th Anniversary Issue* 73 (1970) : 10.

3 Second Corinthians 5:20.

4 Psalms 68:31.

5 Kenneth Scott Latourette, *The Great Century in the Americas, Australia, and Africa, 1800–1914* (New York: Harper, 1943), pp. 1–2, 469.

6 Winthrop S. Hudson, *Religion in America*, 2nd ed. (New York: Scribner's, 1973), pp. 152, 157, 323, 372; Stow Persons, "Religion and Modernity, 1865–1914," in *Religion in American Life* (Princeton: Princeton University Press, 1961), 1:391; Ruth Slade, *English-Speaking Missions in the Congo Independent State, 1878–1908* Brussels: Académie Royale des Sciences D'Outre Mer, 1959), pp. 20, 24.

7 Slade, *English-Speaking Missions*, p. 232.

8 *Missionary Review of the World* 10 (January 1887): 23; ibid., 23 (January 1900) : 544.

9 Hudson, *Religion*, pp. 146, 320–22; Walter LaFeber, *The New Empire: An Interpretation of American Expansion, 1860–1898* (Ithaca, N.Y.: Cornell University Press, 1963), pp. 72–80, 305–8.

10 Hudson *Religion*, pp. 318–22; LaFeber, *New Empire*, pp. 305–8.

11 William E. Strong, *The Story of the American Board* (Boston: Pilgrim Press, 1910), p. 475.

12 *Missionary Review of the World* 10 (May 1887) : 348–49; ibid., 23 (January 1900): 68–69.

13 Oliver Elsbree, *The Rise of the Missionary Spirit in America* (Williamsport, Pa.: Williamsport Printing Co., 1928), pp. 150–52; G. G. Brown, "Missionaries and Cultural Diffusion," *American Journal of Sociology* 50 (November 1944): 214; Paul A. Carter, *The Spiritual Crisis of the Gilded Age* (DeKalb: Northern Illinois University Press, 1971).

14 Ako Adjei, "Imperialism and Spiritual Freedom: An African View," *American Journal of Sociology* 50 (November 1944): 194; Hugh Stuntz, "Christian Missions and Social Cohesion," ibid., p. 184. Good accounts of the disruptive effects of Christian missions are contained in Colin M. Turnbull, *The Lonely African* (Garden City, N.Y.: Doubleday, 1963), and Chinua Achebe, *Things Fall Apart* (Greenwich, Conn.: Fawcett, 1959).

15 *Proceedings of the Southern Baptist Convention*, 1874, p. 63.

16 Ibid., 1877, pp. 16, 40; this encouragement of black missionaries was repeated in the 1879 *Proceedings*, p. 22.

17 Archibald Johnson, "Claimants for Territory on the Congo," *A.M.E. Church Review* 2 (October 1885) : 127–38.

18 C. L. Woodworth, *Historic Correspondences in Africa and America* (Boston: Beacon Press, 1889), pp. 1, 6, 8–11, 13–14.

19 For an early expression of the Theory of Providential Design, see Philip J. Staudenraus, *The African Colonization Movement, 1816–1865* (New York: Columbia University Press, 1961), chaps. 1 and 2. An indication of how thoroughly this theory was accepted by black American mission supporters is contained in St. Clair Drake, *The Redemption of Africa and Black Religion* (Chicago: Third World Press, 1970), pp. 53, 74.

20 Frederick Noble, "The Chicago Congress on Africa," *Our Day* 12 (October 1893) : 300.

21 An excellent summary of the growth of M.E. mission interest in Liberia is contained in Donald F. Roth, "Grace Not Race: Southern Negro Church Leaders, Black Identity, and Missions to West Africa, 1865—1919" (Ph.D. dis., University of Texas at Austin, 1975), pp. 131—56. See also Lewis M. Hagood, *The Colored Man in the Methodist Episcopal Church* (1890; Westport, Conn.: Negro Universities Press, 1970).

22 Alexander Priestley Camphor, *Missionary Story Sketches* (Cincinnati: Jennings and Graham, 1909), pp. 7—8.

23 J. W. E. Bowen, ed., *Africa and the American Negro: Addresses and Proceedings of the Congress on Africa* (1896; Miami: Mnemosyne Publishing, 1969); Willis J. King, "History of the Methodist Church Mission in Liberia," typescript in United Methodist Church Commission on Archives and History (Lake Junaluska, N.C.: Methodist Missions in Africa, ca. 1945); Roth, "Grace Not Race," pp. 143—56.

24 Bowen letter, quoted in *Liberia* 6 (February 1895): 68.

25 Walter L. Yates, "The History of the African Methodist Episcopal Zion Church in West Africa, Liberia and Gold Coast (Ghana), 1880—1900" (M.A. thesis, Hartford Seminary, 1963), p. 49.

26 Wilbur C. Harr, "The Negro as an American Protestant Missionary in Africa" (D.D. diss., University of Chicago Divinity School, 1945), pp. 12, 22, 30, 48—50, 112; William Seraile, "Black American Missionaries in Africa, 1821—1925," *Social Studies* 63 (October 1972) : 198—202.

27 The best study of the founding of Liberia and early American involvement there is Staudenraus, *The African Colonization Movement*.

28 Ibid.; see also J. Gus Liebenow, *Liberia: The Evolution of Privilege* (Ithaca, N.Y.: Cornell University Press, 1969), pp. 1—15.

29 Seraile, "Black American Missionaries," pp. 198—200.

30 Latourette, *Great Century*, pp. 452—53. One of the black American diplomats to Liberia, Charles H. J. Taylor, strongly criticized this emphasis of mission work; see Taylor letter of 11 November 1887, Despatches Received from U.S. Ministers to Liberia, 1863—1908, National Archives Microcopy M170, roll 10, pp. 58, 81, 83.

31 Seraile, "Black American Missionaries," pp. 198—99; Latourette, *Great Century*, pp. 451—52; William H. Heard, *The Bright Side of African Life* (Philadelphia: A.M.E. Publications House, 1898), p. 79.

32 August Meier, *Negro Thought in America, 1880—1915* (Ann Arbor: University of Michigan Press, 1966), pp. 42—43; Robert July, *The Origins of Modern African Thought* (New York: Praeger, 1967), pp. 103—4; Kathleen O. Wahle, "Alexander Crummell: Black Evangelist and Pan-Negro Nationalist," *Phylon* 29 (December 1968): 388—95; Forrest Jack Lance, "The Life and Educational Thought of Alexander Crummell, Black Minister and Educator" (M.A. thesis, University of Georgia, 1972), pp. 10—22; Wilson J. Moses, "Civilizing Missionary: A Study of Alexander Crummell," *Journal of Negro History* 60 (April

1975): 229–40.

33 Ibid.

34 Alexander Crummell, *Civilization the Primal Need of the Race* (Washington: The American Negro Academy, 1898), reprinted in Herbert Aptheker, ed., *A Documentary History of the Negro People in the United states* (New York: Citadel press, 1951), 2:771–74.

35 Sermon to his Washington, D.C. church, ca. 1878, Alexander Crummell Papers, Schomberg Collection of the New York Public Library ms. c. 363, no. 755.

36 Alexander Crummell, "The Destiny of the Negro," *African Repository* 63 (October 1887): 103; Alexander Crummell speech, in Bowen, ed., *Africa and the American Negro*, pp. 119–20.

37 Alexander Crummell, *Africa and America* (Springfield, Mass.: Wiley & Co., 1891, p. v.)

38 Ibid., p. 442.

39 Ibid., p. 421.

40 Heard, *Bright Side*, p. 79; Latourette, *Great Century*, pp. 451–52; George F. Bragg, *History of the Afro-American Group of the Episcopal Church* (Baltimore: Church Advocate Press, 1922), p. 201; Jane J. Martin, "The Dual Legacy: Government Authority and Mission influence among the Glebo of Eastern Liberia, 1834–1910" (Ph.D diss., Boston University, 1968), pp. 322–23, 351. Ferguson's correspondence is in the Liberia papers of the Protestant Episcopal Church Historical Society, Austin, Texas. See also Amanda Smith, *An Autobiography* (Chicago: Meyer, 1893), p. 438.

41 *Lincoln University Biographical Catalogue* (Lancaster, Pa.: New Era Printing Co., 1918), p. 14; Horace Mann Bond, "God Glorified by Africa," typescript, 1955, in Lincoln University (Pa.) Archives, 1955, p. 3; Seraile, "Black American Missionaries," pp. 198–99; Andrew E. Murray, *Presbyterians and the Negro: A History* (Philadelphia: Presbyterian Historical Society, 1966).

42 Hollis R. Lynch, *Edward Wilmot Blyden: Pan-Negro Patriot, 1832–1912* (London: Oxford University Press, 1967); Hollis R. Lynch, *Black Spokesman: Edward Wilmot Blyden* (New York: Humanities Press, 1971).

43 See, for example, Blyden's articles in the *A.M.E. Church Review*: "Mohammedans of Nigritia" 4 (January, April, and July 1887); "The African Problem and the Method of Its Solution" 7 (October 1890); and "A Chapter in the History of Liberia" 9 (July 1892). His major work, originally published in 1887, was *Christianity, Islam and the Negro Race* (Edinburgh: Edinburgh University Press, 1967).

44 *A.M.E. Christian Recorder*, 2 January 1890, quoted in Edith Holden, *Blyden of Liberia* (New York: Vantage Press, 1966), p. 619.

45 Lynch, *Edward Wilmot Blyden*, p. 154; Holden, *Blyden*, p. 485.

46 Lynch, *Edward Wilmot Blyden*, p. 166; Holden, *Blyden*, p. 573; *Lincoln University Biographical Catalogue*, pp. 53, 59; Bond, "God Glorified," pp. 7, 35–36.

47 Smith, *Autobiography*, pp. 365, 438, 464–65.

48 King, "History," pp. 57, 58, 63. See also *Missionary Review of the World* 22 (1909): 563–70; Charles P. Groves, *The Planting of Christianity in Africa* (London: Lutterworth Press, 1948–58), 3:211–12; *Dictionary of American Biography*, vol. 4, p. 2, pp. 370–71; Hagood, *Colored Man*, p. 304.

49 Camphor, *Missionary*, pp. 7–9, 21–22; King, "History," p. 58; Clement Richardson, ed., *National Cyclopedia of the Colored Race* (Montgomery, Ala.: National Publishing Co., 1919), p. 238; *Official Journal of the Liberia Annual Conference, M.E. Church* (2–7 February 1898), pp. 68–71; Holden, *Blyden*, pp. 674, 700; Camphor to A. B. Leonard, 12 July 1899, Missionary Correspondence Papers, Board of Global Ministries of the United Methodist Church, New York, N.Y. (hereafter cited as Methodist Missionary Papers).

50 Camphor, *Missionary*, p. 24: Camphor letters 14 June 1897, 25 January 1898, 13 July 1898, and 23 June 1899, Methodist Missionary Papers. On Camphor's impact on black Americans see Frank Mather, ed., *Who's Who of the Colored Race* (n.p., 1915), p. 58; and Roth, "Grace Not Race," pp. 298–327.

51 Joseph Hartzell to A. B. Leonard, 3 January 1899; and J. A. Simpson to M.E. Board of Foreign Missions, 9 March 1908, Methodist Missionary Papers.

52 Sherrill to Hartzell, 28 October 1898 and 3 December 1898, ibid.

53 Camphor to Leonard, 5 September 1899, ibid.

54 F. M. Allen to Leonard, 13 November 1901, ibid.

55 Camphor to Leonard, 12 July 1899, ibid. Evidently this state of hopefulness had declined within a decade. In 1908 Sherrill wrote that although he had abandoned self-interest in coming to Africa as a missionary, he did not have enough salary to provide for the basic needs of his family and to operate his mission school in Cape Palmas. Despite his family's poor health, however, Sherrill retained his strong mission interest in Africa (Sherrill to Leonard, 1 December 1908). Alexander Camphor was likewise disillusioned. He returned to the United States in 1907 to raise more money for expansion of the mission, but finding little interest in his denomination he accepted the presidency of an M.E. Freedman's Aid school, the Central Alabama Institute. In 1916 Camphor was honored by being chosen as the M.E. Bishop to Africa, and he returned to Liberia. But again money problems plagued his mission, and he died in Liberia in 1919, a discouraged man. (Roth, "Grace Not Race," pp. 313–27.)

56 Latourette, *Great Century*, pp. 455–56.

57 Bond, "God Glorified," p. 50; John B. Rendall, *Historical Sketch of Lincoln University* (Philadelphia: M. C. Wood Printing Co., 1904), pp. 9–10.

58 J. S. Mills, *Africa and Mission Work in Sierra Leone, West Africa* (Dayton: United Brethren Publishing House, 1898), pp. 221–23; *Mis-*

sionary Visitor 12 (6 July 1876). Most of the material on the Gomers can be found in the Evangelical United Brethren Division of the United Methodist Commission on Archives and History in Dayton, Ohio (hereafter cited as Gomer Papers).

59 T. M. Williams, undated report in Gomer Papers.

60 Mills, *Africa*, pp. 202, 221, 230.

61 *Missionary Visitor* 11 (8 April 1876): 74; United Brethren Church, *Annual Report*, 1879, pp. 21–22; Smith, *Autobiography*, p. 423.

62 *Missionary Visitor* 12 (6 July 1876).

63 Mills, *Africa*, pp. 225–31, 237.

64 Ibid., pp. 123, 125, 127, 137, 237; *Search Light*, December 1899, p. 7; *Missionary Visitor* 18 (22 August 1882): 13; United Brethren Church, *Annual Report*, 1875, p. 19.

65 *Indianapolis Freeman*, 5 October 1889, p. 1; C. C. Adams, *Negro Baptists and Foreign Missions* (Philadelphia: Foreign Mission Board of the National Baptist Convention, 1944), p. 26; Edward A. Freeman, *The Epoch of Negro Baptists and the Foreign Mission Board, National Baptist Convention, U.S.A., Inc.* (Kansas City: Central Seminary Press, 1953), p. 70; Latourette, *Great Century* p. 440; *Proceedings of the Southern Baptist Convention*, 1878, pp. 44–46; ibid., 1880, p. 40; Owen Pelt and Ralph Smith, *The Story of the National Baptists* (New York: Vantage Press, 1960), p. 85; Roth, "Grace Not Race," pp. 48, 110–15.

66 Southern Baptist Convention, *Foreign Mission Journal*, August 1877, p. 2; September 1878, p. 3; May 1879, p. 2; January 1880, p. 3; and May 1880, p. 2.

67 Thomas L. Johnson, *Africa for Christ, or Twenty-Eight Years a Slave*, 6th ed. (London: Alexander and Shepheard, 1892), pp. 9, 12, 31, 37–42, 52, 66, 97; *Indianapolis Freeman*, 27 July 1889, pp. 2, 5.

68 Johnson, *Africa for Christ*, pp. 83, 95–96; Groves, *Planting of Christianity*, 3:116.

69 John Brown Myers, *The Congo for Christ: The Story of the Congo Mission* (New York: Fleming R. Revell Co., 1895), pp. 148–54; Slade, *English-Speaking Missions*, p. 97; Congo Mission Papers, American Baptist Foreign Mission Society Archives, Valley Forge, Pa.

70 T. E. S. Scholes, ed., *Industrial Self-Supporting Missionaries* (Colwyn Bay, Wales: Congo Training Institute, [1895]); Immanuel Geiss, *The Pan-African Movement: A History of Pan-Africanism in America, Europe and Africa* (New York: Africana Publishing Co., 1974), pp. 110, 207.

71 *Missionary Review of the World* 10 (1887): 337.

72 Johnson, *Africa for Christ*, pp. 83, 95–96; Lynch, *Edward Wilmot Blyden*, p. 222, 238; E. A. Ayandele, *The Missionary Impact on Modern Nigeria, 1842–1914* (London: Longmans, 1966), pp. 254–55; C. G. Baeta, ed., *Christianity in Tropical Africa* (London: International African Institute, 1968), p. 238; *Mission Herald* 73 (1970): 11.

73 Strong, *The Story of the American Board*, p. 336; Clifton J. Phillips, *Protestant America and the Pagan World: The First Half Century of the American Board of Commissioners for Foreign Missions* (Cambridge: Harvard University Press, 1969); Clarence Clendennen et al., *Americans in Africa, 1865–1900* (Stanford: Stanford University Press, 1966), p. 115; Latourette, *Great Century*, p. 399.

The best ethnographic descriptions of the Ovimbundu are in Fola Soremkun, "A History of the American Board Mission in Angola," 1880–1940" (Ph. D. diss., Northwestern University, 1965), pp. 1–25; and Merran McCullock, *The Ovimbundu of Angola* (London: International African Institute, 1952), pp. 1–9. The Ovimbundu were a central Bantu-speaking people who were divided into twenty-two autonomous chiefdoms. They had developed as major traders between the central African interior and the Portuguese on the Angola coast, especially during the eighteenth century. Ovimbundu trade in slaves, ivory, and rubber continued to expand in the nineteenth century, despite periodic wars with neighboring peoples and with the Portuguese, who were able to occupy the Benguella highlands between 1890 and 1902. They wiped out Ovimbundu trade patterns by ending the slave trade and establishing direct European trade with the interior. This disruption produced a decline in the Ovimbundu economy after 1900.

74 Soremekun, "History," pp. 50–52, 72; Miller letters in the Papers of the American Board of Commissioners for Foreign Missions, Houghton Library of Harvard University, collection 6, vol. 30 (hereafter cited as A.B.C.F.M. Papers).

75 Soremekun, "History," pp. 72–73; Miller letters, 1 May 1881, 2 October 1881, 24 March 1882, 24 June 1884, A.B.C.F.M. Papers, collection 15.1, vol. 6.

76 Miller letters, 23 December 1884, 1 January 1885, 13 February 1886, A.B.C.F.M. Papers, collection 15.1, vol. 6—the last communications between Miller and the American Board.

77 Ousley letters, 28 December 1882 and 25 October 1883; A.B.C.F.M. Papers, collection 15.4, vol. 12; Strong, *Story*, p. 342.

78 Ousley letters, 23 February 1887, 12 December 1892, 13 September 1893; A.B.C.F.M. Papers, collection 15.4, vol. 12.

79 Nancy Jones letters, 19 July 1887; A.B.C.F.M. Papers, collection 6, vol. 35; 2 May 1888, 22 July 1889, collection 15.4, vol. 12; 9 January 1890, 10 June 1891, 25 May 1897, 28 October 1897; collection 15.4, vol. 20; *Indianapolis Freeman*, 5 February 1898, p. 2; Strong, *Story*, pp. 343–44.

80 Stanley Shaloff, *Reform in Leopold's Congo* (Richmond, Va.: John Knox Press, 1970), pp. 13–16, 18; Murray, *Presbyterians and the Negro*.

81 Slade, *English-Speaking Missions*, pp. 104, 233. The idea of African missions as attractions for black American emigration is developed in Shaloff, *Reform*, pp. 13–16, 18; Morgan's motive is an excellent example in support of the thesis of American commercial imperialism

developed by William A. Williams, *The Contours of American History* (Chicago: Quadrangle Books, 1966), and LaFeber, *New Empire*.

82 *Missionary Review of the World* 8 (1895): 327; Shaloff, *Reform*, pp. 17–20; Slade, *English-Speaking Missions*, p. 104; Roth, "Grace Not Race," pp. 262–64.

83 The five ethnic groups near Luebo were the Bakete, Bakuba, Bena Lulua, Baluba, and Zappo-Zap. Slade, *English-Speaking Missions*, pp. 104–6; Shaloff, *Reform*, pp. 23, 26: Groves, *Planting of Christianity*, 3:120.

84 William H. Sheppard, *Pioneers in Congo* (Louisville, Ky.: Pentecostal Publishing Co., 1917), p. 16.

85 Sheppard letter, 17 May 1890, printed in *Missionary*, September 1890, pp. 352–55.

86 Unpublished W. H. Sheppard letter, 5 January 1892, Sheppard Papers, ms. no. 55644, Historical Foundation of the Presbyterian and Reformed Churches, Montreat, N.C. (hereafter cited as Sheppard Papers).

87 Samuel Lapsley letter, printed in *Missionary*, April 1892, p. 151.

88 Photograph collection, Sheppard Papers. Although the others missionaries are shown solemn and unmoving, Sheppard is usually smiling and striking a masterful pose. Many photographs show him involved in various activities with Africans.

89 Shaloff, *Reform*, pp. 26–30; Slade, *English-Speaking Missions*, pp. 104–7, 197; *Annual Report of the Executive Committee of Foreign Missions of the Presbyterian Church in the United States* (Nashville: University Press, 1894), p. xxxvii (hereafter cited as *Annual Report*).

90 Shaloff, *Reform*, pp. 30–31.

91 Ibid., pp. 26–27. While there is a considerable literature in French, the only good Bakuba ethnography in English is Jan Vansina, *The Children of Woot: A History of the Kuba Peoples* (Madison: University of Wisconsin Press, 1978). According to Jan Vansina, in *Les Tribus Ba-Kuba et Les Peuplades Apparentees* (Tervuren, Belgium: Annales du Musée Royal du Congo Belge, 1954), pp. 8–9, the Bakuba king was sacred and powerful. Each tribe within the Bakuba nation paid tribute to the king, but retained autonomy over its own internal affairs. In the nineteenth century, the Bakuba had to repel invasions by neighboring peoples, but they preserved their kingdom. Even though a European trading post was established at Luebo in 1885, and the Presbyterian missionaries came six years later, the Bakuba were not greatly affected by the Europeans until after 1904. See also Vansina's *De la Tradition Orale* (Tervuren, Belgium: Annales du Musée Royal du Congo Belge, 1961); and E. Torday, *Notes ethnographiques sur les peuples communément appelés bakuba* (Brussels: Annales du Musée Royal du Congo Belge, 1910).

92 Shaloff, *Reform*, pp. 31–35; *Missionary Review of the World* 8 (1895): 329–30; Sheppard, *Pioneers*, pp. 93–104.

93 Shaloff, *Reform*, pp. 36–39.

94 *Missionary Review of the World* 8 (1895): 331; *Southern Workman* 29 (April 1900): 221.
95 *Missionary Review of the World* 8 (1895): 327.
96 *Memorial of Dr. William H. Sheppard* (Louisville, Ky.: Presbyterian Colored Mission, n.d.), p. 2, copy in Sheppard Papers.
97 *Missionary*, August 1894, p. 319.
98 William Sheppard letter, *Indianapolis Freeman*, 27 February 1892, p. 7. Sheppard went on to say that he often read the newspaper to the Africans, and he recommended the paper as evidence of "the vast and solid strides of the Negro in material, industrial and spiritual wealth."
99 *Southern Workman* 29 (April 1900): 218–19.
100 Ibid., 22 (December 1893): 182.
101 Groves, *Planting of Christianity*, 3:120n; Julia Lake Kellersberger, *Lucy Gantt Sheppard, Shepherdess of His Sheep on Two Continents* (Atlanta: Committee on Women's Work, Presbyterian Church in the U.S., n.d.), pp. 5–10; Lucien V. Rule, "A Daughter of the Morning," typescript of interviews with Lucy Gantt Sheppard in 1940, Sheppard Papers. Undated wedding clipping is from the Boston *Citizen*, Hampton Institute Clippings Collection, cited in Roth, "Grace Not Race," p. 269.
102 *Missionary*, July 1894, pp. 272–73; *Annual Report*, 1894, p. xxxvi, and 1895, pp. 28–29; Shaloff, *Reform*, p. 39.
103 Kellersberger, *Lucy Gantt Sheppard*, p. 11; *Missionary*, November 1895, p. 491. See also *Annual Report*, 1896, pp. 12–13. Other black American missionaries who later served at the Presbyterian Luebo Mission, and their dates in Africa, were: L. A. De Yampert (1902–18), Althea Brown (1902–37), A. L. Edmiston (1903–41), A. A. Rochester (1906–39), Annie Kate Taylor (1906–14), and Edna May Taylor (1923–39). See Shaloff, *Reform*, p. 39.
104 In 1895 the Mission Board turned down the application of a recent Moody Bible Institute graduate, Mary McLeod, who would later become famous as a civil rights activist. Rackham Holt, *Mary McLeod Bethune: A Biography* (Garden City: Doubleday, 1964), p. 45.
105 Shaloff, *Reform*, pp. 40, 182.
106 Ibid., p. 49.
107 W. H. Sheppard letter, 9 December 1896, in Rosa Gibbons, "Historical Research on Rev. William H. Sheppard, D.D., F.R.G.S.," typescript in Sheppard Papers, p. 52.
108 Shaloff, *Reform*, pp. 47–49.
109 Sheppard letter, 30 November 1896, in Gibbons, Sheppard Papers, p. 54; *Annual Report*, 1897, p. 14; *Missionary Review of the World* 11 (1898): 798; *Southern Workman* 29 (April 1900): 221; Kellersberger, *Lucy Gantt Sheppard*, pp. 20–21. After Mrs. Sheppard rejoined her husband in the Congo, she bore a son who was named William Lapsley Sheppard in honor of Sheppard's first white co-worker. However, the Congolese named him "Maxamalinge," and that became the name by which the son was called even after he returned to America. Photograph

collection, Sheppard Papers.

110 Sheppard Papers. Also in his collection is a silver trophy presented to Sheppard by the white missionaries at Luebo, in tribute to his twenty years of mission work and as evidence of continued close relations in the integrated Congo mission. On his return to the United States Sheppard preached in Louisville, Kentucky, until his death in 1927. *Sheppard* (pamphlet), p. 10, Sheppard Papers.

Chapter 2
The Rise of the African Mission Movement
in the Independent Black Churches

1 J. Minton Batten, "Henry McNeal Turner: Negro Bishop Extraordinary," *Church History* 7 (September 1938): 231.

2 W. E. B. Du Bois, *The Souls of Black Folk* (1903; New York: Washington Square Press, 1970), p. 157.

3 Ibid., pp. 159—60; Eugene Genovese, *Roll, Jordan, Roll: The World the Slaves Made* (New York: Vintage, 1974), pp. 161—284; Donald Mathews, *Religion in the Old South* (Chicago: University of Chicago Press, 1977), pp. 185—236.

4 Joseph R. Washington, *Black Religion: The Negro and Christianity in the United States* (Boston: Beacon Press, 1964), pp. 220—21.

5 Winthrop S. Hudson, *Religion in America*, 2nd ed. (New York: Scribner's, 1973), p. 225.

6 *Liberia* 4 (February 1894): 54. The only white church with a substantial black membership was the Methodist Church, with 246,249.

7 Du Bois, *Souls*, p. 158.

8 Ibid., p. 157.

9 Washington, *Black Religion*, pp. 229—30. Even Booker T. Washington, in writing a tribute to a prominent black clergyman in 1915, emphasized the importance of the black church as the first black social center. In his typical stance, Washington praised the church for being an "organization for general uplift," and for teaching blacks "what was necessary for them to do to become useful citizens. The importance of settling down and going to work, of acquiring property and getting an education was impressed upon them." Quoted in Mungo M. Ponton, *Life and Times of Henry M. Turner* (Atlanta: A. B. Caldwell, 1917), pp. 153—54.

10 Carter Woodson, *A History of the Negro Church* (Washington, D.C.: Associated Publishers, 1945), p. 268.

11 United States Census statistics, 1870—1900, quoted in *The Statistical History of the United States* (Stanford, Conn.: Fairfield Publishers, 1965), pp. 213—14.

12 Woodson, *History*, p. 269.

13 Ibid., pp. 271—78; Richard Bardolph, *The Negro Vanguard* (New York:

Rinehart and Co., 1959), pp. 74, 80; George B. Tindall, *South Carolina Negroes, 1877–1900* (Baton Rouge: Louisiana State University Press, 1966), pp. 202–6; August Meier, *Negro Thought in America, 1880–1915* (Ann Arbor: University of Michigan Press, 1966), p. 130; Washington, *Black Religion*, p. 229.

14 Melvin Small, "Suggestions from the Behavioral Sciences for Historians Interested in the Study of Attitudes," *Societas* 3 (Winter 1973): 18.

15 Washington, *Black Religion*, p. 230.

16 Sheldon H. Harris, *Paul Cuffe: Black America and the African Return* (New York: Simon and Schuster, 1972), pp. 38–42.

17 William J. Simmons, *Men of Mark* (1887; New York: Arno Press, 1968), p. 343. See also Lewis G. Jordan, *Up the Ladder in Foreign Missions* (Nashville: National Baptist Publications Board, 1901 and 1903), pp. 15–16; Owen D. Pelt and Ralph Lee Smith, *The Story of the National Baptists* (New York: Vantage Press, 1960), pp. 69–70; Miles Fisher, "Lott Cary, the Colonizing Missionary," *Journal of Negro History* 7 (October 1922): 380–418.

18 *Indianapolis Freeman*, 30 January 1897, p. 3; Richard R. Wright, *Centennial Encyclopedia of the African Methodist Episcopal Church* (Philadelphia: Book Concern of the A.M.E. Church, 1916), p. 319; Charles S. Smith, *A History of the African Methodist Episcopal Church* (Philadelphia: Book Concern of the A.M.E. Church, 1922), p. 174; Daniel A. Payne, *History of the African Methodist Episcopal Church* (1891; New York: Johnson Reprint Corp., 1968), p. 484; Charles P. Groves, *The Planting of Christianity in Africa* (London: Lutterworth Press, 1948–58), 3:222.

19 Washington, *Black Religion*, pp. 156–57; Horace Mann Bond, "God Glorified by Africa," typescript in Lincoln University (Pa.) Archives, 1955, p. 7.

20 Walter L. Yates, "The History of the African Methodist Episcopal Zion Church in West Africa, Liberia and Gold Coast (Ghana), 1880–1900" (M.A. thesis, Hartford Seminary, 1963), p. 57.

21 Solomon Porter Hood, "What Should Be the Policy of the Colored American toward Africa?" *A.M.E. Church Review* 2 (July 1885): 72.

22 Ibid. For other expressions of this assimilationist philosophy, see Walter L. Williams, "Black Journalism's Opinions about Africa during the Late Nineteenth Century," *Phylon* 34 (September 1973): 224–35; and Walter L. Williams, "Black American Attitudes toward Africa, 1877–1900," *Pan-African Journal* 4 (Spring 1971): 173–94.

23 Frederick P. Noble, "The Chicago Congress on Africa," *Our Day* 12 (October 1893): 285.

24 Quoted in Josephus R. Coan, "The Expansion of Missions of the African Methodist Episcopal Church in South Africa, 1896–1908" (Ph.D. diss., Hartford Seminary, 1961), p. 57.

25 Charles S. Smith, *Glimpses of Africa, West and Southwest Coast* (Nashville: A.M.E. Sunday School Union, 1895), p. 24. The cross-

cultural model is from Philip Curtin, ed., *Africa and the West* (Madison: University of Wisconsin Press, 1972), pp. 242–43.

26 Quoted in Hollis R. Lynch, *Edward Wilmot Blyden: Pan-Negro Patriot, 1832–1912* (London: Oxford University Press, 1967), pp. 150–51.

27 *A.M.E. Church Review* 1 (July 1884): 5, 314, 319; and Coan, "Expansion," pp. 38–40.

28 *A.M.E. Church Review* 4 (April 1888): 401–2.

29 Washington, *Black Religion*, pp. 156–57.

30 H. B. Parks, *Africa, the Problem of the New Century* (New York: Mission Department of the A.M.E. Church, 1899), p. 15; Artishia W. Jordan, *The African Methodist Episcopal Church in Africa* (New York: A.M.E. Department of Foreign Missions, 1964), p. 147; Batten, "Henry M. Turner," p. 244; *Missionary Review of the World* 3 (1880): 343.

31 Thomas L. Johnson, *Africa for Christ, or Twenty-eight Years a Slave*, 6th ed. (London: Alexander and Shepheard, 1892), pp. 80–81.

32 *A.M.E.Z. Star of Zion*, 8 December 1898, p. 1.

33 *A.M.E. Church Review* 1 (July 1884): 5, 314, 319; Payne, *History*, p. 293; Smith, *History*, p. 155; Coan, "Expansion," pp. 38–40; Wesley John Gaines, *African Methodism in the South* (Atlanta: Franklin Publishing House, 1890), p. 120.

34 Alfred Lee Ridgel, *Africa and African Methodism* (Atlanta: Franklin Publishing Co., 1896), pp. 58–60.

35 David H. Bradley, *A History of the A.M.E. Zion Church* (Nashville: Parthenon Press, 1970), pt. 2, p. 226; Idonia E. Rogerson, *Historical Synopsis of the Women's Home and Foreign Missionary Society, African Methodist Episcopal Zion Church* (Charlotte, N.C.: A.M.E. Zion Publishing House, 1967), pp. 18–19; Yates, "History," pp. 49–53, 60.

36 Tindall, *South Carolina Negroes*, pp. 153–61; Henry M. Turner speech in *African Repository* 54 (July 1878): 78, quoted in Cyril E. Griffith, *The African Dream: Martin R. Delany and the Emergence of Pan-African Thought* (University Park: Pennsylvania State University Press, 1975), p. 108.

37 Simmons, *Men of Mark*, pp. 675–76; Jordan, *Up the Ladder*, p. 122; *Mission Herald* 73 (1970): 9.

38 *Indianapolis Freeman*, 30 January 1897, p. 3; Henry McNeal Turner Papers, Howard University Library, folder 1; William H. Heard, *The Bright Side of African Life* (Philadelphia: A.M.E. Publications House, 1898), p. 91; Parks, *Africa*, pp. 15–16; Tindall, *South Carolina Negroes*, pp. 153–68; Smith, *History*, pp. 127–28.

39 Washington, *Black Religion*, p. 229.

40 *Proceedings of the Southern Baptist Convention*, 1877, p. 16.

41 Ibid., 1881, p. 45.

42 Ibid., 1882, p. 69.

43 Ibid., p. 37.

44 Bond, "God Glorified," p. 30, 35.

45 Amanda Smith, *An Autobiography* (Chicago: Meyer, 1893), p. 423.

46 William Seraile, "Black American Missionaries in Africa, 1821—1925," *Social Studies* 63 (October 1972): 201; Emory Ross, *Out of Africa* (New York: Friendship Press, 1936), pp. 154—59. European fear of Afro-American missionaries was greatly increased in the 1920s, in reaction to Marcus Garvey's black nationalist movement.

47 James Dennis et al., eds., *World Atlas of Christian Missions* (New York: Student Volunteer Movement for Foreign Missions, 1911), pp. 87—94.

48 Parks, *Africa*, p. 52.

49 *A.M.E. Church Hymnal* (Philadelphia: A.M.E. Book Concern, 1899), p. 293.

50 Ibid., p. 295.

51 Ridgel, *Africa*, p. 62.

52 Henry M. Turner speech in *A.M.E. Budget*, 1883, 130.

53 *Voice of Missions*, February 1894, p. 1, and June 1893, p. 1.

54 Parks, *Africa*, p. 15.

55 Ponton, *Life and Times of Henry M. Turner*, p. 76.

56 See appendices D—G.

Chapter 3
Mission Organization in Independent
Afro-American Methodist Churches

1 John Hope Franklin, *From Slavery to Freedom*, 3rd ed. (New York: Alfred A. Knopf, 1967), pp. 162—63, 227, 309; Artishia W. Jordan, *The African Methodist Episcopal Church in Africa* (New York: A.M.E. Department of Foreign Missions, 1964), p. 147; J. Minton Batten, "Henry McNeal Turner: Negro Bishop Extraordinary," *Church History* 7 (September 1938): 244; *Missionary Review of the World* 3 (1880): 343.

2 See chapter 2.

3 William J. Simmons, *Men of Mark* (1887; New York: Arno Press, 1968), pp. 1135—38.

4 *A.M.E. Budget*, 1883, p. 130.

5 Wesley John Gaines, *African Methodism in the South* (Atlanta: Franklin Publishing House, 1890), pp. 119—20.

6 *A.M.E. Budget*, 1882, pp. 88—89; 1883, p. 132.

7 H. B. Parks, *Africa, the Problem of the New Century* (New York: Mission Department of the A.M.E. Church, 1899), p. 16. See appendix B.

8 W. F. Dickerson, *The Quadrennial Address of the Bishops of the African Methodist Episcopal Church to the Eighteenth Session of the General Conference* (Baltimore: A.M.E. Church, 1884), pp. 6—7; Archibald Johnson, "Claimants for Territory on the Congo," *A.M.E. Church Review* 2 (October 1885): 127—38; George W. Cook, "Early Discoveries in Africa," ibid., pp. 149—63.

9 Parks, *Africa*, p. 17; Jordan, *A.M.E.* pp. 46–47; Daniel A. Payne, *History of the African Methodist Episcopal Church* (1891; New York: Johnson Reprint Corp., 1968), pp. 487–90; Hollis R. Lynch, *Edward Wilmot Blyden: Pan-Negro Patriot, 1832–1912* (London: Oxford University Press, 1967), p. 219; Edith Holden, *Blyden of Liberia* (New York: Vantage Press, 1966), pp. 600–601; my thanks to Professor Josephus Coan of Interdenominational Theological Center, Atlanta, for kindly providing me with a copy of his unpublished manuscript on A.M.E. missionaries in Sierra Leone, J. R. Frederick, Sarah Gorham, and Alfred L. Ridgel.

10 Parks, *Africa*, pp. 17, 55; *Voice of Missions*, September 1893, p. 1, and October 1894, p. 4; Lewellyn L. Berry, *A Century of Missions of the African Methodist Episcopal Church, 1840–1940* (New York: Gutenberg Printing Co., 1942), pp. 70, 138–39.

11 Charles S. Smith, *A History of the African Methodist Episcopal Church* (Philadelphia: Book Concern of the A.M.E. Church, 1922), p. 155; August Meier, *Negro Thought in America, 1880–1915* (Ann Arbor: University of Michigan Press, 1966), p. 66.

12 *A.M.E. Christian Recorder*, 2 January 1890, quoted in Holden, *Blyden*, p. 619.

13 See, for example, Blyden's articles, "Mohammedans of Nigritia," in vol. 4 (January, April, and July 1887); "The African Problem and the Method of Its Solution," in vol. 7 (October 1890); and "A Chapter in the History of Liberia," in vol. 9 (July 1892).

14 Payne, *History*, p. 492.

15 Mungo M. Ponton, *Life and Times of Henry M. Turner* (Atlanta: A. B. Caldwell, 1917), pp. 33–34.

16 Ibid., pp. 34–36; Batten, "Henry M. Turner," p. 236; Henry Turner Papers, manuscript division, Moorland Collection, Howard University Library, Washington, D.C, folder 1.

17 Turner Papers, folder 1; Ponton, *Life and Times of Henry M. Turner,* pp. 67–71.

18 The best summary of Turner's life and ideas can be found in Edwin Redkey, *Black Exodus: Black Nationalist and Back-to-Africa Movements, 1890–1910* (New Haven: Yale University Press, 1969). See also Jane Walker Herndon, "Henry McNeal Turner: Exponent of American 'Negritude'" (M.A. thesis, Georgia State College, Atlanta, 1967); Meier, *Negro Thought*, pp. 65–66; Ponton, *Life and Times of Henry M. Turner*; Batten, "Henry M. Turner"; and Turner's newspaper, *Voice of Missions* (1893–99).

19 *Voice of Missions*, March 1893, p. 2.

20 Turner letter to *A.M.E. Christian Recorder*, 8 December 1881, quoted in Edwin Redkey, ed., *Respect Black: The Writings and Speeches of Henry McNeal Turner* (New York: Arno Press, 1971), pp. 50–51.

21 Alfred Lee Ridgel, *Africa and African Methodism* (Atlanta: Franklin Publishing Co., 1896), p. 107.

22 *Indianapolis Freeman*, 19 February 1898, p. 4.

23 Ponton, *Life and Times of Henry M. Turner*, pp. 47, 75, 82, 85–86, 114.

24 Simmons, *Men of Mark*, pp. 567, 575.

25 *Missionary Review of the World* 2 (1889): 707; Redkey, *Black Exodus*, p. 36; Batten, "Henry M. Turner," p. 244.

26 Henry M. Turner to John P. Turner, 5 March 1880, quoted in Redkey, ed., *Respect Black*, pp. 47–48.

27 Henry M. Turner, letter to *Christian Recorder*, 21 June 1883, quoted in Redkey, ed., *Respect Black*, p. 58.

28 *A.M.E. Church Review* 8 (April 1892): 446–98. For background on Derrick, see Simmons, *Men of Mark*, pp. 88–97. Derrick was born in the West Indies, but came to the United States as a child with his family. During the Civil War he served in the Union navy, and dabbled in politics during Reconstruction. By the 1880s he was prospering as a New York City businessman, so it is not surprising that he was uninterested in emigration.

29 *A.M.E. Church Review* 8 (April 1892): 467–68.

30 Ibid., pp. 469, 472; see also Smith, *History*, pp. 175–76.

31 *A.M.E. Church Review* 8 (April 1892): 446–98; Parks, *Africa*, p. 53; Turner Papers, folder 1; *Indianapolis Freeman*, 30 January 1897, p. 3; Smith, *History*, pp. 175–78; William H. Heard, *The Bright Side of African Life* (Philadelphia: A.M.E. Publications House, 1898), pp. 91–92.

32 Ridgel, *Africa; Voice of Missions*, December 1896, p. 1.

33 Berry, *Century*, p. 137; Jordan, *A.M.E.*, p. 47; William H. Heard, *The Missionary Fields of West Africa* (Philadelphia: A.M.E. Book Concern, n.d.); Lynch, *Edward Wilmot Blyden*, p. 246; *A.M.E.Z. Star of Zion*, 6 January 1898, p. 1, and 27 January 1898, p. 2.

34 Parks, *Africa*, p. 55; Jordan, *A.M.E.*, p. 48.

35 William H. Heard, *From Slavery to the Bishopric in the A.M.E. Church* (1924; New York: Arno Press, 1969), pp. ii–iv; William H. Heard, *Africa: Verse and Song* (Atlanta: Union Publishing Co., [1896]), pp. 6–7; Heard, *Missionary Fields*; Heard, *Bright Side*; Richard Bardolph, *The Negro Vanguard* (New York: Rinehart and Co., 1959), pp. 72–73; James A. Padgett, "The Ministers to Liberia and Their Diplomacy," *Journal of Negro History* 22 (January 1937): 59–60, 78.

36 Ibid.; *A.M.E. Church Review* 13 (January 1897): 336–37; W. H. Heard to U.S. Department of State, Despatches Received from U.S. Ministers to Liberia, 1863–1908, National Archives Microcopy M170, rolls 11 and 12.

37 Parks, *Africa*, p. 53.

38 Joseph R. Coan, "The Expansion of Missions of the African Methodist Episcopal Church in South Africa, 1896–1908" (Ph.D. diss., Hartford Seminary, 1961), p. 42; Batten, "Henry M. Turner," p. 245; *Voice of Missions*, March 1893, p. 2.

39 Batten, "Henry M. Turner," p. 245; Turner Papers, folder 1.
40 *Voice of Missions*, October 1893, p. 2; see also Frederick R. Noble, "The Chicago Congress on Africa," *Our Day* 12 (October 1893): 284.
41 *A.M.E. Church Review* 16 (January 1900): 314.
42 *A.M.E. Church Hymnal* (Philadelphia: A.M.E. Book Concern, 1899), p. 358, verses 1 and 4; copy in Turner Papers, folder 14.
43 Quoted in Coan, "Expansion," p. 57.
44 Gaines, *African Methodism*, p. 71.
45 Quoted in Ponton, *Life and Times of Henry M. Turner*, p. 78.
46 Batten, "Henry M. Turner," p. 232.
47 Charles S. Smith, *Glimpses of Africa, West and Southwest Coast* (Nashville: A.M.E. Sunday School Union, 1895), pp. 5, 147–49; see also Smith's *History*.
48 *Voice of Missions*, March 1896, p. 1.
49 Parks, *Africa*, p. 61.
50 Ibid.
51 Charles P. Groves, *The Planting of Christianity in Africa* (London: Lutterworth Press, 1948–58), 3:177; Kenneth Scott Latourette, *The Great Century in the Americas, Australia, and Africa, 1800–1914* (New York: Harper and Brothers, 1943), p. 338.
52 Coan, "Expansion," pp. 107–13. This study is the best work on the topic, and I wish to acknowledge the generous assistance of Professor Coan, through correspondence and conversations, in the formulation of ideas in this chapter.
53 Smith, *History*, p. 181.
54 Bengt G. M. Sundkler, *The Bantu Prophets of South Africa* (London: Lutterworth Press, 1948); Thomas Hodgkin, *Nationalism in Colonial Africa* (New York: New York University Press, 1957), pp. 98–99.
55 This closeness is perhaps a good example of the ideological similarity between England and the United States. Even when passed in two directions (from the English to white Americans to black Americans; from the English to the Africans) the cultural similarities were astounding.
56 Coan, "Expansion," p. 100–101; Jordan, *A.M.E.*, pp. 59–60.
57 Richard R. Wright, *Centennial Encyclopedia of the African Methodist Episcopal Church* (Philadelphia: Book Concern of the A.M.E. Church, 1916), p. 285.
58 See, for example, *Voice of Missions*, December 1895, pp. 1, 3; March 1896, p. 2; 1 December 1897, p. 1; 1 October 1898, p. 3; 1 July 1899, p. 2; and 1 December 1899, p. 1.
59 Berry, *Century*, p. 75; Parks, *Africa*, p. 26.
60 Wright, *Centennial*, p. 285.
61 *Voice of Missions*, 1 December 1899, p. 2.
62 Wright, *Centennial*, pp. 11, 285; C. G. Baeta, ed., *Christianity in Tropical Africa* (London: International African Institute, 1968), p. 251; Sundkler, *Bantu*, p. 40.

63 Wright, *Centennial*, p. 285.
64 *Voice of Missions*, 1 June 1898, p. 2; "Resolution of Welcome," presented to Bishop Turner by the A.M.E. leaders of Pretoria and Johannesburg, Turner Papers, folders 15, 16.
65 *Voice of Missions*, 1 June 1898, pp. 2, 6; 1 July 1898, p. 2.
66 Turner Papers, folder 1; Wright, *Centennial*, pp. 285–86, 319; Sundkler, *Bantu*, p. 41; Adelaide Cromwell Hill and Martin Kilson, eds., *Apropos of Africa: Sentiments of Negro American Leaders on Africa from the 1800s to the 1950s* (London: Frank Cass, 1969), p. 43.
67 *Voice of Missions*, 1 June 1898, p. 2; 1 December 1898, p. 2.
68 Latourette, *Great Century*, p. 361; Sundkler, *Bantu*, p. 40.
69 Wright, *Centennial*, p. 286.
70 Ibid.; Latourette, *Great Century*, pp. 358–61; Sundkler, *Bantu*, pp. 41–42; *Voice of Missions*, 1 December 1899, p. 2.
71 Totals computed by the author from congregational reports in the *Voice of Missions*, September 1893; 1 July 1897; 1 June 1898; and 1 June 1899. See appendix C.
72 Ibid.
73 *Voice of Missions*, 1 February 1899, p. 4.
74 See appendices D–G, and following chapters on missionaries and African students.
75 James W. Hood, *One Hundred Years of the African Methodist Episcopal Zion Church* (New York: A.M.E. Zion Book Concern, 1895); Meier, *Negro Thought*, pp. 6, 14, 131–32, 218–21, 252.
76 Walter L. Yates, "The History of the African Methodist Episcopal Zion Church in West Africa, Liberia and Gold Coast (Ghana), 1880–1900" (M.A. thesis, Hartford Seminary, 1963), pp. 65–70. This thesis, written by the Dean of the Theology School of Livingstone College, is the best summary of the rise of the missionary movement in the A.M.E.Z. Church.
77 Ibid., p. 74; Idonia E. Rogerson, *Historical Synopsis of the Woman's Home and Foreign Missionary Society, African Methodist Episcopal Zion Church* (Charlotte, N.C.: A.M.E. Zion Publishing House, 1967), pp. 18, 40–41.
78 David H. Bradley, *A History of the A.M.E. Zion Church* (Nashville: Parthenon Press, 1970), pt 2, p. 226; Rogerson, *Historical*, pp. 18–19; Yates, "History," p. 60.
79 Yates, "History," pp. 60, 63, 71, 76, 79; Rogerson, *Historical*, p. 20; Bradley, *History*, p. 228.
80 Yates, "History," pp. 51, 55–60.
81 Rogerson, *Historical*, pp. 41, 84.
82 *A.M.E.Z. Star of Zion*, 29 October 1896, p. 1.
83 *A.M.E.Z. Church Quarterly* 2 (July 1892): 405–6; Alexander Walters, *My Life and Work* (New York: Fleming H. Revell Co., 1917), pp. 253–60; Meier, *Negro Thought*, pp. 128–31, 172, 218; Simmons, *Men of Mark*, p. 340.

84 *A.M.E.Z. Star of Zion*, 21 January 1897, p. 1.

85 Ibid., 22 October 1896, p. 1.

86 Ibid., 11 February 1897, p. 2.

87 Ibid., 6 January 1898, p. 1; see also 15 July 1897, p. 1; 4 November 1897, p. 2; and 27 January 1898, p. 2.

88 Cameron C. Alleyne, *Gold Coast at a Glance* (New York: Hunt Printing Co., 1931), pp. 100–103; David Kimble, *A Political History of Ghana: The Rise of Gold Coast Nationalism, 1850–1928* (Oxford: Clarendon Press, 1963), p. 163; Yates, "History," pp. 84–89.

89 *A.M.E.Z. Star of Zion*, 15 July 1897, p. 1.

90 Ibid.; also 27 January 1898, p. 1.

91 Yates, "History," p. 89; Rogerson, *Historical*, pp. 23, 26; *A.M.E.Z. Star of Zion*, 16 September 1897, p. 1.

92 *A.M.E.Z. Star of Zion*, 21 October 1897, p. 1; Yates, "History," p. 92.

93 Yates, "History," pp. 89–92; Alleyne, *Gold Coast*, pp. 101–103, 115. See chapter 8 on African students in the United States.

94 *The Gold Coast Aborigines*, 26 November 1898, quoted in Kimble, *Political History*, p. 163. See also Yates, "History," pp. 109–10; and Baeta, *Christianity in Tropical Africa*, p. 260.

95 *The Gold Coast Aborigines*, 25 February 1899, quoted in Kimble, *Political History*, p. 163. See also Rosalynde Ainslie, *The Press in Africa* (London: Victor Gollancz, 1966), p. 24.

96 Yates, "History," p. 110; Alleyne, *Gold Coast*, p. 114.

97 Charles Henry Phillips, *The History of the Colored Methodist Episcopal Church in America* (Jackson, Tenn.: Publishing House of the C.M.E. Church, 1898), pp. 26–42.

98 Ibid., pp. 89–90.

99 Ibid., p. 247. According to Rev. John M. Exum, editor of the *C.M.E. Christian Index*, the C.M.E. Church did not send any missionaries to Africa until the twentieth century (when Dr. John Wesley Gilbert, of Paine College in Augusta, Georgia, was sent): personal communication to the author, 30 May 1973. See also Donald F. Roth, "Grace Not Race: Southern Negro Church Leaders, Black Identity, and Missions to West Africa, 1865–1919" (Ph.D. diss., University of Texas at Austin, 1975), pp. 342–45.

Chapter 4
Mission Organization in Independent Afro-American Baptist Churches

1 Melville Herskovits, *The Myth of the Negro Past* (Boston: Beacon Press, 1958). For a discussion of this hypothesis, see Hart M. Nelson et al., eds., *The Black Church in America* (New York: Basic Books, 1971); Eugene Genovese, *Roll, Jordon, Roll: The World the Slaves Made*

(New York: Vintage, 1974), pp. 232—35; and Donald Mathews, *Religion in the Old South* (Chicago: University of Chicago Press, 1977), pp. 192—94.

2 Richard Bardolph, *The Negro Vanguard* (New York: Rinehart and Co., 1959), p. 75; Winthrop S. Hudson, *Religion in America*, 2nd ed. (New York: Scribner's 1973), pp. 223—25; *Liberia* 4 (February 1894): 54.

3 Lewis G. Jordan, *Up the Ladder in Foreign Missions* (Nashville: National Baptist Publications Board, 1901 and 1903), pp. 15—16; Owen D. Pelt and Ralph Lee Smith, *The Story of the National Baptists* (New York: Vantage Press, 1960), pp. 69—70.

4 Thomas L. Johnson, *Africa for Christ, or Twenty-Eight Years a Slave*, 6th ed. (London: Alexander and Shepheard, 1892), pp. 68—69.

5 Ibid., p. 68.

6 Ibid., p. 70.

7 Ibid., p. 71.

8 Ibid., p. 80.

9 Ibid., p. 83; *Missionary Review of the World* 10 (1887): 337.

10 *Indianapolis Freeman*, 27 July 1889, pp. 2, 5.

11 Edward M. Brawley, ed., *The Negro Baptist Pulpit* (Philadelphia: American Baptist Publishing Society, 1890), p. 269; National Baptist Convention *Mission Herald* 73 (1970): 9; William J. Simmons, *Men of Mark* (1887; New York: Arno Press, 1968), p. 675—76; Jordan, *Up the Ladder*, p. 122.

12 Southern Baptist Convention, *Foreign Mission Journal*, November 1878, p. 2; November 1879, p. 4; May 1880, p. 2. Brawley, *Negro Baptist*, p. 268; Jordan, *Up the Ladder*, p. 18; Baker J. Cauther, *Advance: A History of Southern Baptist Foreign Missions* (Nashville: Broadman Press, 1970), pp. 143—44; *Proceedings of the Southern Baptist Convention*, 1882, p. 69; C. C. Adams, *Negro Baptists and Foreign Missions* (Philadelphia: Foreign Mission Board of the National Baptist Convention, 1944), p. 22.

13 Brawley, *Negro Baptist*, p. 268.

14 *Proceedings of the Southern Baptist Convention*, 1875, p. 36.

15 John J. Coles, *Africa in Brief* (New York: Freeman Steam Printing Establishment, 1886), pp. 13—14; Lewis G. Jordan, *Negro Baptist History, U.S.A.* (Nashville: Sunday School Publishing Board, 1930), pp. 193, 206, 228—29; Adams, *Negro Baptists*, pp. 32—34; Pelt, *Story*, pp. 85—86; Jordan, *Up the Ladder*, pp. 88—93, 121.

16 Jordan, *Up the Ladder*, p. 95; Coles, *Africa*, p. 15.

17 W. W. Colley letter [March 1886], American Colonization Society Papers, Library of Congress Manuscript Department, reel 167, item 17; *Missionary Review of the World* 9 (1886): 304; *Indianapolis Freeman*, 5 October 1889, p. 1.

18 *Indianapolis Freeman*, 27 April 1889, p. 5.

19 Colley letter [March 1886], American Colonization Society Papers.

20 Jordan, *Up the Ladder*, pp. 18—20.

21 *Washington Bee*, 6 November 1886, p. 1; S. P. Fullinwider, *The Mind and Mood of Black America* (Homewood, Ill.: Dorsey Press, 1969), p. 32.

22 Coles, *Africa in Brief*, p. 17; Jordan, *Up the Ladder*, p. 99; Adams, *Negro Baptists*, p. 23.

23 Jordan, *Up the Ladder*, pp. 122–23; *Indianapolis Freeman*, 27 April 1889, p. 5.

24 Jordan, *Up the Ladder*, pp. 20, 97–101; Pelt, *Story*, pp. 86, 154.

25 Jordan, *Up the Ladder*, pp. 103, 110–11.

26 Ibid., p. 103; *Mission Herald* 73 (1970): 4, 7, 10.

27 Jordan, *Up the Ladder*, p. 124.

28 Ibid., p. 125.

29 *Voice of Missions*, 1 July 1898, p. 3.

30 Ibid.

31 *Richmond Planet*, 5 March 1898, p. 1.

32 The two South African Baptist ministers were John Tule and E. B. P. Koti. Jordan, *Up the Ladder*, pp. 20–22, 111, 115, 124.

33 Ibid., p. 125.

34 Donald F. Roth, "Grace Not Race: Southern Negro Church Leaders, Black Identity, and Missions to West Africa, 1865–1919" (Ph.D. diss., University of Texas at Austin, 1975), chap. 3, 5, 6. Even R. A. Jackson defected to the Lott Cary group temporarily in 1898, because of inadequate financial support from the N.B.C. See *Voice of Missions*, 1 July 1898, p. 4.

35 Jordan, *Up the Ladder*, p. 3.

36 Ibid., pp. 21–22, 111, 115.

37 Ibid., pp. 24, 128; *Richmond Planet*, 4 November 1899, p. 1.

38 Charles Morris speech, quoted in *Ecumenical Missionary Conference Report* (New York: American Tract Society, 1900), p. 469.

39 *Voice of Missions*, 1 December 1899, p. 2.

40 Quoted in Jordan, *Up the Ladder*, p. 204.

41 Hollis Lynch, *Edward Wilmot Blyden: Pan-Negro Patriot, 1832–1912* (London: Oxford University Press, 1967), pp. 222–38; E. A. Ayandele, *The Missionary Impact on Modern Nigeria, 1842–1914* (London: Longmans, 1966), pp. 217–81; James Coleman, *Nigeria: Background to Nationalism* (Berkeley: University of California Press, 1958), pp. 176–77.

42 E. A. Ayandele, *Holy Johnson: Pioneer of African Nationalism, 1836–1917* (London: Frank Cass, 1970), pp. 203, 288; Ayandele, *Missionary Impact*, pp. 186, 252.

43 C. G. Baeta, ed., *Christianity in Tropical Africa* (London: International African Institute, 1968), p. 238; Ayandele, *Missionary Impact*, pp. 254–55; Lynch, *Edward Wilmot Blyden*, pp. 222, 238; *Mission Herald* 73 (1970): 11.

44 *Missionary Review of the World* 23 (1900): 305.

45 Jordan, *Up the Ladder*, p. 103. A good summary of the entire National

Baptist mission effort is contained in the Nineteenth Anniversary Issue of the church's *Mission Herald* (vol. 73, 1970).

Chapter 5
Motivation of Black American
Missionaries in Africa

1 See appendices D—F. There is some overlap of numbers in these statistics, because some individuals represented different church bodies, or served in different areas, at various periods of their time in Africa.

2 Wilson J. Moses, "Civilizing Missionary: A Study of Alexander Crummell," *Journal of Negro History* 60 (April 1975): 233.

3 William H. Sheppard, *Pioneers in Congo* (Louisville, Ky.: Pentecostal Publishing Co. 1917), p. 11; Stanley Shaloff, *Reform in Leopold's Congo* (Richmond, VA: John Knox Press, 1970), p. 16; *Southern Workman* 29 (April 1900): 218.

4 Benjamin Ousley to A.B.C.F.M., 24 September 1883 (letter 171), A.B.C.F.M. Papers, collection 6, vol. 37, no. 466.

5 Alfred Lee Ridgel, *Africa and African Methodism* (Atlanta: Franklin Publishing Co., 1896), pp. 112—13.

6 Joseph C. Sherrill to Joseph Hartzell, 3 December 1898, Methodist Missionary Papers.

7 Ibid.; Moses, "Civilizing Missionary," p. 233; Rackham Holt, *Mary McLeod Bethune: A Biography* (Garden City: Doubleday, 1964), p. 31; Amanda Smith, *An Autobiography* (Chicago: Meyer, 1893), p. 17; Ridgel, *Africa*, pp. 112—13. The author is indebted to Professor Josephus Coan of Atlanta University Interdenominational Theological Center for biographical data on Alfred Ridgel.

8 See appendices D—F for colleges attended. For more specific biographical data from a person-by-person and mission-by-mission approach, see Walter L. Williams, "Black American Attitudes toward Africa: The Missionary Movement 1877—1900" (Ph.D. diss., University of North Carolina at Chapel Hill, 1974).

9 Ousley letter, 24 September 1883 (letter 171), A.B.C.F.M. Papers, collection 6, vol. 37, no. 466.

10 Bailey letter, 2 November 1883 (letter 181), ibid.

11 Fisk Professor Helen C. Freesfan letter, 3 November 1883 (letter 177), ibid.

12 Professor J. M. Cox to Joseph Hartzell, 26 July 1898, Methodist Missionary Papers.

13 Alexander Priestley Camphor, *Missionary Story Sketches* (Cincinnati: Jennings and Graham, 1909), pp. 7—9, 21—22; Clement Richardson, ed., *National Cyclopedia of the Colored Race* (Montgomery, Ala.: National Publishing Co., 1919), p. 238; Willis J. King, "History of the

Methodist Church Mission in Liberia," typescript in United Methodist Church Commission on Archives and History (Lake Junaluska, N.C.: Methodist Missions in Africa, ca. 1945), p. 58; Donald F. Roth, "Grace Not Race: Southern Negro Church Leaders, Black Identity, and Missions to West Africa, 1865—1919" (Ph.D. diss., University of Texas at Austin, 1975), pp. 305—9.

14 William H. Sheppard, *William H. Sheppard, Pioneer Missionary to the Congo* (Nashville: Presbyterian Church Educational Department, ca. 1928), pp. 3—7; Sheppard, *Pioneers*, p. 13; *Southern Workman* 12 (January 1883): 9; Kenneth J. King, *Pan-Africanism and Education* (Oxford: Oxford University Press, 1971), p. 3; Roth, "Grace Not Race," pp. 250—53, 259.

15 *Voice of Missions*, October 1894, p. 4; H. B. Parks, *Africa, the Problem of the New Century* (New York: Mission Department of the A.M.E. Church, 1899), p. 55; Lewellyn L. Berry, *A Century of Missions of the African Methodist Episcopal Church, 1840—1940* (New York: Gutenberg Printing Co., 1942), pp. 70, 138—39.

16 John B. Rendall, *Historical Sketch of Lincoln University* (Philadelphia: M. C. Wood Printing Co., 1904), pp. 9—10; Horace Mann Bond, "God Glorified by Africa," typescript in Lincoln University (Pa.) Archives 1955, p. 50.

17 Camphor, *Missionary*, pp. 21—22; *Official Journal of the Liberia Annual Conference, M.E. Church* (2—7 February 1898), p. 68.

18 F. M. Allen to Joseph Hartzell, letter, ca. December 1898, Methodist Missionary Papers.

19 F. M. Allen to Joseph Hartzell, 4 June 1898, 23 June 1898, 7 July 1898, Methodist Missionary Papers.

20 Joseph A. Davis to Joseph Hartzell, 8 November 1898, and J. C. Sherrill to Hartzell, 28 October 1898 and 3 December 1898, Methodist Missionary Papers.

21 Samuel Miller to General Samuel Armstrong, 11 January 1880 (letter 98), A.B.C.F.M. Papers, collection 6, vol. 30, no. 344; J. H. Presley, "Missionaries' Farewell," quoted in John J. Coles, *Africa in Brief* (New York: Freeman Steam Printing Establishment, 1886), p. xiii.

22 *Voice of Missions*, January 1895, p. 1. See also Ridgel, *Africa*.

23 Nancy Jones letter, 20 March 1887 (letter 610), and 19 July 1887 (letter 612), A.B.C.F.M. Papers, collection 6, vol. 35, no. 464. See also *Indianapolis Freeman*, 5 February 1898, p. 2.

24 Samuel Miller to J. O. Means, 24 April 1880 (letter 100), A.B.C.F.M. Papers, collection 6, vol. 30, no. 344.

25 Camphor, *Missionary*, pp. 86—87.

26 Holt, *Mary McLeod Bethune*, p. 31. In 1895 she applied to the southern board to be assigned as an African missionary, but the board replied that there were no openings for Negro missionaries (p. 45). This was, ironically, at the same time that William Sheppard was trying to attract more missionaries. See Andrew E. Murray, *Presbyterians and the Negro:*

A History (Philadelphia: Presbyterian Historical Society, 1966), p. 78. Mrs. Bethune went on to become a leading civil rights activist in twentieth-century America, with the same strong sense of social duty that she felt for mission work.

27 Smith, *Autobiography*, pp. 215–16.

28 Ibid., pp. 219, 283–85.

29 Joseph Sherrill to Joseph Hartzell, 3 December 1898 and 28 October 1898, Methodist Missionary Papers.

30 Walter L. Yates, "The History of the African Methodist Episcopal Zion Church in West Africa, Liberia and Gold Coast (Ghana), 1880–1900" (M.A. thesis, Hartford Seminary, 1963), pp. 49–56.

31 William J. Simmons, *Men of Mark* (1887; New York: Arno Press, 1968), pp. 675–76.

32 Smith, *Autobiography*, pp. 17–25, 219.

33 Ibid., pp. 453, 446.

34 Sheppard, *Pioneers*, p. 11; *Southern Workman* 29 (April 1900): 218; Shaloff, *Reform*, p. 16.

35 Shaloff, *Reform*, pp. 18–20; Roth, "Grace Not Race," pp. 7, 260; *Missionary Review of the World* 8 (1895): 327.

36 Photograph Collection, Sheppard Papers.

37 Shaloff, *Reform*, p. 49.

38 Abraham Maslow, "A Theory of Metamotivation," *Journal of Humanistic Psychology* 7 (1967): 93–127; Abraham Maslow, *Toward a Psychology of Being* (Princeton: Van Nostrand, 1968). For references to this and following psychological theories, I wish to express appreciation to several psychologists at the University of Cincinnati, especially Amuzie Chimezie and William Seeman.

39 Calvin S. Hall and Gardner Lindzey, *Theories of Personality* (New York: John Wiley and Sons, 1970), p. 463; Samuel H. Osipow, *Theories of Career Development* (Englewood Cliffs: Prentice-Hall, 1973), pp. 215–20.

40 Gordon Allport, P. E. Vernon, and Gardner Lindzey, in *The Study of Values* (Boston: Houghton-Mifflin, 1960), developed the test, which was applied to white United Methodist missionary candidates between 1956 and 1976 by William Seeman, Department of Psychology, University of Cincinnati. I wish to thank Professor Seeman for generously sharing the results of this unpublished research. While the test was administered to a group which was racially different and of a different time period, its results correlate closely with historical evidence about the nineteenth-century Afro-American missionaries.

41 Hall and Lindzey, *Theories*, pp. 32–35.

42 Osipow, *Theories*, p. 220; Kieth Barton and G. M. Vaughan, "Church Membership and personality: A Longitudinal Study," *Social Behavior and Personality* 4 (January 1976): 11–15.

43 William T. Alexander, *History of the Colored Race in America* (Kansas City, Mo.: Palmetto Publishing Co., 1888), pp. 530–31.

44 Coles, *Africa in Brief*, p. 89.

45 *Voice of Missions*, February 1894, p. 2.

46 *Missionary*, November 1895, p. 491; *Annual Report*, 1896, pp. 12–13.

47 Moses, "Civilizing Missionary," p. 233.

48 Camphor, *Missionary*, pp. 7–9, 21–22; King, "History," p. 58; *National Cyclopedia of the Colored Race*, p. 238. On Gorham, see *Voice of Missions*, October 1894, p. 4; Parks, *Africa*, p. 55; Berry, *Century of Missions*, pp. 70, 138–39.

49 Thomas L. Johnson, *Africa for Christ, or Twenty-Eight Years a Slave*, 6th ed. (London: Alexander and Shepheard, 1892), pp. 9, 12, 31, 37.

50 Ibid., p. 31.

51 Smith, *Autobiography*, pp. 215, 217.

52 Samuel Miller to Samuel Armstrong, 11 January 1880 (letter 98), A.B.C.F.M. Papers, collection 6, vol. 30, no. 344.

53 Johnson, *Africa for Christ*, p. 69.

54 Ibid., pp. 97–98. Evidently the Africans to whom Johnson had preached in the Cameroons did not share this feeling, because they did not distinguish among the missionaries and called all of them, including Johnson, "white men" (p. 59).

55 *Voice of Mission*, October 1893, p. 2; see also February 1896, p. 3.

56 E. A. Ayandele, *Holy Johnson: Pioneer of African Nationalism, 1836–1917* (London: Frank Cass, 1970) pp. 203, 288; E. A. Ayandele, *The Missionary Impact on Modern Nigeria, 1842–1914* (London: Longmans, 1966), pp. 186, 252.

57 Quoted in Josephus R. Coan, "The Expansion of Missions of the African Methodist Episcopal Church in South Africa, 1896–1908" (Ph.D. diss., Hartford Seminary, 1961), pp. 49–51.

58 H. B. Parks letters in *Voice of Missions*, December 1896, p. 3, and September 1896, p. 1.

59 Lewis Garnett Jordan, *Up the Ladder in Foreign Missions* (Nashville: National Baptist Publications Board, 1901 and 1903), p. 204.

60 Interview by the author with William Jacob Walls, retired Senior Bishop of the A.M.E. Zion Church, Salisbury, N.C., 25 May 1971.

61 *American Citizen*, 8 January 1897, p. 2.

62 William H. Heard, *The Bright Side of African Life* (Philadelphia: A.M.E. Publishing House, 1898), pp. 87, 95.

63 George Wilson Brent, "The Ancient Glory of the Hamitic Race," *A.M.E. Church Review* 12 (October 1895): 272–74.

64 This argument is well developed in James W. Hood, *One Hundred Years of the African Methodist Episcopal Zion Church* (New York: A.M.E. Zion Book Concern, 1895), pp. 28, 37, 41, 55. See also St. Clair Drake, *The Redemption of Africa and Black Religion* (Chicago: Third World Press, 1970), pp. 49–50.

65 *A.M.E.Z. Star of Zion*, 22 October 1896, p. 1.

66 *Voice of Missions*, 1 November 1898, p. 4.

67 Ibid., February 1896, p. 3.

68 Camphor, *Missionary*, pp. 21—22; *Official Journal of the Liberia Annual Conference*, p. 68.
69 Samuel Miller to J. O. Means, 2 October 1881 (letter 238), A.B.C.F.M. Papers, collection 15.1, vol. 6.
70 Miller to Means, 30 December 1881 (letter 239), ibid.
71 Miller to Means, 24 March 1882 (letter 242), ibid.
72 *Voice of Missions*, May 1894, p. 3. See also February 1893, p. 2, and July 1895, p. 1.
73 Ibid., August 1895, p. 4.
74 Ibid., March 1896, p. 3.
75 Ibid., 1 October 1898, p. 4.
76 Alexander Camphor to A. B. Leonard, M.E. Church Board of Missions, 23 June 1899, Methodist Missionary Papers.
77 E. C. Morris address, quoted in Jordan, *Up the Ladder*, p. 204..
78 E. W. S. Hammond, quoted in J. W. E. Bowen, ed., *Africa and the American Negro: Addresses and Proceedings of the Congress on Africa* (1896; Miami: Mnemosyne Publishing, 1969), p. 207.
79 *Voice of Missions*, October 1896, p. 2.
80 Parks, *Africa*, p. 52. See also Bowen, *Africa*, p. 148.
81 Henry M. Turner, letter to the *A.M.E. Christian Recorder*, 4 June 1891, quoted in Edwin Redkey, ed., *Respect Black: The Writings and Speeches of Henry McNeal Turner* (New York: Arno Press, 1971), p. 83.
82 *Voice of Missions*, 1 September 1899, p. 4; Parks, *Africa*, pp. 43—44.

Chapter 6
Missionary Attitudes toward African Cultures

1 Philip D. Curtin, *The Image of Africa: British Ideas and Action 1780— 1850* (Madison: University of Wisconsin Press, 1964); Felix N. Okoye, *The American Image of Africa: Myth and Reality* (Buffalo, N.Y.: Black Academy Press, 1971).
2 H. B. Parks letter, *Voice of Missions*, Septmber 1896, p. 1. The Methodist missionary Amanda Smith also used the term "heathen darkness"; Amanda Smith, *An Autobiography* (Chicago: Meyer, 1893), p. 346.
3 William H. Sheppard, *Pioneers in Congo* (Louisville, Ky.: Pentecostal Publishing Co., 1917), p. 87.
4 Lewis Garnett Jordan, *Up the Ladder in Foreign Missions* (Nashville: National Baptist Publications Board, 1901 and 1903), p. 95.
5 *Voice of Missions*, January 1893, p. 1.
6 H. B. Parks, *Africa, the Problem of the New Century* (New York: Mission Department of the A.M.E. Church, 1899), p. 43.
7 Charles S. Smith, *Glimpses of Africa, West and Southwest Coast* (Nashville: A.M.E. Sunday School Union, 1895), p. 78.
8 Ibid., p. 164.

9 Alexander Crummell, *The Greatness of Christ and Other Sermons* (New York: n.p., 1882), p. 343; as quoted in Wilson J. Moses, "Civilizing Missionary: A Study of Alexander Crummell," *Journal of Negro History* 60 (April 1975): 229. For a review of the American notion of inevitable conflict between cultures, see Roy Harvey Pearce, *Savagism and Civilization* (Baltimore: Johns Hopkins Press, 1967).

10 Alexander Crummell, *Africa and America* (1891; Miami, Fla.: Mnemosyne Publishing, 1969), pp. 129–30.

11 Annual Report of the Baptist General Association of Western States and Territories, 1884, quoted in Thomas L. Johnson, *Africa for Christ, or Twenty-Eight Years a Slave*, 6th ed. (London: Alexander and Shepheard, 1892), p. 81.

12 John J. Coles, *Africa in Brief* (New York: Freeman Steam Printing Establishment, 1886), pp. 58–59.

13 *Voice of Missions*, 1 September 1899, p. 4.

14 Ibid.; Parks, *Africa*, p. 9.

15 Johnson, *Africa for Christ*, pp. 52, 66. See also *Indianapolis Freeman*, 27 July 1889, p. 5.

16 Jordan, *Up the Ladder*, pp. 88–90.

17 H. B. Parks letter, *Voice of Missions*, December 1895, p. 3; see also September 1896, p. 1.

18 Alexander Priestley Camphor, *Missionary Story Sketches* (Cincinnati: Jennings and Graham, 1909), p. 78.

19 Nathan B. Young, "A Race without an Ideal," *A.M.E. Church Review* 15 (October 1898): 606.

20 Coles, *Africa in Brief*, p. xii.

21 Camphor, *Missionary*, p. 77.

22 Samuel Ferguson to C. T. O. King, 20 November 1888, American Colonization Society Papers, Library of Congress Manuscript Department, reel 170, item 23.

23 Johnson, *Africa for Christ*, p. 60.

24 Daniel A. Payne, *History of the African Methodist Episcopal Church* (1891; Nashville: A.M.E. Sunday School Union, 1968), p. 483.

25 Turner letter, 4 December 1891, quoted in Charles S. Smith, *A History of the African Methodist Episcopal Church* (1922; New York: Johnson Reprint Corp., 1968), p. 179; and in Adelaide Cromwell Hill and Martin Kilson, eds., *Apropos of Africa: Sentiments of Negro American Leaders on Africa from the 1800s to the 1950s* (London: Frank Cass, 1969), p. 236. See also Turner letter quoted in J. W. E. Bowen, ed., *Africa and the American Negro: Addresses and Proceedings of the Congress on Africa* (1896; Miami: Mnemosyne Publishing, 1969), p. 195.

26 Carrie Lee, "The Future of Africa," *Voice of Missions*, 1 July 1899, p. 4.

27 Parks, *Africa*, p. 7.

28 Coles, *Africa in Brief*, p. 74.

29 Camphor, *Missionary*, pp. 65–66.

30 Benjamin Ousley letter, 26 July 1885 (letter 98), A.B.C.F.M. Papers, collection 15.4, vol. 12, no. 400.

31 Alfred Lee Ridgel, *Africa and African Methodism* (Atlanta: Franklin Publishing Co., 1896), p. 72; see also p. 69.

32 Crummell speech, in Bowen, ed., *Africa*, pp. 119–20.

33 Crummell, *Africa*, p. 195. See also Moses, "Civilizing Missionary," pp. 236–37.

34 M. C. B. Mason speech, in Bowen, ed., *Africa*, p. 148.

35 H. B. Parks letter, *Voice of Missions*, September 1896, p. 1.

36 Smith, *Glimpses*, pp. 113–14; see also William H. Heard, *The Missionary Fields of West Africa* (Philadelphia: A.M.E. Book Concern, n.d.); and Camphor, *Missionary*, p. 61.

37 See, for example, Henry Turner's letter from Liberia, 11 May 1895, in *Voice of Missions*, August 1895, p. 4.

38 Sheppard letter, *Southern Workman* 22 (December 1893): 184–87; Sheppard, *Pioneers*, p. 135; Sheppard letter, *Missionary*, June 1896, pp. 48–49.

39 Sheppard letter, *Southern Workman* 22 (December 1893): 182.

40 Crummell, *Africa*, pp. 131, 136.

41 Johnson, *Africa for Christ*, pp. 46–49.

42 Smith, *Autobiography*, pp. 378–79.

43 Ridgel letter, *Indianapolis Freeman*, 5 August 1893, p. 2.

44 C. W. Cole letter, *Voice of Missions*, 1 June 1897, p. 5.

45 Benjamin Ousley letter, 26 July 1885 (letter 98), A.B.C.F.M. Papers, collection 15.4, vol. 12, no. 400.

46 Coles, *Africa in Brief*, p. 93.

47 Smith, *Autobiography*, p. 390.

48 Nancy Jones letter, 26 October 1896 (letter 84), A.B.C.F.M. Papers, collection 15.4, vol. 20, no. 500; Nancy Jones letter, *Indianapolis Freeman*, 5 February 1898, p. 2; Coles, *Africa in Brief*, p. 66.

49 Smith, *Autobiography*, p. 389.

50 Benjamin Ousley letter, 26 July 1885 (letter 98), A.B.C.F.M. Papers, collection 15.4, vol. 12, no. 400.

51 Smith, *Glimpses*, pp. 95–96, 104, 110.

52 A.M.E. Rev. Floyd G. Snelson letter, from Sierra Leone, *A.M.E.Z. Star of Zion*, 16 September 1897, p. 1.

53 Nancy Jones letter, 2 April 1890 (letter 65), vol. 20, no. 500, and 29 May 1888 (letter 71), vol. 12, no. 400, A.B.C.F.M. Papers, collection 15.4.

54 Johnson, *Africa for Christ*, pp. 56, 61, 63.

55 Smith, *Autobiography*, pp. 386–89.

56 Sheppard, *Pioneers*, pp. 149, 135, 137.

57 Sheppard letter, *Southern Workman* 22 (December 1893): 184–87.

58 Johnson, *Africa for Christ*, pp. 56, 59, 61–63.

59 Smith, *Autobiography*, p. 383.

60 Camphor, *Missionary*, pp. 43–46, 56–58, 111.

61 Edward Blyden, *Christianity, Islam and the Negro Race* (1887; Edinburgh: Edinburgh University Press, 1967).
62 Coles, *Africa in Brief*, p. 38.
63 Rev. J. Allen Viney letter, *Voice of Missions*, July 1896, p. 2.
64 H. B. Parks letter, *Voice of Missions*, 15 March 1899, p. 6; Parks, *Africa*, p. 38.
65 Crummell, *Africa*, p. 319. See also Kathleen O. Wahle, "Alexander Crummell: Black Evangelist and Pan-Negro Nationalist," *Phylon* 29 (December 1968): 394.
66 Ridgel, *Africa*, pp. 66–67, 70.
67 Ibid., pp. 68–69.
68 Ibid., p. 71.
69 Edith Holden, *Blyden of Liberia* (New York: Vantage Press, 1966), pp. 5, 486. See also Edward Blyden, "America and Africa's Evangelization," *African Repository* 64 (October 1888): 109.
70 Blyden, *Christianity*; Blyden, "Mohammedans of Nigritia," *A.M.E. Church Review* 3 (January 1887): 241; *A.M.E. Church Review* 3 (April 1887): 415–17; *A.M.E. Church Review* 4 (July 1887): 534–36; Blyden letter, *African Repository* 62 (July 1887): 89; *African Repository* 62 (October 1887): 110. See also Holden, *Blyden*, pp. 121, 573; and Hollis Lynch, *Edward Wilmot Blyden: Pan-Negro Patriot, 1832–1912* (London: Oxford University Press, 1967), p. 166.
71 Blyden letter, 16 March 1887, American Colonization Society Papers, quoted in Holden, *Blyden*, p. 578.
72 Blyden, *Christiantiy*, pp. 62, 64, 186–88; Blyden speech, *Southern Workman* 12 (January 1883): 9; Blyden, "The Mohammedans of Nigritia," *A.M.E. Church Review* 3 (April 1887): 415–17; *A.M.E. Church Review* 4 (July 1887): 534–36.
73 Blyden letters, *African Repository* 63 (July 1887): 89, and 63 (October 1887): 110. See also Blyden letters, 1 October 1888 and 16 March 1887, American Colonization Society Papers, quoted in Holden, *Blyden*, pp. 121, 578, 588.
74 *Voice of Missions*, 1 September 1898, p. 2.
75 Quoted in Holden, *Blyden*, pp. 600–601.
76 Frederick letter, *Voice of Missions*, March 1893, p. 1.
77 Turner letter, 16 November 1891, *A.M.E. Church Review* 8 (April 1892): 476–77.
78 Turner letter, 9 December 1891, Sherbro River of Sierra Leone, quoted in Hill and Kilson, *Apropos*, p. 242.
79 Ibid.
80 Payne, *History*, pp. 489–90.
81 Johnson, *Africa for Christ*, pp. 56–57.
82 Philip Curtin, ed., *Africa and the West* (Madison: University of Wisconsin Press, 1972), pp. 231–36.
83 For example, ethnographers up to the 1950s reported that the Kpe people of the Cameroons, who cooperated with the missionaries of

Afro-American Baptist Thomas Johnson's group, still followed their traditional religion. Edwin Ardener, *Coastal Bantu of the Cameroons* (London: International African Institute, 1956), p. 108.

84 Ousley letter, 26 July 1885 (letter 98), A.B.C.F.M. Papers, collection 15.4, vol. 12, no. 400.

85 Nancy Jones letter, *Indianapolis Freeman*, 5 February 1898, p. 2; Jones letter, 22 July 1889, (letter 75), A.B.C.F.M. Papers, collection 15.4, vol. 12, no. 400.

86 William H. Heard, *The Bright Side of African Life* (Philadelphia: A.M.E. Publications House, 1898), p. 8.

87 *Missionary Visitor* 12 (22 July 1876): 6.

88 Henry Hawkins letter, *Annual Report*, 1900, p. 25.

89 Johnson, *Africa for Christ*, pp. 59, 62–63; Stanley Shaloff, *Reform in Leopold's Congo* (Richmond, Va.: John Knox Press, 1970), p. 48.

90 Jeanne Davis, et. al., "Negro Missionary Reaction to Africa," *Practical Anthropology* 11 (March-April 1964): 62–68.

91 Turner letter, *A.M.E. Church Review* 8 (April 1892): 446–98.

92 Quoted in Edwin Redkey, *Black Exodus: Black Nationalist and Back-to-Africa Movements, 1890–1910* (New Haven: Yale University Press, 1969), p. 44.

93 Quoted in Smith, *History*, p. 179; and in Hill and Kilson, eds., *Apropos*, p. 236.

94 Johnson, *Africa for Christ*, pp. 49–51, 63–64.

95 Smith, *Autobiography*, pp. 399, 451.

96 Jones letter, *Indianapolis Freeman*, 5 February 1898, p. 2.

97 Crummell, *Africa*, pp. 316–17.

98 Ibid., pp. 182–83 and 193–94.

99 Alexander Crummell, "The Destiny of the Negro," *African Repository* 63 (October 1887): 103.

100 For example, see Parks, *Africa*, p. 38, on the Zulu; Smith, *Glimpses*, p. 203, on the Mpongwe of Gabon; and *A.M.E.Z. Star of Zion*, 2 September 1897, p. 3, on the Hausa.

101 Johnson, *Africa for Christ*, pp. 56, 61.

102 Turner letter, *A.M.E. Church Review* 8 (April 1892): 476.

103 Henry Turner Papers, manuscript division, Moorland Collection, Howard University Library, Washington, D.C., folder 1. Typescript reference to Turner's 1891 trip to West Africa.

104 W. H. Sheppard letter, 17 May 1890, printed in *Missionary* (September 1890): 352–55; Sheppard, *Pioneers*, pp. 29–30.

105 W. H. Sheppard journal, December 1890–February 1891, printed in *Missionary*, July 1891, pp. 254–59.

106 Ibid.; Sheppard letter, 5 January 1892, Sheppard Papers.

107 Photograph collection, Sheppard Papers.

108 Sheppard, *Pioneers*, pp. 59–61.

109 Ibid., pp. 101, 96–97, 123.

110 Ibid., pp. 76–77.

111 Ibid., pp. 93–94, 134.
112 Ibid., pp. 37–38.
113 Ibid., pp. 127–29, 140; *Missionary Review of the World* 8 (1895): 330.
114 Sheppard, *Pioneers*, p. 143.
115 *Southern Workman* 22 (December 1893): 184–87.

Chapter 7
Missionary Attitudes toward
Emigration and Imperialism

1 Philip Staudenraus, *The African Colonization Movement, 1816–1865*
   (New York: Columbia University Press, 1961); Willis Boyd, "Negro
   Colonization in the National Crisis" (Ph.D. diss., University of California
   at Los Angeles, 1953); and Floyd Miller, *The Search for a Black
   Nationality: Black Emigration and Colonization, 1787–1863* (Urbana:
   University of Illinois Press, 1975).
2 Cyril Griffith, *The African Dream: Martin R. Delany and the Emergence
   of Pan-African Thought* (University Park: Pennsylvania State University
   Press, 1975); Howard Bell, ed., *Search for a Place: Black Separatism
   and Africa* (Ann Arbor: University of Michigan Press, 1969); Richard
   MacMaster, "Henry Highland Garnet and the African Civilization
   Society," *Journal of Presbyterian History* 48 (Summer 1970): 95–112;
   Joel Schor, *Henry Highland Garnet: A Voice of Black Radicalism in
   the Nineteenth Century* (Westport: Greenwood Press, 1977); and St.
   Clair Drake, "Negro Americans and the Africa Interest," in *The American Negro Reference Book*, ed. John P. Davis (Englewood Cliffs, N.J.:
   Prentice-Hall, 1966), p. 675.
3 Benjamin Quarles, *The Negro in the Civil War* (Boston: Little Brown,
   1969), pp. 145–57.
4 Edwin Redkey, *Black Exodus: Black Nationalist and Back-to-Africa
   Movements, 1890–1910* (New Haven: Yale University Press, 1969),
   pp. 22, 41.
5 Hollis R. Lynch, *Edward Wilmot Blyden: Pan-Negro Patriot, 1832–
   1912* (London: Oxford University Press, 1967), p. 107.
6 Redkey, *Black Exodus*, p. x; August Meier and Elliott M. Rudwick,
   From Plantation to Ghetto (New York: Hill and Wang, 1966), p. 202.
7 Walter L. Williams, "Black Journalism's Opinions about Africa during
   the Late Nineteenth Century," *Phylon* 34 (September 1973): 224–35;
   and Walter L. Williams, "Black American Attitudes toward Africa,
   1877–1900," *Pan-African Journal* 4 (Spring 1971): 173–94.
8 George Tindall, *South Carolina Negroes, 1877–1900* (Baton Rouge:
   Louisiana State University Press, 1966), pp. 153–61.
9 Redkey, *Black Exodus*, p. 74.
10 Lynch, *Edward Wilmot Blyden*, pp. 109–10; Frenise Logan, *The Negro*

in North Carolina, 1876—1894 (Chapel Hill: University of North Carolina Press, 1964), p. 121.

11 Redkey, *Black Exodus*, pp. 7, 92.

12 Tindall, *South Carolina Negroes*, pp. 157, 160. See also Henry Turner Papers, manuscripts division, Howard University Library, Washington, D.C., folder 1.

13 C. W. Johnson letter, *Liberia* 10 (February 1897): 56—57.

14 *African Repository* 64 (July 1888): 96, 99.

15 J. G. Robinson, "Africa, and the Educated and Wealthy Negroes of America," *A.M.E. Church Review* 10 (July 1893): 161, 163; see also Rev. R. L. Coffey letter, *Voice of Missions*, February 1896, p. 1.

16 Rev. C. H. Thompson letter, *African Repository* 61 (October 1885): 117—19.

17 Alexander Crummell, *Africa and America* (1891; Miami, Fla.: Mnemosyne Publishers, 1969), p. 14.

18 Ibid., pp. 162—63.

19 Ibid., p. 150.

20 Ibid., pp. 184—85.

21 Ibid., p. 158.

22 Ibid., p. 195.

23 Ibid., p. 427. Crummell expressed similar sentiments in his sermons on Africa; see for example a [post-1873] sermon in the Alexander Crummell Papers, Schomberg Collection of the New York Public Library, ms. c. 17, vol. A. no. 729.

24 Turner letters, *A.M.E. Church Review* 8 (April 1892): 446—98.

25 Redkey, *Black Exodus*, p. 7 ff.

26 *A.M.E. Christian Recorder*, 4 January 1883, quoted in Edward Blyden, *Christianity, Islam and the Negro Race* (1887; Edinburgh: Edinburgh University Press, 1967), p. 107.

27 *Voice of Missions*, 1 November 1899, p. 6.

28 Turner interview, *North Carolina Republican* (Waldon, N.C.), 22 May 1884, p. 2.

29 *Voice of Missions*, 1 June 1899, p. 2.

30 *Indianapolis Freeman*, 2 April 1892, p. 1.

31 Redkey, *Black Exodus*, pp. 70—71.

32 *Indianapolis Freeman*, 25 November 1893, pp. 2, 3, 5, 6. Those who expressed a lack of opposition to emigration included A.M.E. Zion Bishop Alexander Walters, A.M.E. Rev. T. W. Henderson, Ida B. Wells, and P. B. S. Pinchback.

33 R. L. Coffey letter, *Voice of Missions*, February 1896, p. 1.

34 Ibid., June 1894, p. 1.

35 William H. Heard, *The Bright Side of African Life* (Philadelphia: A.M.E. Publications House, 1898), p. 8.

36 Andrew Cartwright letters, American Colonization Society Papers, Library of Congress Manuscript Department, reel 165, items 36, 42, and reel 166, items 21, 41, 66.

37 Thomas Johnson, *Africa for Christ, or Twenty-Eight Years a Slave*, 6th ed. (London: Alexander and Shepheard, 1892), pp. 96—97.

38 John J. Coles, *Africa in Brief* (New York: Freeman Steam Printing Establishment, 1886), p. 9. Although he was less consistent on emigration by the end of the century, Edward Blyden shared such views: he wrote that Afro-American colonists were "indispensable" to the success of missions, and that the two movements should be intimately connected. See Edith Holden, *Blyden of Liberia* (New York: Vantage Press, 1966), p. 704.

39 Charles S. Morris speech to the Interdenominational Association of Colored Clergymen, Boston, January 1899, quoted in Herbert Aptheker, ed., *A Documentary History of the Negro People in the United States* (New York: Citadel Press, 1951), pp. 812—14; see also Jordan, *Up the Ladder in Foreign Missions* (Nashville: National Baptist Publications Board, 1901 and 1903), pp. 22—24.

40 Charles S. Morris letters, *Voice of Missions*, 1 November 1899, p. 6, and 1 December 1899, p. 2; see also Charles Morris speech quoted in *Ecumenical Missionary Conference Report* (New York: American Tract Society, 1900), p. 471.

41 Daniel Warner letter, 4 December 1879, quoted in Jane Martin, "The Dual Legacy: Government Authority and Mission Influence among the Glebo of Eastern Liberia, 1834—1910" (Ph.D. diss., Boston University, 1968), p. 291.

42 Anderson letter, 15 February 1886, quoted in Martin, "The Dual Legacy," p. 417.

43 Martin, "The Dual Legacy," chaps. 2, 7, 8, and esp. pp. 290—99; Clarence Clendennen et al., *Americans in Africa, 1865—1900* (Stanford: Stanford University Press, 1966) pp. 32—38.

44 J. Gus Liebenow, *Liberia: The Evolution of Privilege* (Ithaca, N.Y.: Cornell University Press, 1969), pp. 1—15, 22—23; Martin, "Dual Legacy."

45 *Indianapolis Freeman*, 5 August 1893, p. 2.

46 See Amanda Smith, *An Autobiography* (Chicago: Meyer, 1893), pp. 347, 451—52, 458—64; Nancy Jones letter, *Indianapolis Freeman* 5 February 1898, p. 2; Charles S. Smith, *Glimpses of Africa, West and Southwest Coast* (Nashville: A.M.E. Sunday School Union, 1895), pp. 131, 135, 143.

47 Lynch, *Edward Wilmot Blyden*, pp. 110, 121—22, 133, 144, 165—66; Blyden, *Christianity*, p. 204; Blyden letter, *A.M.E. Church Review* 16 (January 1900): 309—15; Blyden letter to Francis Grimké, 4 November 1889, in Carter Woodson, ed., *The Works of Francis Grimké* (Washington, D.C.: Associated Publishers, 1942), 4:15—17.

48 *Voice of Missions*, July 1896, p. 2; 15 March 1899, p. 2; July 1898, p. 4. H. B. Parks, *Africa, the Problem of the New Century* (New York: Mission Department of the A.M.E. Church, 1899), pp. 20—21. Smith *Glimpses*, pp. 50, 54, 89—91, 102, 285. Thomas McCants Stewart,

Liberia: The Americo-African Republic (New York: E. O. Jenkins Sons, 1886), p. 10.

49 Crummell, *Africa*, pp. 214, 311, 314—15; Kathleen Wahle, "Alexander Crummell: Black Evangelist and Pan-Negro Nationalist," *Phylon* 29 (December 1968): 393—94; Crummell Papers, ms. c. 17, vol. A, and ms. c. 37, vol. C.

50 Crummell, *Africa*, pp. 320—21.

51 Sylvia Jacobs, in *The African Nexus: Black American Perspectives on the European Partitioning of Africa, 1870—1920* (Westport, Conn.: Greenwood Press, 1981), points out that it was not until after 1900 that most black American spokespeople began opposing imperialism.

52 Coles, *Africa in Brief*, pp. 7—8, 74.

53 Alfred Lee Ridgel, *Africa and African Methodism* (Atlanta: Franklin Publishing Co., 1896), pp. 38, 41, 52, 57.

54 Wilfred Cartey and Martin Kilson, eds., *The African Reader: Colonial Africa* (New York: Random House, 1970), pp. 62—69.

55 *Voice of Missions*, 1 October 1898, p. 4.

56 Ibid., March 1899, p. 5.

57 Robert I. Rotberg and Ali A. Mazrui, eds., *Protest and Power in Black Africa* (New York: Oxford University Press, 1970), p. 175.

58 *Voice of Missions*, January 1895, p. 1.

59 Ibid., 1 December 1899, p. 2.

60 *Missionary Visitor* 11 (8 April 1876), p. 74; United Brethren Church, *Annual Report*, 1879, p. 22.

61 Nancy Jones letter, *Indianapolis Freeman*, 5 February 1898, p. 2.

62 Parks, *Africa*, p. 30.

63 Lynch, *Edward Wilmot Blyden*, pp. 66, 191—200, 209, 231, 237; Blyden, *Christianity*, pp. 240, 348; Edward Blyden, "Mohammedans of Nigritia," *A.M.E. Church Review* 3 (January 1887): 241; Edward Blyden, "A Chapter in the History of Liberia," *A.M.E. Church Review* 9 (July 1892): 68—70; Blyden letter in J. W. E. Bowen, ed., *Africa and the American Negro: Addresses and Proceedings of the Congress on Africa* (1896; Miami: Mnemosyne Publishing, 1969), p. 16.

64 Samuel Miller letter, 24 June 1884 (letter 261), A.B.C.F.M. Papers, collection 15.1, vol. 6.

65 Benjamin Ousley letters, 22 December 1884 (letter 88), 26 July 1885 (letter 98), and 25 October 1885 (letter 103), A.B.C.F.M. Papers, collection 15.4, vol. 12, no. 400.

66 Nancy Jones letter, 6 February 1890 (letter 64), A.B.C.F.M. Papers, collection 15.4, vol. 20, no. 500; *Indianapolis Freeman*, 5 February 1898, p. 2.

67 Mrs. C. C. Pettey letter, *A.M.E.Z. Church Quarterly* 7 (April 1897): 30.

68 J. M. Henderson letter, *Voice of Missions*, 1 October 1898, p. 4.

69 E. W. S. Hammond speech, quoted in Bowen, ed., *Africa*, p. 205.

70 *Voice of Missions*, May 1896, p. 3.

71 Turner letter, *Voice of Missions*, April 1893, p. 2; June 1893, p. 3;

October 1894, p. 2.

72 *Voice of Missions*, July 1895, p. 1.

73 Turner letter, *A.M.E. Church Review* 8 (April 1892): 472.

74 *Voice of Missions*, June 1898, p. 6; and July 1898, p. 2.

75 R. A. Jackson letter, *Voice of Missions*, 1 April 1899, p. 4.

76 Henry Hawkins letter, *Annual Report*, 1900, p. 21; see also Ruth Slade, *English-Speaking Missions in the Congo Independent State, 1878-1908* (Brussels: Académie Royal des Sciences d'Outre Mer, 1959), pp. 240-42; and Stanley Shaloff, *Reform in Leopold's Congo* (Richmond, Va.: John Knox Press, 1970).

77 *Southern Workman* 29 (April 1900): 220-21; *Missionary Review of the World* 13 (1900): 340-44; Slade, *English-Speaking Missions*, pp. 244, 254; Shaloff, *Reform*; Charles Groves, *The Planting of Christianity in Africa*, (London: Lutterworth Press, 1948-58), 3:268; William H. Sheppard, *Pioneers in Congo* (Louisville, Ky.: Pentecostal Publishing Co., 1917).

78 William Sheppard and William Morrison letter, *Missionary*, February 1900.

79 Slade, *English-Speaking Missions*, pp. 254, 306.

80 *Southern Workman* 29 (April 1900): 221.

81 Slade, *English-Speaking Missions*, pp. 359, 367-72; Sheppard, *Pioneers*.

82 Benjamin Arnett, "Africa and the Descendants of Africa," *A.M.E. Church Review* 11 (October 1894): 232-33, 235.

Chapter 8
Mission Relations with Westernized Africans
and African Students in the United States

1 Valuable essays on westernized Africans are contained in Philip Curtin, ed., *Africa and the West* (Madison: University of Wisconsin Press, 1972), pp. 99-138, 231-44. This chapter is not meant to suggest that black Americans originated nationalism among Africans. In most cases Afro-American contacts merely accentuated tendencies that were already present among the educated African elite. In all the areas where Afro-American churches had an impact—Sierra Leone, Gold Coast, Nigeria, and South Africa—the African separatist churches had already established their independence from white control *before* they affiliated with Afro-American denominations. The inter-ethnic and Pan-African vision of some black Americans, however, and indeed the very presence of black missionaries in positions of authority, showed Africans what they could aspire to if they received an education. This realization was crucial in the rise of African nationalism. See St. Clair Drake, "Negro Americans and the African Interest," in John P. Davis, ed., *The American Negro Reference Book* (Englewood Cliffs, N.J.: Prentice

Hall, 1966), p. 668; George Shepperson and Thomas Price, *Independent African* (Edinburgh: Edinburgh University Press, 1958), p. 73; C. G. Baeta, ed., *Christianity in Tropical Africa* (London: International African Institute, 1968), p. 251; G. C. Oosthuizen, *Post-Christianity in Africa* (Grand Rapids, Mich.: William B. Eardmans Publishing Co., 1968), p. 80.

2 Charles Morris letters, *Voice of Missions*, 1 December 1899, p. 2; and 1 November 1899, p. 6.

3 Turner letter, *A.M.E. Church Review* 8 (April 1892): 455; see also pp. 476, 482, 484–85.

4 Ridgel letters, *Indianapolis Freeman*, 28 July 1894, p. 1; and 1 September 1894, p. 6.

5 Samuel Ferguson letters, 10 August 1887, 6 December 1887, and 20 November 1888, American Colonization Society Papers, Library of Congress Manuscript Department, reel 168, items, 153, 190 and reel 170, item 23.

6 Ferguson letters, 27 December 1886 and 6 December 1887, ibid., reel 167, item 147, and reel 168, item 190.

7 George F. Bragg, *History of the Afro-American Group of the Episcopal Church* (Baltimore: Church Advocate Press, 1922), p. 214.

8 Thomas Johnson, *Africa for Christ, or Twenty-Eight Years a Slave*, 6th ed. (London: Alexander and Shepheard, 1892), p. 46; see also pp. 39–42, 97.

9 Charles Morris letters, *Voice of Missions*, 1 November 1899, p. 6; and *Richmond Planet*, 2 December 1899, p. 1.

10 D. B. Vincent letter, *Voice of Missions*, July 1894, p. 3.

11 *Gold Coast Aborigines*, 10 November 1898, p. 3; and 26 November 1898, p. 1; quoted in Imanuel Geiss, *The Pan-African Movement: A History of Pan-Africanism in America, Europe and Africa* (New York: Africana Publishing Co., 1974), p. 148.

12 William Grant, "Negro Creed," quoted in Hollis R. Lynch, *Edward Wilmot Blyden: Pan-Negro Patriot, 1832–1912* (London: Oxford University Press, 1967), p. 213.

13 E. A. Ayandele, *Holy Johnson: Pioneer of African Nationalism, 1836–1917* (London: Frank Cass, 1970), pp. 43–45, 60, 286–89. This biography proves that Johnson's ideology was formulated entirely from West African thought, influenced by Christianity brought by early English missionaries. While his ideas did not grow out of black American thought, the similarities between the two groups' attitudes are striking.

14 See chapter 3.

15 James Dwane letter, *Voice of Missions*, 1 December 1897, p. 1; H. B. Parks, *Africa, the Problem of the New Century* (New York: Mission Department of the A.M.E. Church, 1899), p. 26.

16 J. G. Xaba letter, *Voice of Missions*, December 1895, p. 3.

17 *Voice of Missions*, 1 July 1899, p. 2; 1 December 1899, p. 1.

18 *A.M.E. Church Review* 15 (April 1899): 810.

1891, p. 2.

47 *Indianapolis Freeman*, 8 April 1893, p. 4; and 3 June 1893, p. 5.

48 H. M. Turner editorial, *Voice of Missions*, February 1897, p. 2.

49 T. A. Johns letters, *Washington Bee*, 17 March 1888, p. 1; 10 November 1888, p. 1, through 15 December 1888, p. 1.

50 George Barh-Fofoe Peabody, *Barh-Fofoe: A Bassa Boy* (Lancaster, Pa.: New Era Printing House, 1891), p. 68.

51 E. Mayfield Boyle letter, *Voice of Missions*, 1 June 1897, p. 1.

52 George Peabody to Reverend Edward Webb, 7 July 1891, Webb Papers, Lincoln University (Pa.) Archives.

53 Yates, "History," pp. 106–8.

54 Johnson, *Africa for Christ*, pp. 43–45.

55 *Indianapolis Freeman*, 29 October 1892, p. 2; see also 24 June 1893, p. 1.

56 Shepperson and Price, *Independent African*, p. 93; Jordan, *Up the Ladder*, p. 132.

57 Anne Spencer, a black American student at Virginia Theological Seminary in the late 1890s: personal communication quoted in Shepperson and Price, *Independent African*, pp. 114–15.

58 Bond, "God Glorified." This pattern, of some culture conflict but generally good relations, seems to hold for twentieth-century African students in the United States; see Ralston, "Second Middle Passage."

59 Coan, "Expansion of Missions," pp. 99–100; Jordan, *A.M.E.* pp. 59–67; Berry, *Century of Missions*, pp. 158, 186, 189.

60 *Voice of Missions*, 1 February 1895, p. 4; July 1898, p. 2.

61 Carrie Belle Lee, "The Future of Africa," *Voice of Missions*, 1 July 1899, p. 4.

62 Yates, "History," p. 90.

63 Smith, *Aggrey*, pp. 59–61.

64 See appendix G for specific information on each student.

65 J. W. N. Hilton essay, enclosed in Samuel S. Sevier to Reverend Edward Webb, 16 November 1885, in Webb Papers.

66 Peabody, *Barh-Fofoe*, pp. 44, 34.

67 Ibid., p. 87.

68 Ibid., p. 77.

69 George Peabody, "The Hope of Africa," *A.M.E. Church Review* (July 1890): 58–60.

70 E. Mayfield Boyle letter, *Voice of Missions*, June 1897, p. 1.

71 Ibid., November 1899, p. 1.

72 Dube, "Zululand and the Zulus," pp. 435–40.

73 Ibid., pp. 438, 441–43.

74 Bowen, ed., *Africa*, pp. 31–35. See also (pp. 113–14) the speech of Etna Holderness, a Bassa woman from Liberia who was being educated in Asheville, North Carolina.

75 Ibid., pp. 133–34; O. Faduma letter, *A.M.E. Church Review* (July

1892): 3–6.

76 Bowen, ed., *Africa*, pp. 31–35.

77 Ibid., pp. 127–28; see also pp. 125, 130, 132, 136. Faduma later authored *The Defects of the Negro Church* (Washington, D.C.: The Academy, 1904).

78 T. A. Johns letters, *Washington Bee*, 17 March 1888, p. 1; 10 November 1888, p. 1, through 15 December 1888, p. 1.

79 Jordan, *Up the Ladder*, p. 129; see also Shepperson and Price, *Independent African*, pp. 113, 118, 122.

80 Quoted in Shepperson and Price, *Independent African*, pp. 113, 118.

81 *Voice of Missions*, 1 October 1899, p. 3.

82 A.M.E.Z. Senior Bishop William Jacob Walls, quoted from a personal interview by the author, Salisbury, North Carolina, 25 May 1971. See also Smith, *Aggrey*, p. 60.

83 *Eighth General Catalogue of the Yale Divinity School*, p. 323; and Shepperson, "External Factors," p. 209.

84 Bond, "God Glorified," p. 29.

85 Smith, *Aggrey*.

86 Bond, "God Glorified," p. 6.

87 References to Luke Anthony and Charles Dunbar; ibid., pp. 6, 19, 23, 29–34, 40–41.

88 The full story of Chilembwe's 1915 Nyasaland Revolt is told in Shepperson and Price, *Independent African*; Robert Rotberg, "Psychological Stress and the Question of Identity: Chilembwe's Revolt Reconsidered," in *Protest and Power in Black Africa*, ed. Robert Rotberg and Ali Mazrui (New York: Oxford University Press, 1970), pp. 355–59; and Okon Edet Uya, ed., *Black Brotherhood: Afro-Americans and Africa* (Lexington, Mass.: D. C. Heath, 1971), p. 162.

89 Shepperson, "External Factors," p. 209; William Bittle and Gilbert Geis, in their *The Longest Way Home: Chief Alfred C. Sam's Back-to-Africa Movement* (Detroit: Wayne State University Press, 1964), briefly mention Faduma on pp. 164, 183, 185, 186.

90 Berry, *Century*, pp. 158, 186, 189; Jordan, *A.M.E.*, pp. 66–67; and Marshall Maxeke, "How the Boars Treat the Natives," *The Independent* 51 (2 November 1899): 2946–48.

91 Dube's impact is analyzed in W. Manning Marable, "Black Skin, Bourgeois Masks," in *Profiles of Self-Determination: African Responses to European Colonialism in Southern Africa*, ed. David Chanaiwa (Northside: California State University Foundation, 1976), pp. 320–45; Marable, "African Nationalist"; Marable, "A Black School in South Africa," *Negro History Bulletin* 37 (June-July 1974): 258–61; and Davis, "John L. Dube."

92 Smith, *Aggrey*, pp. 61–62; Kimble, *Political History of Ghana*, pp. 113, 115–17, 548; King, "Aggrey," pp. 527–30.

93 Ralston," Second Middle Passage," p. 192.

Chapter 9
The Impact of the Mission Movement on
the Rise of Pan-African Sentiment

1 D. Augustus Straker, "The Congo Valley: Its Redemption," *A.M.E. Church Review* 2 (January 1886): 157.

2 Imanuel Geiss, *The Pan-African Movement: A History of Pan-Africanism in America, Europe and Africa* (New York: Africana Publishing Co., 1974) pp. 3–6.

3 Edward Blyden, *Christianity, Islam and the Negro Race* (1887; Edinburgh: Edinburgh University Press, 1967), p. 122; Hollis R. Lynch, *Edward Wilmot Blyden: Pan-Negro Patriot, 1832–1912* (London: Oxford University Press, 1967), pp. 54–55, 62–63.

4 Geiss, *Pan-African*, pp. 164–69.

5 *Voice of Missions*, August 1895, p. 3.

6 Cora Wigg, "My Home Across the Sea," *Voice of Missions*, 1 1895, p. 8.

7 See chapter 5 on the missionaries' sense of race responsibility, especially the references to Thomas Johnson, *Africa for Christ, or Twenty-Eight Years a Slave*, 6th ed. (London: Alexander and Shepheard, 1892), pp. 69, 97–98.

8 Alfred Lee Ridgel, *Africa and African Methodism* (Atlanta: Franklin Publishing Co., 1896), pp. 42–43.

9 *Voice of Missions*, 1 September 1899, p. 1.

10 Amanda Smith, *An Autobiography* (Chicago: Meyer, 1893), p. 295.

11 Samuel Miller letter, 1 January 1885 (letter 265), A.B.C.F.M. Papers, collection 15.1, vol. 6.

12 Ibid., 13 February 1886 (letter 273).

13 Quoted in Fola Soremekun, "A History of the American Board Mission in Angola, 1880–1940" (Ph.D diss., Northwestern University, 1965), pp. 72–73; see also *Missionary Herald*, October 1883, p. 272.

14 Charles Morris speech, quoted in *Ecumenical Missionary Conference Report* (New York: American Tract Society, 1900), p. 470.

15 Nancy Jones letter, 27 June 1890 (letter 67), A.B.C.F.M. Papers, collection 15.4, vol. 20, no. 500; *Indianapolis Freeman*, 5 February 1898, p. 2.

16 J. S. Mills, *Africa and Mission Work in Sierra Leone, West Africa* (Dayton: United Brethren Publishing House, 1898), pp. 230–31, 237.

17 See chapter 6.

18 Ridgel, *Africa*, pp. 45, 48, 56. See also Ridgel's letter in *Voice of Missions*, June 1895, p. 1.

19 Blyden speech at Hampton Institute, quoted in *Southern Workman* 12 (January 1883): 9. See also Blyden, *Christianity*, pp. 220–21.

20 Blyden, *Christianity*, pp. 317–18, 400; Robert July, *The Origins of Modern African Thought* (New York: Praeger, 1967), pp. 215–19. The best analysis of Blyden's ideas is Lynch, *Edward Wilmot Blyden*.

21 See chapter 6.
22 Quoted in Henry Wilson, *Origins of West African Nationalism* (London: Macmillan, St. Martin's Press, 1969), p. 241.
23 Blyden, *Christianity*, pp. 138–39, 266–70, 272; Lynch, *Edward Wilmot Blyden*, pp. 143, 147, 151. After 1900 Blyden's praise of African culture involved a greater rejection of Western society; see Wilson, *Origins*, pp. 254–62.
24 Quoted in Wilson, *Origins*, pp. 242, 246.
25 L. C. Curtis letter, *Voice of Missions*, 2 May 1898, p. 2.
26 Quoted in Daniel Payne, *History of the African Methodist Episcopal Church* (1891; New York: Johnson Reprint, 1968), pp. 489–90.
27 Lynch, *Edward Wilmot Blyden*, p. 219.
28 Of course Turner was not the only Afro-American of his time who encouraged feelings of identity with indigenous Africans. For a secular advocacy of black unity see Walter Williams, "Nineteenth Century Pan-Africanist: John Henry Smyth, United States Minister to Liberia, 1878–1885," *Journal of Negro History* 63 (January 1978): 18–25. See also concluding sections of two other articles by Walter Williams, "Black Journalism's Opinions about Africa during the Late Nineteenth Century," *Phylon* 34 (September 1973): 224–35; and "Black American Attitudes toward Africa, 1877–1900," *Pan-African Journal* 4 (Spring 1971): 173–94.
29 Henry Turner, "My Trip to South Africa," *A.M.E. Church Review* 15 (April 1899): 809; see also *Voice of Missions*, August 1895, p. 4.
30 Turner letter, *A.M.E. Church Review* 8 (April 1892): 455, 476, 482–85.
31 *Voice of Missions*, December 1896, p. 4.
32 Ibid., April 1893, p. 2; *A.M.E. Church Review* 8 (April 1892): 488.
33 *Voice of Missions*, July 1895, p. 1.
34 Quoted in *Indianapolis Freeman*, 30 December 1893, p. 5.
35 *A.M.E. Church Review* 15 (April 1899): 810; see also *Voice of Missions*, February 1896, p. 2.
36 *Voice of Missions*, November 1895, p. 3.
37 See chapter 7.
38 John Tule letter, *Voice of Missions*, March 1896, p. 2.
39 Turner letter, ibid., July 1896, p. 2.
40 Quoted in Daniel Thwaite, *The Seething African Pot: A Study of Black Nationalism, 1882–1935* (London: Constable, 1936), pp. 37–38.
41 T. A. Dunlap letter, *Voice of Missions*, February 1895, p. 4.
42 Geiss, *Pan-African*, pp. 110–12. Scholes' books, all published in London, are *The British Empire and Alliances* (1899), *Chamberlain and Chamberlainism* (1903), and *Glimpses of the Ages* (2 vols., 1905, 1908).
43 Geiss, *Pan-African*, pp. 176–80. The other two United States participants at the 1899 planning session were August Straker, a federal judge who possibly was the author of an 1886 mission treatise in the *A.M.E. Church Review* (see note 1), and Tuskegee Institute President

Booker T. Washington. The most thorough study of the conference is Owen Mathurin, *Henry Sylvester Williams and the Origins of the Pan-African Movement* (Westport, Conn.: Greenwood Press, 1976).

44 Alexander Walters, *My Life and Work* (New York: Fleming Revell Co., 1917), pp. 253—60; Geiss, *Pan-African*, p. 182; and Mathurin, *Henry Sylvester Williams*.

45 Clarence Contee, "The Emergence of Du Bois as an African Nationalist," *Journal of Negro History* 54 (January 1969): 48—53; Francis Broderick, *W. E. B. Du Bois: Negro Leader in a Time of Crisis* (Stanford, Calif.: Stanford University Press, 1959).

46 W. E. B. Du Bois, *The Souls of Black Folk* (1903; New York: Washington Square Press, 1970), pp. 177, 185.

47 See chapter 6, especially the references to Alexander Crummell, *Africa and America* (Springfield, Mass.: Wiley and Co., 1891).

48 W. E. B. Du Bois, *The Conservation of the Race* (Washington: American Negro Academy, 1897), p. 10; Geiss, *Pan-African*, p. 173.

49 Du Bois to Paul Hageman, 1897, Du Bois Papers, quoted in Elliott Rudwick, *W. E. B. Du Bois: Propagandist of the Negro Protest* (New York: Atheneum, 1968), p. 210.

Conclusion

1 Edwin Redkey, *Black Exodus, Black Nationalist and Back-to-Africa Movements, 1890—1910* (New Haven: Yale University Press, 1969), pp. 289—301.

2 *Voice of Missions*, May 1895, p. 4.

3 A.M.E. Reverend J. M. Henderson letter, *Indianapolis Freeman*, 27 August 1898, p. 5.

4 Carrie Lee, "The Future of Africa," *Voice of Missions*, 1 July 1899, p. 4.

5 Alfred Ridgel, *Africa and African Methodism* (Atlanta: Franklin Publishing Co., 1896), pp. 42—43.

Bibliography

In a study of this type of the bibliography is much more than a reference list. Since primary sources were written or spoken by black people, it is also an extension of the thesis itself, in that it indicates the amount and type of attention which Africa received from black Americans.

Without attempting to evaluate every source in this bibliography, I wish to note the most important historical works. For background on white attitudes, see: Winthrop Jordan, *White Over Black*; Felix Okoye, *The American Image of Africa*; Philip Curtin, *The Image of Africa*; and Clarence Clendennen, et al., *Americans in Africa*. Twentieth-century Afro-American attitudes toward Africa have been well covered in Imanuel Geiss, *The Pan-African Movement*; Robert Weisbord, *Ebony Kinship*; John A. Davis, ed., *Africa from the Point of View of American Negro Scholars*; Sylvia Jacobs, *The African Nexus*; Harold Isaacs, *The New World of Negro Americans*; David Cronen, *Black Moses*; and Francis Broderick, *W. E. B. Du Bois*. The most valuable works on late nineteenth-century black Americans, without which this study would have been a great deal more difficult, are August Meier, *Negro Thought in America*, and Edwin Redkey, *Black Exodus*. The best book of readings is Adelaide C. Hill and Martin Kilson, eds., *Apropos of Africa*.

Locations of rare books are indicated in brackets.

Primary Sources

Manuscript Collections

Cambridge, Mass. Houghton Library of Harvard University. American Board of Commissioners for Foreign Missions Papers. Collections of Samuel Miller, Mr. and Mrs. Benjamin Ousley, and Nancy Jones: collection 6, vols. 30, 35, 37; collection 15.1, vol. 6; collection 15.4, vols. 12, 20.

Dayton, Ohio. Evangelical United Brethren Division of the United Methodist Commission on Archives and History. Joseph and Mary Gomer Papers.

Lincoln, Pa. University Archives of Lincoln University. Edward Webb Papers. Letters from Lincoln graduates in Africa, 1877—1900.

Montreat, N.C. Historical Foundation of the Presbyterian and Reformed Churches. William Henry Sheppard Papers. Various letters, photographs, and artifacts of Sheppard, plus several typescripts and pamphlets about him and other Afro-American members of the Presbyterian Congo Mission.

New York, N.Y. Schomburg Center for Research in Black Culture, New York City Public Library. Alexander Crummell Papers. ms. c. 17, vol. A (729), and ms. c. 363 (755).

New York, N.Y. United Methodist Church, Board of Global Ministries. Missionary Correspondence Papers. Papers of black American Methodist Episcopal missionaries in Liberia, 1897—1900.

Raleigh, N.C. Manuscript Department of the North Carolina Department of Archives and History. Superintendent of Public Instruction Papers. Correspondence and letter-books, 1885—89.

Washington, D.C. Manuscript Department of the Moorland Collection of Howard University Library. Henry M. Turner Papers. Folders 1, 14—16.

Washington, D.C. Manuscripts Department of the Library of Congress. American Colonization Society Papers. Microfilm reels 164—70.

Newspapers and Periodicals

A.M.E. Church Review. Philadelphia: African Methodist Episcopal Church, 1884—99.

A.M.E. Zion Church Quarterly. Wilmington, N.C.: A.M.E. Zion Church, 1890—1901.

A.M.E.Z. Star of Zion. Charlotte, N.C.: A.M.E. Zion Church, 1896—99.

African Repository. Washington, D.C.: American Colonization Society, 1877—92.

Afro-American Sentinel. Omaha, Nebr.: 1888—99.

American Citizen. Kansas City, Kans.: 1888—99.

Foreign Mission Journal. Richmond, Va.: Southern Baptist Convention, 1877—80.

Grit. Washington, D.C.: 1883—84.

Indianapolis Freeman. Indianapolis, Ind.: 1888—99.

Liberia. Washington, D.C.: American Colonization Society, 1892—99.

Mission Herald. Philadelphia: National Baptist Convention, Ninetieth Anniversary Issue, 1970.

Missionary. Nashville, Tenn.: Mission Board of the Presbyterian Church in the United States (South), 1890—1900.

Missionary Review of the World. New York: 1878—1906.

Missionary Visitor. Dayton, Ohio: United Brethren Church, 1876—82.

Official Journals of the Liberian Annual Conferences, Methodist Episcopal Church. New York: Methodist Episcopal Church, 1885—1900.

People's Advocate. Alexandria, Va.: 1876—86.

Planet. Richmond, Va.: 1895—99.

Proceedings of the Southern Baptist Convention. 1874—82.

Southern Workman. Hampton Institute, Va.: 1877—1905.

Voice of Missions. Atlanta, Ga.: A.M.E. Church, 1893—99.

Washington Bee. Washington, D.C.: 1882—99.

Books, Pamphlets, Articles, and
Edited Collections of Documents

Adams, C. C. *Negro Baptists and Foreign Missions.* Philadelphia: Foreign
Mission Board of the National Baptist Convention, 1944.
African Methodist Episcopal Church Hymnal. Philadelphia: A.M.E. Book
Concern, 1899. [Howard University]
Alexander, William T., *History of the Colored Race in America.* Kansas
City, Mo.: Palmetto Publishing Co., 1888.
Annual Report of the Missionary Society of the Methodist Episcopal Church.
New York: M.E. Church, 1895–1900.
*Annual Reports of the Executive Committee of Foreign Missions of the
Presbyterian Church in the United States.* Nashville: University Press,
1891–1900.
Aptheker, Herbert, ed. *A Documentary History of the Negro People in the
United States.* New York: Citadel Press, 1951.
Arnett, Benjamin W., ed. *The Centennial Budget . . . [of the A.M.E. Church
for 1887–88].* N.p.: A.M.E. Church, 1888.
Blyden, Edward. *Christianity, Islam and the Negro Race.* 1887. Edinburgh:
Edinburgh University Press, 1967.
Bowen, John Wesley Edward, ed. *Africa and the American Negro: Addresses
and Proceedings of the Congress on Africa.* 1896. Miami: Mnemosyne
Publishing, 1969.
Bowen, John Wesley Edward, ed. *What Shall the Harvest Be? A National
Sermon; or, a Series of Plain Talks to the Colored People of America
on Their Problems.* Washington, D.C.: Stafford Printing Co., 1892.
[Interdenominational Theological Center, Atlanta University]
Bracey, John H., August Meier, and Elliott Rudwick, eds. *Black Nationalism
in America.* Indianapolis and New York: Bobbs-Merrill Co., 1970.
Brawley, Edward M., ed. *The Negro Baptist Pulpit.* Philadelphia: American
Baptist Publishing Society, 1890.
Brotz, Howard, ed. *Negro Social and Political Thought 1850–1920, Repre-
sentative Texts.* New York: Basic Books, 1966.
Camphor, Alexander Priestley. *Missionary Story Sketches: Folklore from
Africa.* Cincinnati: Jennings and Graham, 1909.
Coles, John J. *Africa in Brief.* New York: Freeman Steam Printing Establish-
ment, 1886. [Schomburg Center, New York Public Library]
Crummell, Alexander. *Africa and America.* 1891. Miami, Fla.: Mnemosyne
Publishing, 1969.
Delany, Martin. *Principia of Ethnology: The Origin of Races and Color,
with an Archaeological Compendium of Ethiopean and Egyptian Civiliza-
tion from Years of Careful Examination and Enquiry.* Philadelphia:
Harper and Bros., 1879. [Howard University]
Delany, Martin, and Robert Campbell. *Search for a Place: Black Separatism*

and Africa. Ann Arbor: University of Michigan Press, 1969.

Dickerson, W. F. *The Quadrennial Address of the Bishops of the African Methodist Episcopal Church to the Eighteenth Session of the General Conference*. Baltimore: A.M.E. Church, 1884. [University of North Carolina]

Du Bois, W. E. B. *The Conservation of the Race*. Washington: American Negro Academy, 1897.

Du Bois, W. E. B. *The Souls of Black Folk*. 1903. New York: Washington Square Press 1970.

Ecumenical Missionary Conference Report. New York: American Tract Society, 1900.

Gaines, Wesley John. *African Methodism in the South*. Atlanta: Franklin Publishing House, 1890. [Atlanta University]

Haley, James T., ed. *Afro-American Encyclopaedia; or the Thoughts, Doings, and Sayings of the Race*. Nashville: Haley and Florida, 1896.

Hayne, Joseph E. *The Black Man: Or, the Natural History of the Hametic Race*. Raleigh, N.C.: Edwards, 1894.

Heard, William H. *Africa: Verse and Song*. Atlanta: Union Publishing Co., [1896]. [Atlanta University]

Heard, William H. *The Bright Side of African Life*. Philadelphia: A.M.E. Publications House, 1898. [Atlanta University]

Heard, William H. *From Slavery to the Bishopric in the A.M.E. Church*. 1924. New York: Arno Press, 1969.

Heard, William H. *The Missionary Fields of West Africa*. Philadelphia: A.M.E. Book Concern, n.d. [Howard University]

Hill, Adelaide Cromwell, and Martin Kilson, eds. *Apropos of Africa: Sentiments of Negro American Leaders on Africa from the 1800s to the 1950s*. London: Frank Cass and Co., 1969.

Hood, James W. *One Hundred Years of the African Methodist Episcopal Zion Church*. New York: A.M.E. Zion Book Concern, 1895.

Johnson, Edward A. *A School History of the Negro Race in America*. Raleigh, N.C.: Edwards and Broughton, 1890.

Johnson, Thomas L. *Africa for Christ, or Twenty-Eight Years a Slave*. 6th ed. London: Alexander and Shepheard, 1892. [Atlanta University]

Jordan, Lewis Garnett. *Up the Ladder in Foreign Missions*. Nashville: National Baptist Publications Board, 1901 and 1903.

Kletzing, H[enry] F., and W. H. Crogman. *Progress of a Race, or, the Remarkable Advancement of the Afro-American*. 1897. New York: Negro Universities Press, 1969.

Noble, Frederick Perry, ed. "The Chicago Congress on Africa." *Our Day* 12 (October 1893): 279–300.

Parks, H. B. *Africa, the Problem of the New Century*. New York: Mission Department of the A.M.E. Church, 1899. [Howard University]

Payne, Daniel A. *History of the African Methodist Episcopal Church*. 1891. New York: Johnson Reprint Corp., 1968.

Peabody, George Barh-Fofoe. *Barh-Fofoe: A Bassa Boy*. Lancaster, Pa.:

New Era Printing House, 1891. [Atlanta University]

Peabody, George Barh-Fofoe. "The Hope of Africa." *A.M.E. Church Review* 7 (July 1890): 58—61.

Penn, Irvine Garland. *The Afro-American Press and Its Editors*. Springfield, Mass.: Willey and Co., 1891.

Perry, Rufus L. *The Cushite: Or, the Children of Ham*. Springfield, Mass.: Willey and Co., 1893.

Phillips, Charles Henry. *The History of the Colored Methodist Episcopal Church in America*. Jackson, Tenn.: Publishing House of the C.M.E. Church, 1898.

Richardson, Clement, ed. *National Cyclopedia of the Colored Race*. Montgomery, Ala: National Publishing Co., 1919.

Ridgel, Alfred Lee. *Africa and African Methodism*. Atlanta: Franklin Publishing Co., 1896. [Atlanta University]

Sheppard, William H. *Pioneers in Congo*. Louisville, Ky.: Pentecostal Publishing Co., 1917. [University of North Carolina[

Simmons, William J. *Men of Mark*. 1887. New York: Arno Press, 1968.

Smith, Amanda. *An Autobiography*. Chicago: Meyer, 1893.

Smith, Charles S. *Glimpses of Africa, West and Southwest Coast*. Nashville: A.M.E. Sunday School Union, 1895.

Smith, Charles S. *A History of the African Methodist Episcopal Church*. 1922. New York: Johnson Reprint Corp., 1968.

[Smith, Owen Lun West], *Biographical Sketch of Rev. Owen L. W. Smith, D.D., U.S. Minister to Liberia*. N.p.: n.p., [ca 1900]. [University of North Carolina, Carolina Collection]

Stewart, Thomas McCants. *Liberia: The Americo-African Republic*. New York: E. O. Jenkins Sons, 1886. [Oberlin College]

Walters, Bishop Alexander. *My Life and Work*. New York: Fleming H. Revell Co., 1917.

Washington, Booker T. *Up from Slavery*. New York: Doubleday, 1901.

William H. Sheppard, Pioneer Missionary to the Congo. Nashville: Presbyterian Church Educational Department, n.d. [Presbyterian Historical Foundation]

Williams, George W. *History of the Negro Race in America*. 2 vols. New York: G. P. Putnam's Sons, 1883.

Wilson, Joseph T. *Emancipation: Its Course and Progress from 1481 B.C. to A.D. 1875*. 1882. New York: Negro Universities Press, 1969.

Woodson, Carter, ed. *The Works of Francis Grimké*. Washington, D.C.: Associated Publishers, 1942.

Woodworth, Reverend C. L. *Historic Correspondences in Africa and America*. Boston: Beacon Press, 1889. [Schomburg Center, New York Public Library]

Wright, Richard R. *Centennial Encyclopedia of the African Methodist Episcopal Church*. Philadelphia: Book Concern of the A.M.E. Church, 1916.

Secondary Sources

Ainslie, Rosalynde. *The Press in Africa: Communications Past and Present.* London: Victor Gollancz, 1966.

Alleyne, Cameron C. *Gold Coast at a Glance.* New York: Hunt Printing Co., 1931.

American Society of African Culture. *Pan-Africanism Reconsidered.* Berkeley and Los Angeles: University of California Press, 1962.

Ardener, Edwin. *Coastal Bantu of the Cameroons.* London: International African Institute, 1956.

Ayandele, E. A. *Holy Johnson: Pioneer of African Nationalism, 1836–1917.* London: Frank Cass and Co., 1970.

Ayendele, E. A. *The Missionary Impact on Modern Nigeria, 1842–1914.* London: Longmans, 1966.

Bacote, C. A. "Negro Proscription, Protest, and Proposed Solutions in Georgia, 1880–1908." *Journal of Southern History* 21 (November 1959): 471–98.

Baeta, C. G., ed. *Christianity in Tropical Africa.* London: International African Institute, 1968.

Bardolph, Richard. *The Negro Vanguard.* New York: Rinehart and Co., 1959.

Barrett, David B. *Schism and Renewal in Africa.* Nairobi: Oxford University Press, 1968.

Batten, J. Minton. "Henry McNeal Turner: Negro Bishop Extraordinary." *Church History* 7 (September 1938): 231–46.

Berkhofer, Robert K., Jr. *Salvation and the Savage: An Analysis of Protestant Missions and American Indian Response, 1787–1862.* Lexington: University of Kentucky Press, 1965.

Berry, Lewellyn L. *A Century of Missions of the African Methodist Episcopal Church, 1840–1940.* New York: Gutenberg Printing Co., 1942.

Bittle, William, and Gilbert Geis. *The Longest Way Home: Chief Alfred C. Sam's Back-to-Africa Movement.* Detroit: Wayne State University Press, 1964.

Bond, Horace Mann. "God Glorified by Africa: The Story of Lincoln University and the Providence of God in the Ancestral Continent." Typescript. Archives, Lincoln University, Pennsylvania, 1955.

Boyd, Willis D. "Negro Colonization in the National Crisis." Ph.D. dissertation, University of California, Los Angeles, 1953.

Bradley, David H. *A History of the A.M.E. Zion Church.* Nashville: Parthenon Press, 1970.

Bragg, George F. *History of the Afro-American Group of the Episcopal Church.* Baltimore: Church Advocate Press, 1922.

Broderick, Francis L. *W. E. B. Du Bois: Negro Leader in a Time of Crisis.* Stanford: Stanford University Press, 1959.

Brown, G. G. "Missionaries and Cultural Diffusion." *American Journal of Sociology* 50 (November 1944): 214–19.

Cauther, Baker J. *Advance: A History of Southern Baptist Foreign Missions*. Nashville: Broadman Press, 1970.

Chanaiwa, David, ed. *Profiles of Self-Determination: African Responses to European Colonialism in Southern Africa*. Northside: California State University Foundation, 1976.

Clendennen, Clarence, et al. *Americans in Africa, 1865—1900*. Hoover Institution Studies, vol. 17. Stanford: Stanford University Press, 1966.

Clowes, W. Laird. *Black America: A Study of the Ex-Slave and His Late Master*. London: Cassell and Co., 1891.

Coan, Josephus R. "The Expansion of Missions of the African Methodist Episcopal Church in South Africa, 1896—1908." Ph.D. dissertation, Hartford Seminary, 1961.

Coleman, James. *Nigeria: Background to Nationalism*. Berkeley and Los Angeles: University of California Press, 1958.

Collins, Robert and Peter Duignan. *Americans in Africa: A Preliminary Guide to American Missionary Archives and Library Manuscript Collections on Africa*. Stanford: Hoover Institution on War, Revolution, and Peace, 1963.

Contee, Clarence. "Afro-Americans and Early Pan-Africanism." *Negro Digest* (February 1970): 24—30.

Contee, Clarence. "The Emergence of Du Bois as an African Nationalist." *Journal of Negro History* 54 (January 1969): 48—63.

Cornell, William Glenn. "The Life and Thought of John Edward Bruce." M.A. thesis, University of North Carolina, Chapel Hill, 1970.

Cronon, Edmund David. *Black Moses: The Story of Marcus Garvey and the Universal Negro Improvement Association*. Madison: University of Wisconsin Press, 1955, 1968.

Curtin, Philip D., ed. *Africa and The West*. Madison: University of Wisconsin Press, 1972.

Curtin, Philip D. *The Image of Africa: British Ideas and Action, 1780—1850*. Madison: University of Wisconsin Press, 1964.

Davis, John A., ed. *Africa from the Point of View of American Negro Scholars*. Paris: Présence Africaine, 1958.

Davis, Jeanne, et al. "Negro Missionary Reaction to Africa." *Practical Anthropology* 11 (March-April 1964): 61—70.

Davis, R. Hunt. "John L. Dube: A South African Exponent of Booker T. Washington." *Journal of African Studies* 2 (December 1975).

Drake, St. Clair. "Negro Americans and the Africa Interest." In *The American Negro Reference Book*, ed. John P. Davis. Englewood Cliffs, N.J.: Prentice-Hall, 1966.

Drake, St. Clair. *The Redemption of Africa and Black Religion*. Chicago: Third World Press, 1970.

Drimmer, Melvin. "Black Exodus, Review Article." *Journal of American Studies* 4 (February 1971): 249—56.

Duignan, Peter. *Handbook of American Resources for African Studies*. Stanford: Hoover Institution on War, Revolution, and Peace, 1967.

Dyer, Brainerd. "The Persistence of the Idea of Negro Colonization." *Pacific Historical Review* 12 (1943): 53—65.

Elsbree, Oliver. *The Rise of the Missionary Spirit in America.* Williamsport, Pa.: Williamsport Printing Co., 1928.

Esedebe, P. O. "Origins and Meaning of Pan-Africanism." *Présence Africaine* 73 (1970): 108—27.

Essien-Udom, E. U. *Black Nationalism: A Search for an Identity in America.* New York: Dell, 1964.

Fisher, Miles. "Lott Cary, the Colonizing Missionary." *Journal of Negro History* 7 (October 1922): 380—418.

Fleming, Walter. "Pap Singleton, the Moses of the Colored Exodus." *American Journal of Sociology* (July 1909): 61—82.

Franklin, John Hope. *From Slavery to Freedom.* 3d ed. New York: Alfred A. Knopf, 1967.

Franklin, John Hope. *George Washington Williams and Africa.* Washington, D.C.: History Department, Howard University, 1971.

Freeman, Edward A. *The Epoch of Negro Baptists and the Foreign Mission Board, National Baptist Convention, U.S.A., Inc.* Kansas City: Central Seminary Press, 1953.

Geiss, Imanuel. *The Pan-African Movement: A History of Pan-Africanism in America, Europe and Africa.* New York: Africana Publishing Co., 1974.

Gibbons, Rosa. "Historical Research on Rev. William H. Sheppard, D.D., F.R.G.S." Typescript. Montreat, North Carolina: Historical Foundation, 1939.

Gordon, Robert. "Black Man's Burden." *Evangelical Missions Quarterly* 9 (Fall 1973): 267—76.

Griffith, Cyril E. *The African Dream: Martin R. Delany and the Emergence of Pan-African Thought.* University Park: Pennsylvania State University Press, 1975.

Groves, Charles P. *The Planting of Christianity in Africa.* 4 vols. London: Lutterworth Press, 1948—58.

Harlan, Louis R. "Booker T. Washington and the White Man's Burden." *The American Historical Review* 71 (January 1966): 441—67.

Harlan, Louis R. *Booker T. Washington: The Making of a Black Leader, 1856—1901.* London: Oxford University Press, 1972.

Harr, Wilbur C. "The Negro as an American Protestant Missionary in Africa." Ph.D. dissertation, University of Chicago Divinity School, 1945.

Herndon, Jane Walker. "Henry McNeal Turner: Exponent of American 'Negritude.'" M.A. thesis, Georgia State College, Atlanta, 1967.

Hodgkin, Thomas. *Nationalism in Colonial Africa.* New York: New York University Press, 1957.

Holden, Edith. *Blyden of Liberia.* New York: Vantage Press, 1966.

Hudson, Winthrop S. *Religion in America.* 2nd ed. New York: Scribner's, 1973.

Isaacs, Harold R. "The American Negro and Africa: Some Notes." *The*

Phylon Quarterly 20 (Fall 1959): 219—33.

Isaacs, Harold R. *The New World of Negro Americans*. New York: John Day Co., 1963.

Jacobs, Sylvia M. *The African Nexus: Black American Perspectives on the European Partitioning of Africa, 1880—1920*. Westport, Conn.: Greenwood Press, 1981.

Johnston, Harry H. *Liberia*. 2 vols. London: Hutchinson and Co., 1906.

Jordan, Artishia W. *The African Methodist Episcopal Church in Africa*. New York: A.M.E. Department of Foreign Missions, 1964.

Jordan, Lewis G. *Negro Baptist History, U.S.A*. Nashville: Sunday School Publishing Board, 1930.

Jordan, Winthrop D. *White over Black: American Attitudes toward the Negro, 1550—1812*. Chapel Hill: University of North Carolina Press, 1968.

July, Robert. *The Origins of Modern African Thought*. New York: Praeger, 1967.

Kellersberger, Julia Lake. *Lucy Gantt Sheppard, Shepherdess of His Sheep on Two Continents*. Atlanta: Committee on Women's Work, Presbyterian Church in the United States, n.d.

Kimble, David. *A Political History of Ghana: The Rise of Gold Coast Nationalism, 1850—1928*. Oxford: Clarendon Press, 1963.

King, Kenneth. "James E. K. Aggrey: Collaborator, Nationalist, Pan-African." *Canadian Journal of African Studies* 3 (Fall 1970): 511—30.

King, Kenneth J. *Pan-Africanism and Education*. London: Oxford University Press, 1971.

King, Willis J. "History of the Methodist Church Mission in Liberia." Typescript. Lake Junaluska, North Carolina: United Methodist Commission on Archives and History, box 266, n.d.

LaFeber, Walter. *The New Empire: An Interpretation of American Expansion, 1860—1898*. Ithaca, N.Y.: Cornell University Press, 1963.

Lance, Forrest Jack. "The Life and Educational Thought of Alexander Crummell, Black Minister and Educator." M.A. thesis, University of Georgia, 1972.

Latourette, Kenneth Scott. *The Great Century in the Americas, Australia, and Africa, 1880—1914*. A History of the Expansion of Christianity, vol. 5. New York: Harper and Bros., 1943.

Legum, Colin. *Pan-Africanism: A Short Political Guide*. London: Pall Mall Press, 1962.

Lewis, Elsie M. "The Political Mind of the Negro, 1865—1900." *Journal of Southern History* 21 (May 1955): 189—202.

Liebenow, J. Gus. *Liberia: The Evolution of Privilege*. Ithaca, N.Y.: Cornell University Press, 1969.

Lincoln University Biographical Catalogue. Lancaster, Pa.: New Era Printing Co., 1918.

Logan, Frenise A. *The Negro in North Carolina, 1876—1894*. Chapel Hill: University of North Carolina Press, 1964.

Logan, Rayford W. *The Betrayal of the Negro*. London: Collier Books, 1965.

Lynch, Hollis R., ed. *Black Spokesman: Edward Wilmot Blyden*. New York: Humanities Press, 1971.

Lynch, Hollis R. *Edward Wilmot Blyden: Pan-Negro Patriot, 1832–1912*. London: Oxford University Press, 1967.

McBride, David. "Africa's Elevation and Changing Racial Thought at Lincoln University, 1854–1886." *Journal of Negro History* 62 (October 1977): 363–77.

McCulloch, Merran. *The Ovimbundu of Angola*. West Central Africa Ethnographic Survey, pt. 2. London: International African Institute, 1952.

MacMaster, Richard R. "Henry Highland Garnet and the African Civilization Society." *Journal of Presbyterian History* 48 (Summer 1970): 95–112.

Magubane, Bernard. "The American Negro's Conception of Africa." Ph.D. dissertation, University of California, Los Angeles, 1967.

Marable, W. Manning. "African Nationalist: The Life of John Langalibalele Dube." Ph.D. dissertation, University of Maryland, 1976.

Marable, W. Manning. "A Black School in South Africa." *Negro History Bulletin* 37 (June-July 1974): 258–61.

Marable, W. Manning. "Booker T. Washington and African Nationalism." *Phylon* 35 (December 1974): 398–406.

Martin, Jane J. "The Dual Legacy: Government Authority and Mission Influence among the Glebo of Eastern Liberia, 1834–1910." Ph.D. Dissertation, Boston University, 1968.

Martin, Jane J. "How to Build a Nation: Liberian Ideas about National Integration in the Later Nineteenth Century." *Liberian Studies Journal* 2 (1969): 15–42.

Mathurin, Owen. *Henry Sylvester Williams and the Origins of the Pan-African Movement*. Westport, Conn.: Greenwood Press, 1976.

Medford, Hampton T. *Zion Methodism Abroad*. Washington, D.C.: n.p., 1937.

Meier, August. "The Emergence of Negro Nationalism." *Midwest Journal* 4 (1951–52): no. 1, pp. 96–104; no. 2, pp. 95–111.

Meier, August. *Negro Thought in America, 1880–1915: Racial Ideologies in the Age of Booker T. Washington*. Ann Arbor: University of Michigan Press, 1966.

Meier, August, and Elliott M. Rudwick. *From Plantation to Ghetto: An Interpretive History of American Negroes*. American Century Series. New York: Hill and Wang, 1966.

Mills, J. S. *Africa and Mission Work in Sierra Leone, West Africa*. Dayton: United Brethren Publishing House, 1898.

Moses, Wilson. "Civilizing Missionary: A Study of Alexander Crummell." *Journal of Negro History* 60 (April 1975): 229–51.

Murdock, George. *Africa: Its Peoples and Their Culture History*. New York: McGraw-Hill, 1959.

Murray, Andrew E. *Presbyterians and the Negro: A History*. Philadelphia: Presbyterian Historical Society, 1966.

Myers, John Brown. *The Congo for Christ: The Story of the Congo Mission*.

New York: Fleming H. Revell Co., 1895.

Nelson, Hart M., et al., eds. *The Black Church in America*. New York: Basic Books, 1971.

Nicol, Davidson, ed. *Black Nationalism, 1867: The Writings of Africanus Horton*. New York: Africana Publishing Corp., 1969.

Okoye, Felix N. *The American Image of Africa: Myth and Reality*. Buffalo, N.Y.: Black Academy Press, 1971.

Oosthuizen, G. C. *Post-Christianity in Africa*. Grand Rapids, Mich.: William B. Eerdmans Publishing Co., 1968.

Padgett, James A. "The Ministers to Liberia and Their Diplomacy." *Journal of Negro History* 22 (January 1937): 50—92.

Pelt, Owen D., and Ralph Lee Smith. *The Story of the National Baptists*. New York: Vantage Press, 1960.

Ponton, Mungo M. *Life and Times of Henry M. Turner* . . . Atlanta: A. B. Caldwell, 1917.

Presbyterian Colored Missions. *Memorial of Dr. William H. Sheppard*. Louisville, Ky.: Presbyterian Church in the United States, [ca. 1927].

Pride, Armistad. "Register and History of the Negro Newspaper in the United States, 1827—1950." Ph.D. dissertation, Northwestern University, 1950.

Quarles, Benjamin. *Black Abolitionists*. London: Oxford University Press, 1969.

Ralston, Richard. "A Second Middle Passage: African Student Sojourns in the United States during the Colonial Period and Their Influence upon the Character of African Leadership." Ph.D. dissertation, University of California, Los Angeles, 1972.

Redkey, Edwin S. *Black Exodus: Black Nationalist and Back-to-Africa Movements, 1890—1910*. New Haven: Yale University Press, 1969.

Redkey, Edwin S., ed. *Respect Black: The Writings and Speeches of Henry McNeal Turner*. New York: Arno Press, 1971.

Rendall, John B. *Historical Sketch of Lincoln University*. Philadelphia: M. C. Wood Printing Co., 1904.

Richardson, Nathaniel R. *Liberia's Past and Present*. London: Diplomatic Press and Publishing Co., 1959.

Rogerson, Idonia E. *Historical Synopsis of the Women's Home and Foreign Missionary Society, African Methodist Episcopal Zion Church*. Charlotte, N.C.: A.M.E. Zion Publishing House, 1967.

Ross, Emory. *Out of Africa*. New York: Friendship Press, 1936.

Rotberg, Robert I., and Ali A. Mazrui, eds. *Protest and Power in Black Africa*. New York: Oxford University Press, 1970.

Roth, Donald R. "Grace Not Race: Southern Negro Church Leaders, Black Identity, and Missions to West Africa, 1865—1919." Ph.D. dissertation, University of Texas, Austin, 1975.

Rudwick, Elliott M. *W. E. B. Du Bois: Propagandist of the Negro Protest*. New York: Atheneum, 1969.

Rule, Lucien V. "A Daughter of the Morning: Lucy G. Sheppard." Typescript. Montreat, North Carolina: Presbyterian Historical Foundation, n.d.

Saunders, Davis Lee. "A History of Baptists in Central and Southern Africa." Ph.D. dissertation, Southern Baptist Theological Seminary, Louisville, Kentucky, 1973.

Schatz, Walter. *Directory of Afro-American Resources*. New York: Bowker, 1970.

Seraile, William. "Black American Missionaries in Africa, 1821—1925." *Social Studies* 63 (October 1972): 198—202.

Shaloff, Stanley. *Reform in Leopold's Congo*. Richmond, Va.: John Knox Press, 1970.

Shepperson, George. "External Factors in the Development of African Nationalism." *Phylon* 22 (Fall 1961): 207—25.

Shepperson, George. "Notes on Negro American Influences on the Emergence of African Nationalism." *Journal of African History* 1:2 (1960): 299—312.

Shepperson, George. "The Politics of African Church Separatist Movements in British Central Africa, 1892—1916." *Africa* 24 (July 1954): 233—47.

Shepperson, George, and Thomas Price. *Independent African*. Edinburgh: Edinburgh University Press, 1958.

Slade, Ruth. *English-Speaking Missions in the Congo Independent State, 1878—1908*. Brussels: Académie Royale des Sciences d'Outre Mer, 1959.

Small, Melvin. "Suggestions from the Behavioral Sciences for Historians Interested in the Study of Attitudes." *Societas* 3 (Winter 1973): 1—19.

Smith, E. W. *Aggrey of Africa: A Study in Black and White*. New York: R. R. Smith, 1930.

Smith, James W., and A. L. Jameson, eds. *Religion in American Life*. Princeton, N.J.: Princeton University Press, 1961.

Soremekun, Fola. "A History of the American Board Mission in Angola, 1880—1940." Ph.D. dissertation, Northwestern University, 1965.

Staudenraus, Philip J. *The African Colonization Movement, 1816—1865*. New York: Columbia University Press, 1961.

Strong, William E. *The Story of the American Board*. Boston: Pilgrim Press, 1910.

Sundkler, Bengt G. M. *The Bantu Prophets of South Africa*. London: Lutterworth Press, 1948.

Thorpe, Earl E. "Africa in the Thought of Negro Americans." *Negro History Bulletin* 23 (October 1959): 5—10, 22.

Thorpe, Earl E. *The Mind of the Negro*. Groton, Conn.: Negro Universities Press, 1961.

Thorpe, Earl E. *Negro Historians in the United States*. Baton Rouge, La.: Fraternal Press, 1958.

Thwaite, Daniel. *The Seething African Pot: A Study of Black Nationalism, 1882—1935*. London: Constable and Co., 1936.

Tindall, George B. *South Carolina Negroes, 1877—1900*. Baton Rouge: Louisiana State University Press, 1966.

Torbet, Robert G. *A History of the Baptists*. Philadelphia: Judson Press, 1963.

Torday, E. *Notes ethnographiques sur les peuples communément appelés bakuba*. Brussels: Annales du Musée Royal du Congo Belge, 1910.

Uya, Okon Edet, ed. *Black Brotherhood: Afro-Americans and Africa*. Lexington, Mass.: D. C. Heath and Co., 1971.

Vansina, Jan. *The Children of Woot: A History of the Kuba Peoples*. Madison: University of Wisconsin Press, 1978.

Vansina, Jan. *De la Tradition Orale*. Tervuren, Belgium: Annales du Musée Royal du Congo Belge, 1961.

Vansina, Jan. *Les Tribus Ba-Kuba et les Peuplades Apparentees*. Tervuren, Belgium: Annales du Musee Royal du Congo Belge, 1954.

Wahle, Kathleen O. "Alexander Crummell: Black Evangelist and Pan-Negro Nationalist." *Phylon* 29 (December 1968): 388−95.

Walls, William Jacob, Senior Bishop of the African Methodist Episcopal Zion Church. Interview on African Students at Livingstone College in 1899, where Walls was a student. Salisbury, North Carolina, May 25, 1971.

Washington, Joseph R. *Black Religion: The Negro and Christianity in the United States*. Boston: Beacon Press, 1964.

Weisbord, Robert G. *Ebony Kinship: Africa, Africans, and the Afro-American*. Westport, Conn.: Greenwood Press, 1973.

Williams, Ethel L. *Afro-American Religious Studies: A Comprehensive Bibliography with Locations in American Libraries*. Metuchen, N.J.: Scarecrow Press, 1972.

Williams, Walter L. "Black American Attitudes toward Africa, 1877−1900." *Pan-African Journal* 4 (Spring 1971): 173−94.

Williams, Walter L. "Black American Attitudes toward Africa: The Missionary Movement, 1877−1900." Ph.D. dissertation, University of North Carolina, Chapel Hill, 1974.

Williams, Walter L. "Black American Attitudes toward Emigration to Africa, 1877−1900." M.A. thesis, University of North Carolina, Chapel Hill, 1972.

Williams, Walter L. "Black Journalism's Opinions about Africa during the Late Nineteenth Century." *Phylon* 34 (September 1973): 224−35.

Williams, Walter L. "Ethnic Relations of African Students in the United States, with Black Americans, 1870−1900." *Journal of Negro History* 65 (Summer 1980): 228−49.

Williams, Walter L. "Nineteenth Century Pan-Africanist: John Henry Smyth, United States Minister to Liberia, 1878−1885." *Journal of Negro History* 63 (January 1978): 18−25.

Williamson, Joel. *After Slavery: The Negro in South Carolina during Reconstruction, 1861−1877*. Chapel Hill: University of North Carolina Press, 1965.

Wilson, Henry S. *Origins of West African Nationalism*. London: MacMillan, St. Martin's Press, 1969.

Woodson, Carter. *A History of the Negro Church*. Washington, D.C.: Associated Publishers, 1921 and 1945.

Work, Monroe. *A Bibliography of the Negro in Africa and America*. New York: H. W. Wilson Co., 1928.

Yates, Walter L. "The History of the African Methodist Episcopal Zion Church in West Africa, Liberia and Gold Coast (Ghana) 1880—1900." M.A. thesis, Hartford Seminary, 1963.

Index

JACKET DESIGNED BY CAROLINE BECKETT
COMPOSED BY FIVE STAR PHOTO TYPESETTING, INC.,
NEENAH, WISCONSIN
MANUFACTURED BY THOMSON-SHORE, INC., DEXTER, MICHIGAN
TEXT IS SET IN TIMES ROMAN, DISPLAY LINES IN BASKERVILLE

Library of Congress Cataloging in Publication Data
Williams, Walter L., 1948—
Black Americans and the evangelization of Africa,
1877—1900.
Bibliography: pp. 237—250.
Includes index.
1. Missions—Africa, Sub-Saharan. 2. Afro-American
missionaries—Africa, Sub-Saharan. 3. Afro-Americans—
Religion. I. Title.
BV3520.W49   266′.023′73067   81—69830
ISBN 0-299-08920-7   AACR2